Mainstreaming Gays

Mainstreaming Gays

● ●

Critical Convergences of Queer Media, Fan Cultures, and Commercial Television

EVE NG

Rutgers University Press
New Brunswick, Camden, and Newark, New Jersey
London and Oxford

Rutgers University Press is a department of Rutgers, The State University of New Jersey, one of the leading public research universities in the nation. By publishing worldwide, it furthers the University's mission of dedication to excellence in teaching, scholarship, research, and clinical care.

Library of Congress Cataloging-in-Publication Data
Names: Ng, Eve, author.
Title: Mainstreaming gays : critical convergences of queer media, fan cultures, and commercial television / Eve Ng.
Description: New Brunswick : Rutgers University Press, [2023] | Includes bibliographical references and index.
Identifiers: LCCN 2023004711 | ISBN 9781978831339 (paperback) | ISBN 9781978831346 (hardcover) | ISBN 9781978831353 (epub) | ISBN 9781978831360 (pdf)
Subjects: LCSH: Sexual minorities in mass media. | Sexual minorities in popular culture.
Classification: LCC P96.S58 N44 2023 | DDC 306.76/8—dc23/eng/20230410
LC record available at https://lccn.loc.gov/2023004711

A British Cataloging-in-Publication record for this book is available from the British Library.

References to internet websites (URLs) were accurate at the time of writing. Neither the author nor Rutgers University Press is responsible for URLs that may have expired or changed since the manuscript was prepared.

♾ The paper used in this publication meets the requirements of the American National Standard for Information Sciences—Permanence of Paper for Printed Library Materials, ANSI Z39.48-1992.

rutgersuniversitypress.org

For Quinn

Contents

Mainstreaming Gays

Introduction

• •

Between Legacy and
Streaming

In a 2010 episode of *The Simpsons* (Fox, 1989–) where the top executives of America's major television networks are assembled, the two male-presenting representatives of Bravo and Logo are shown to be making out, a sly commentary about the fact that these two networks were seen as "gay" channels (figure 1). Logo's programming specifically targeted LGBTQ viewers at the time of its launch in 2005 and for several years afterward, while Bravo, which had premiered both the gay dating show *Boy Meets Boy* and the phenomenally popular makeover show *Queer Eye for the Straight Guy* in 2003, was seen as the "gayest channel" for some time even though it never branded itself as such, distinctly situating both networks with respect to LGBTQ media.[1]

Today, with scores of LGBTQ narratives on television as well as multiple digital platforms that facilitate interaction among LGBTQ-identified users, queer content and community has never seemed so at home in commercial media spaces—so much so that it is easy to overlook the complex set of processes that produced the contemporary landscape, including the roles of Bravo and Logo. Antecedents for these developments arose in the 1990s when commercial networks began producing gay-themed programming to appeal to (mostly heterosexual) audience segments identified as interested in edgier content.[2] In the next decade, a gay and lesbian media market was constructed in the United States,[3] and nascent online spaces for LGBTQ users arose as digital media became increasingly widespread.

FIGURE 1 Bravo and Logo executives kissing on *The Simpsons* (episode S22E06), produced by Gracie Films and 20th Television, first aired November 21, 2010, on Fox.

Another key period spanning the 2000s and 2010s occurred when Bravo and Logo, having broken new ground in LGBTQ-themed programming on their linear channels, then expanded their digital footprints into queer and queer-friendly media. Besides its eponymous website BravoTV.com, Bravo had also established OutZoneTV.com in 2005, which the network intended to be "the first online broadband destination for entertaining, thought-provoking content about and for the LGBT audience,"[4] while a year or so later, Logo, in addition to LogoONLINE.com (later LogoTV.com), purchased three LGBTQ-focused digital properties that brought it the entertainment websites AfterEllen and AfterElton and the news site 365gay in June 2006[5] and the social networking site Downelink in August 2007. Also noteworthy was Bravo's March 2007 acquisition of Television Without Pity, the most prolific website for detailed episode recaps and a thriving message board that included numerous "HoYay" ("homo-eroticism, yay!") threads celebrating (usually subtextually) queer readings of television characters. Thus, before shows with LGBTQ lead characters like *Orange Is the New Black* (Netflix, 2013) or *Transparent* (Amazon, 2014) began streaming and before the dominance of Facebook, Twitter, and gay dating apps like Grindr, Bravo and Logo transformed commercial LGBTQ media, as well as being home to sites for queer engagement online prior to the dominance of social media platforms.

What was the significance of these two major U.S. networks expanding their LGBTQ content online at a time when digital spaces were being touted in popular and scholarly commentary as full of potential for traditionally marginalized groups? What were the outcomes for content creators and site users, as well as the websites and the networks themselves? How did Bravo's and Logo's LGBTQ channel content change as both networks moved to multiplatform programming strategies? And what do answers to these questions tell us about the trajectory from legacy television to the streaming era, specifically with respect to the production and distribution of LGBTQ media? The title of this book, *Mainstreaming Gays*, encapsulates two sides of these developments, both in the sense of LGBTQ media and its producers being incorporated into mainstream domains, and of LGBTQ cultural agents who, having been thus integrated, also reshaped those contexts in important ways.[6] Through the lens of what Henry Jenkins theorized as "convergence culture," as well as scholarship about media platforms, content, and producers, this book examines the changes in production cultures, digital community, and LGBTQ content at a moment when the commercialization of queer media intersected with the rise of fan cultures and the emergence of new digital platforms, and explains how these changes have shaped current conditions of LGBTQ media. The account I present includes both gains and losses, highlighting substantial integrations into the mainstream that could not fully counter continuing precarities for queer expression and participation in media spaces.

The "convergence" of convergence culture pertains to multiple elements of media production. One strand involves cultural agents, with industry changes leading to some increased permeability of the traditional producer-consumer demarcation. In this vein, Bravo's and Logo's forays into digital media ended up bringing a new cohort of queer cultural producers, many of whom had originally been fans rather than industry insiders, into the commercial sphere. Notably, it was the first time that there were so many LGBTQ-identified cultural workers involved in the commercial production and distribution of LGBTQ media. The support of Logo in particular also contributed to a growth of independently produced queer media, which benefited from being hosted or promoted on the networks' websites. However, as the first wave of new LGBTQ producers at the networks became professionalized, opportunities for additional outsiders diminished, demonstrating the limits of such convergence trajectories for those who had traditionally been excluded. Still, what happened at Bravo and Logo remains an important legacy for mainstream integrations of LGBTQ media and cultural agents, not just for the precedents it set for later shifts but also the crucial picture it provides for theorizing how production cultures change: through processes that are incomplete and uneven, yet nevertheless leave their mark.

Bravo's and Logo's digital outlets also served as new spaces for queer engagement online. At a time when the major social networks were not yet as widely used, several of these websites underwent processes of what I call "social mediafication." Since these sites revolved around LGBTQ content and were frequented by LGBTQ users, they became distinctive, relatively centralized spaces for queer community: neither just another social media platform for a broader general public nor simply a dating/hookup site. The ultimate demise of the websites thus constitutes a loss, even as they were replaced by numerous other, much more dispersed digital spaces, and illustrate the risks of relying on commercial media for community formation and engagement. In explicating the trajectories of the sites, the analysis provides a piece missing from the existing literature on queer interaction online, which has shifted more and more to accounts of social media and mobile apps, and it situates those newer developments against what had come just a few years earlier.

As the digital properties were reshaping LGBTQ media, Bravo's and Logo's linear channels also underwent significant changes. Reality television featuring gay and lesbian principals, most notably *Queer Eye*, were prominent shows on Bravo, while Logo had begun as an LGBTQ network with an eclectic mix of documentary, reality, and scripted series intended to reflect the community's diversity. Yet, as Logo's channel content converged with Bravo's in a bid to garner slices of the same gay men-straight women "Will and Graces" demographic, its executives leaned into "post-gay" discourses about acceptance and evolution, thus moving away from the queer front-and-center programming that had been its launching pad, and eventually dispensed with any LGBTQ-centric content altogether. At a broader level, then, these shifts illustrate the contingent empowerment offered by the "mainstream." That is, following a long history of marginalization and omission from the commercial domain, the inclusion of LGBTQ media by networks staking out brand distinctiveness did not end up as a sustained model. Instead, the programming strategies of Bravo and Logo contrast with those of streaming platforms that rose to prominence shortly after, where LGBTQ content is now one strand of a wider slate intended to appeal to multiple viewer segments.

Each of these kinds of changes—concerning who the producers of commercial LGBTQ content were, new spaces of queer interaction online, and where LGBTQ media was being produced and circulated—were significant to what Pierre Bourdieu termed the "field of cultural production."[7] Bourdieu's work on the media, written largely in the 1970s and 1980s, did not deal much with television[8] and said nothing about digital media. There has been a substantial amount of scholarship on production since then, including ethnographic studies of cultural producers and the effects of new technologies on media production and consumption, but little in the way of how to represent the complexities of the cultural field. What this book also offers is a revision of Bourdieu's original model that preserves the relational mapping reflecting power differentials between cultural agents, while accounting for contemporary media in substantially improved ways, particularly the characteristics of digital media and the more mixed configurations of capital and viewership size for a range of media texts.

As the following sections discuss, scholarship on convergence culture; digital technologies, LGBTQ media, and queer community; LGBTQ content, television programming, and brand distinction; and media producers and production are each relevant to the account to be presented. Upcoming chapters discuss the integration of new LGBTQ cultural agents into Bravo and Logo, how digital technologies facilitated the production of LGBTQ video and the creation of new spaces for queer engagement, the shifts of LGBTQ content within Bravo's and Logo's television programming both toward and away from queer specificity, and theorizing the mainstreaming of LGBTQ media and cultural agents in the cultural field as a whole.

Convergence Culture and Mainstream/Subculture Dynamics

Discussing developments that became prominent in the 1990s, Jenkins theorized convergence culture as emergent from "the intersections of various media technologies, industries and consumers,"[9] with significant shifts in the industrial structures and modes of media production and consumption compared to those associated with the earlier era of what has come to be called "legacy" media. The notion of convergence applied in a number of distinct though interrelated ways, including the concentration of media ownership, the use of multiple media platforms, and changes to earlier boundaries between producer and consumer, all of which were in play for Bravo and Logo during the period that this book covers. Importantly, these various forms of convergence were key to bringing LGBTQ production, producers, and consumers more centrally into the commercial domain, processes that changed both mainstream media and the place of queer content and cultural agents vis-à-vis the mainstream.

At the time of Bravo's and Logo's purchases of Television Without Pity, AfterEllen/AfterElton, 365gay, and Downelink, media conglomeration, involving both horizontal convergence—the same corporation owning multiple properties across different mediums—and vertical convergence—a corporation owning the production companies as well as the outlets where media content is distributed, for example—had already been occurring for print, music, television, film, and increasingly for digital media as well:[10] music label Bertelsmann purchased a $50 million controlling interest in the music-sharing company Napster in 2000, NewsCorp acquired social networking site MySpace for $580 million in 2005, and Google bought YouTube for what was then an eye-popping $1.65 billion in 2006.[11] Beyond the motivation simply of acquiring rivals, a major reason for consolidations was the interest of legacy media in facilitating what Jenkins called the "transmedia" distribution of content across multiple platforms.

With just a few corporations controlling the vast majority of production studios, television networks and radio stations, music labels and concert vendors, and cable and internet services, there was academic and popular concern about the effects on content diversity, including critical political perspectives. And for digital media more specifically, its potential in offering spaces for a greater range of expression, particularly by groups long marginalized by legacy media, seemed under threat by these consolidations. However, the Bravo and Logo website purchases were also examples of longtime corporate interest in acquiring smaller labels and enterprises seen as diverging from the mainstream, to continue as units within the parent company whose distinctiveness relative to dominant culture would endow them with a profitable cachet.[12] Here, then, the concern was less about losing diversity in media content—at least not immediately—and more about the takeover of independent production by major media corporations.

Assumptions and arguments that the commercial is necessarily counterposed to authentic and politically resistive expression—something that Lisa Henderson termed the "commercial repressive hypothesis"[13]—have a long history in discussions about popular media and culture, but have also been challenged by research demonstrating complex entanglements between dominant culture and subcultures rather than straightforward co-optation. Examining the British context, Dick Hebdige discussed how dominant culture routinely draws from the repertoire of subcultures, perhaps most obviously in fashion and music, while at the same time subcultures produce their identities partly through the incorporation of symbolic and material elements from mass culture, re-creating hybrid but distinct forms of expression and practice.[14] Furthermore, in an account discussing American dance club subcultures, Sarah Thornton described how the prestige of what participants valued was produced in part through being disparaged in the mass media; that is, these subcultures depended crucially on mainstream culture, even as they purported to be removed from it.[15] Thus, even as various scholars have conceptualized mainstream and subculture as defined in opposition to each other—and the youth patrons of club music also imagined the mainstream as clearly separate from (and inferior to) their own subculture—Thornton argued that there were complex intertwinings of the two, both economically and culturally. Although the media forms and user communities she studied were rather different from those being discussed in this book, Thornton's broader analytical arguments about the complex relations and contestations of cultural and subcultural capital also apply here.

Through more contemporary perspectives incorporating the presence of digital media, convergence culture provides a framework to continue nuanced examinations of the bidirectional, though uneven, flows between (more) subcultural and (more) mainstream domains. Jenkins argued that a key characteristic of convergence culture were new modes of participation drawing in consumers who had not previously been central to mainstream media production. Digital technologies facilitated a "participatory culture" that included circuits of production involving both industrial agents and ordinary media users, often across different platforms.[16] Jenkins acknowledged a tension between the opportunities for users who had previously been marginalized to gain visibility and the risks of being commodified by economically powerful corporations, thus losing "control over their own culture, since it is mass produced and mass marketed."[17] Still, his focus was on how new forms of user-producer engagement were enriching the media industries creatively and materially without necessarily diminishing fan cultures.

Jenkins's original account of convergence culture has been criticized along several dimensions. One is setting too low a bar for meaningful "participation" and not sufficiently acknowledging the advantages that industry producers have in terms of capital and other resources compared to media consumers.[18] Scholars of public access and community media have argued that ordinary citizens should be "effectively involved in the mediated production of meaning (content-related participation) or even in the management and policy-development of content producing organizations (structural participation)"[19] in order to challenge existing media power structures. Outside of advocating for such substantial changes, another line of critique about unequal power dynamics in industry-user engagements concerns the strictures that are typically placed on fan content submitted to official websites. Historically, fan videos and fan fiction produced in mostly female communities have provided alternative narratives, including homoerotic pairings not in the canonical texts.[20] However, as Suzanne Scott detailed, industry solicitations of fan submissions often limit the video clips available for fans to edit together, as well as prohibiting sexually explicit content, in ways that diminish the ability to produce the kind of "feminist cultural products" that circulated in fan-centric spaces.[21]

Other issues arise from the absorption of fan practices into commercial spaces. There is the financial benefit that industry media reap from the unpaid labor of "participatory" users, whether through tangible content, such as additional animations, narratives, and game versions via "modding" in online game worlds,[22] or the "immaterial labor" of information, communication, and relationships at social networking sites and elsewhere that are crucial to the digital economy.[23] Indeed, as Alex Lothian argued from a neo-Marxist perspective regarding industry efforts to tap into fan creativity, "Rather than fans stealing commodified culture to make works for their own purposes, capital steals their labor—as, we might consider, it stole ideas from the cultural commons and fenced them off in the first place—to add to its surplus."[24] At another level, the commercialization of fan engagement is at variance with the gift economy that had been typical of earlier fan cultures, in which content was produced and shared for free.[25] There has been some disagreement about characterizing this shift solely or primarily as negative; for example, Abigail De Kosnik cautioned against unduly valorizing fans writing without expectations of payment, and thus "institutionalizing a lack of compensation" as an unchanging norm.[26] However, while acknowledging that some fans benefit from being compensated, Suzanne Scott has critiqued the ways that the "convergence culture industry" has produced a "regifting economy" in which a stratum of regulated fan creativity is repackaged and presented back to fans for the benefit of commercial media entities.[27]

A more critical application of the convergence culture framework must also recognize how disparate levels of privilege among fans shape which forms of user engagement are favored by commercial media producers. For example, Suzanne Scott discussed how fan practices are problematically gendered and (de)valued, including differentiations between "affirmational" practices associated with "fan boys" that reaffirm the key elements of the primary text and its universe, versus transformative "fan girl" practices such as producing fan fiction and fan videos that did not circulate in the same economies as official products.[28] And, examining the realm of commercial gaming, Megan Condis argued that although there was indeed significant producer-user interaction, much of it consisted of straight male gamers seeking to maintain the heterocentricity of mainstream games in the face of increasingly common official forays into more diverse character representations.[29] In more recent work, Jenkins has also been more explicit about how intersectional identities inform the extent to which mainstream media serves as a domain for progressive change and activism, acknowledging "that popular culture does not speak for everyone, that not everyone feels comfortable within its imaginary worlds or has access to the means of production and circulation, and that certain toxic elements in popular culture repel many whom social movements might seek to attract."[30]

One significant outcome of Bravo's and Logo's website purchases is how they led to a new cohort of LGBTQ cultural agents who had not previously worked within major commercial media becoming regular staff members and, in a few cases, executives within the network hierarchies. As such, this illustrates a different depth of convergence from what Jenkins, Suzanne Scott, and others have discussed for the possibilities of ordinary users to take on roles as industry producers, which have generally been confined to a few high-profile successes of "big name fans," such as a fan author being invited to contribute a script for a television show.[31] In contrast, at Bravo and Logo, staff who had formerly been network outsiders also attained roles as content gatekeepers, thus reconfiguring some of the power relations that earlier critiques of convergence culture had pointed to as favoring industry players.

Digital Spaces for Queer Expression and Community

Besides their role for content production, digital media has also offered the potential for new forms of expression and community formation, as it made it much cheaper and easier to produce content and to interact across geographical distance. Initial utopian discourses about "cyberspace" and online community soon gave way to more nuanced accounts recognizing limitations such as inequalities of access to digital technology, as the internet was rapidly commercialized. Digital surveillance that tracked user activities, along with the effects of the shift to online media on face-to-face interaction, could work against cultivating safe(r) queer spaces, given that many users might need or assume anonymity, and the historical importance of physical sites for meeting, such as bars.[32] Furthermore, for LGBTQ communities, which had traditionally formed outside of or on the margins of major commercial domains, the conglomerations of LGBTQ digital media preceding Bravo's and Logo's actions already had implications for queer interaction online, both with respect to the shift of queer media from traditional media to digital forms and the commercialization of previously independent queer spaces.

For news and commentary, historically, gay and lesbian print publications in the United States were produced and consumed in geographically based queer communities from which creative, financial, and organizational resources were drawn when mainstream corporations shunned LGBTQ publications. The development of national magazines in the United States—*The Advocate*, *Out*, and *Curve* in the 1980s and 1990s—began a process of the most highly circulated LGBTQ media coming to depend on corporate advertising support, even when these publications were still independently owned.[33] Commercially significant LGBTQ websites began with the multicategory informational site PlanetOut, founded in 1995, which merged in 2000 with Gay.com, at the time a personals ads and chat site, to create what was then the most highly trafficked website aimed at LGBTQ users.[34] Other consolidations followed, with Here Media becoming the parent company of PlanetOut and then purchasing additional websites, including Pride.com, in the mid-2000s, although most of those soon became inactive. Many gay and lesbian newspapers and magazines, like print more generally, suffered from the shift to digital, and as Travers Scott cautioned, the ascendance of new media at a moment when so many LGBTQ print publications and bars—with their more material visibility—had shuttered, risked the rise of "[a] new kind of virtual closet . . . , even if not one actually hidden," since few people who were not looking for LGBTQ websites would come across them.[35]

Still, as this book discusses, Logo's websites in particular served as spaces unique within commercial media for the forms of LGBTQ expression and engagement they facilitated. While sites like PlanetOut catered to dating and hookup activities, a key distinction of Bravo's and Logo's sites, with the exception of the social networking site Downelink, was that they were not established for dating per se but for queer users to interact around shared interests in entertainment fandoms, LGBTQ media, and news, something that had been occurring in various other spaces online but not, until this moment, within major commercial media.

The interactivity that the sites facilitated was, of course, attractive to the network owners; as Ben Aslinger noted, part of Logo's early digital strategy was to "make its content more interactive,"[36] and Bravo was already an industry leader in multiplatform user engagement.[37] Beyond Downelink, several of the websites, which had begun as places where commentary and analysis posts were hosted, underwent "social mediafication," adding features that made them more similar to nascent social networking sites. Most successfully, after their purchase by Logo,

AfterEllen and AfterElton developed what editor in chief Sarah Warn called a "hybrid model," augmenting the message boards and comment threads on site posts with the ability to create user accounts with personal profiles, mailboxes for communicating privately with other users, and other features such as the ability to "like" other users' posts. These changes occurred partly in parallel to the emergence of Facebook (founded in 2005) and Twitter (founded in 2006), as well as other websites such as FanFiction.net or YouTube that were becoming more social mediafied themselves,[38] but those sites were not targeted specifically to LGBTQ users. Bravo's and Logo's websites thus became new online spaces for queer social networking, distinct from both the more hookup-based practices of other sites and the larger mainstream-oriented social network platforms, and available free of charge to users as advertising rather than subscription-supported sites.

Furthermore, in being the properties of content-producing networks, After-Ellen and AfterElton in particular also came to solicit and host numerous web series. Such content was central in reshaping digital spaces for LGBTQ interaction: it drew many more users to the sites than the non-video posts alone had and further augmented user engagement, since they were consuming and commenting on content in the same place. As Aymar Jean Christian has discussed, digital media had been enabling the production of independent web series from the late 2000s onward, offering narratives about marginalized sexual, racial, and class communities that mainstream outlets assumed could not draw a large enough viewership.[39] However, before the widespread use of social media, it was hard to publicize independent queer content. In contrast, sites belonging to Bravo and Logo had online traffic already partly established through preexisting brand recognition for LGBTQ media as well as other marketing efforts. Thus, the websites also served to form new networks of queer content creators and their viewers. It is true that the corporate parent companies profited from the traffic that this content drew, but as Aslinger argued in discussing Logo, visibility for LGBTQ media through commercial channels should not be regarded as either unadulterated success or total exploitation.[40] The successes of the web series were tied to the new cohort of LGBTQ site staff mentioned above, who were now serving as gatekeepers facilitating a burgeoning of independent queer production.

In short, Bravo and Logo being major commercial networks did not preclude noteworthy developments for queer engagement online, though the trajectory of the websites demonstrated the risks of being subject to commercial imperatives. As Trish Bendix, one of AfterEllen's former contributors and editors, noted in a reflection essay,[41] there was a period where Logo's websites flourished alongside several other sites devoted to LGBTQ content, such as Towleroad and Queerty, as well as more general websites that had dedicated columns for LGBTQ news and commentary, including Buzzfeed and The Huffington Post (later rebranded as HuffPost). Yet longevity is contingent on being financially sustainable, and there have been cycles of boom and bust for LGBTQ digital media, including a recent downturn.

LGBTQ Content and the Branding of Television Programming

Bravo's and Logo's establishment and acquisition of digital outlets were central to how LGBTQ media, producers, and users became part of commercial networks, while still comprising spaces of production and interaction separate from the legacy television channels. Yet, as multiplatform strategies became increasingly the norm, network policies that determined television content also ended up reshaping the websites. The characteristics of Bravo's and Logo's linear programming vis-à-vis LGBTQ content and how these related to their websites should be contextualized within changes to the television industry in the past few decades, involving content distribution methods (e.g., broadcast, cable, streaming), regulatory conditions, revenue sources (e.g., advertising, provider subscription fees, and station licensing fees), and the narrative characteristics of television programming.[42] With the shift to the post-network era, cable networks staking out distinct identities sought new forms of content, including LGBTQ narratives and personalities. The rise of reality TV was significant to first Bravo and then Logo in terms of their strategies for drawing viewers, as well as being consonant with the kinds of content that could be produced relatively cheaply for the websites.

In the United States, the post-network era emerged with a transition from having just a few broadcast networks—originally ABC, CBS, and NBC, and later Fox and the CW[43]—to the period after the introduction of cable networks enabled by new transmission technologies in the 1980s. Whereas the longtime strategy of broadcast networks had been scheduling programs that would each ideally draw a broad mass audience, cable channels aimed to carve out subsections of the overall viewership. Some cable networks targeted interest areas, either more generally or more specifically—ESPN's overall sports coverage, for example, compared to the Golf Channel—while others aimed for demographic groups by age, gender, ethnicity, and so forth with a range of program types, such as Oxygen defining itself as "TV for Women," Spike as "The First Network for Men," and BET as the "Black Entertainment Network." Advertisers also shifted away from mass-marketing approaches toward the targeting of consumer segments identified on the basis of increasingly specific demographic categories.[44]

For LGBTQ representation, broadcast networks had begun including gays and lesbians on prime-time shows such as *Friends* and *NYPD Blue*, primarily as secondary or recurring characters, in the 1990s. As Ron Becker argued, this programming, while increasing LGBTQ visibility on mainstream media, was designed to appeal to a straight, affluent, white, and politically liberal viewership drawn to programming that was "hip," including by virtue of its gay content, but the gay characters on these broadcast series tended to be desexualized and serve as narrative fodder for the heterosexual characters.[45] In a similar vein, Bonnie Dow discussed Ellen DeGeneres and her *Ellen* sitcom (ABC, 1995–1998) in which the lead character came out as a lesbian during the fourth season, as "foregrounding . . . the personal" alongside a "concomitant repression of the political," with the show presenting Ellen's lesbian identity without addressing structural conditions of homophobia and intersecting inequalities.[46] From a different angle, Lynne Joyrich analyzed Ellen's coming out as part of a more general phenomenon of the closet functioning as "an implicit TV form—a logic governing not only the ways in which gays and lesbians are represented but also the generation of narratives and positions on and for TV even in the absence of openly gay characters (or gay characters at all)";[47] thus, such mainstream programming did not in fact signify television moving "beyond" the closet.

More changes occurred when subscriber-supported ("premium") cable channels, led by HBO beginning in the early 1990s, sought to brand themselves with programming that viewers could not find elsewhere on television, including greater sexual explicitness and more representations of minority groups. For the first time, shows with multiple LGBTQ lead characters aired on U.S. television, including *Queer as Folk* (Showtime, 2000–2005) and *The L Word* (Showtime, 2004–2009). They exemplified improved queer representation along several dimensions, including increases in the number of LGBTQ characters and more nuanced depictions that avoided both old tropes of associating queerness with criminality, sickness, and tragedy and the "safe" narratives of coming out and homophobia faced by faultless gay characters, as noted by Larry Gross and others.[48]

Advertiser-supported ("basic") cable television took longer to follow suit in terms of distinctive scripted programming. Initially, original series on these cable channels were more cheaply produced imitations of broadcast network shows. After FX's police drama *The Shield* (2002–2008) broke through in gaining critical recognition (including notice for one main character being a closeted gay police officer), it was followed by higher profile shows such as AMC's *Mad Men* (2007–2015) and *The Walking Dead* (2010–), ushering in an era dubbed "peak TV" in which multiple cable networks sought critically acclaimed programming on which to build their brands.[49] However, for Bravo's and Logo's LGBTQ content, another key trend in television during the same period, the rise of reality television, was even more important.

Distinguished from scripted programming in having people "being themselves" rather than explicitly acting out the role of a character,[50] early examples of reality series existed in the 1970s, but it was the late 1980s onward that saw the genre expand significantly, both with candid reality shows that typically showed several people living and/or interacting with each other regularly (e.g., MTV's *The Real World* series or *Big Brother* on CBS [2000–]), and with competitive reality shows, spurred by the enormous ratings for CBS's *Survivor* (2000–) and *The Amazing Race* (2001–).[51] Although lacking the prestige of well-reviewed scripted series and not as well suited for syndication, reality shows have been both cheaper to produce and able to draw the coveted 18–49-year-old viewer demographic. Successful reality shows could "generate as much or more buzz than" scripted series, and shows like the singing competition show *American*

Idol (Fox, 2002–2016) built in multiplatform viewer engagement through systems to vote for favorite contestants, cultivating the kind of intensely engaged viewer that was particularly attractive to advertisers.[52]

Both Bravo and Logo had signature programming in the 2000s that demonstrated both the use of LGBTQ content and the ascendance of reality shows: Bravo's makeover show *Queer Eye for the Straight Guy* (later just called *Queer Eye*) and the drag competition series *RuPaul's Drag Race* on Logo. These were not the networks' first or only shows with LGBTQ principals, but they became central to the ways that Bravo and Logo steered away from a broader range of queer representation, a change especially striking for Logo, which had launched as a network showcasing more LGBTQ diversity than had ever been available on commercial television. How branding and rebranding played out on Bravo's and Logo's channels thus demonstrated mixed outcomes: an earlier, promising measure of more diverse representation was not ultimately sustained.

Such developments pertain to long-standing questions in queer television studies of how queerly distinct LGBTQ media and cultural agents could remain as they were incorporated into the most "mass" of mass media. As Joyrich has pointed out, television is a deeply mainstream medium that "tends to reflect, refract, and produce dominant ideologies," while queer approaches to culture and politics "are committed to challenging and troubling ideological norms."[53] Simply having LGBTQ representations on television shows—even sustained, nuanced ones—does not necessarily mitigate mainstream ideologies around integration and progress that may also obscure how sexuality intersects with other axes of inequality, such as class and race.[54] Yet the mass media status of television also endows its programming with the potential to contribute to changing mainstream attitudes, including in progressive ways with respect to gender and sexuality. Discussing how gay and lesbian consumers have been targeted by commercial media, Hollis Griffin noted that "the processes of commerce always court minorities as citizens *and* consumers," and thus even problematic instances of mainstream content "have value functions that are related to and different from their economic functions."[55]

A New Cultural Field of Media Production

The developments at Bravo and Logo discussed in this book illustrate shifts involving LGBTQ cultural agents and content moving from more marginal to more mainstream spaces and digital media facilitating processes of production and reaching viewers. Existing research on media production, particularly by Bourdieu and in production studies scholarship, provides important theoretical underpinnings for contextualizing the significance of these changes, but require elaboration and revision to account for the expansions of LGBTQ media into the commercial sphere and the inclusions of a range of content distribution modes, including broadcast, cable, and digital media.

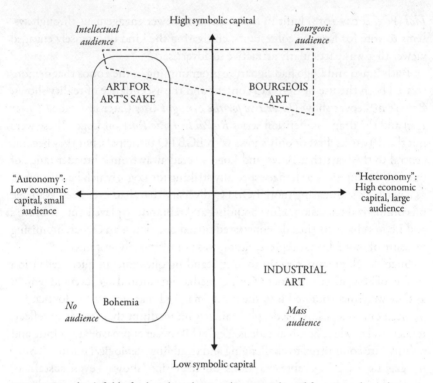

FIGURE 2 Bourdieu's field of cultural production. (Source: Adapted from Bourdieu's diagram, Pierre Bourdieu, *The Field of Cultural Production: Essays on Art and Literature*, trans. R. Johnson (New York: Columbia University Press, 1993), 49.)

Bourdieu proposed a model for the field of cultural production to account for the structure and relationships within domains for producing art, music, media, and similar cultural items.[56] Different forms of capital help structure the cultural field, including economic capital (money and other financial resources), cultural capital in the sense of cultural knowledge, transmitted through upbringing and social institutions, that confer status,[57] and symbolic capital, referring to prestige or recognition (e.g., industry awards). The field itself is social space structured by the positions of cultural agents within it who possess varying amounts of capital. In accounting for differences across the field, Bourdieu distinguished two contrasting subfields: the subfield of small-scale or restricted production, structured by low economic capital and high symbolic capital, and the field of large-scale production, characterized by high economic capital and low symbolic capital. Thus, in figure 2, diagramming the French art world in the nineteenth century, the top-left quadrant represents art with the highest prestige, "art for art's sake" with just a small, "intellectual" audience, while the bottom-right quadrant, "industrial art," maps the space of work supported by substantial resources and enjoying a "mass" audience but garnering little elite cultural recognition—part of what could also be called popular culture. In the top-right quadrant, "bourgeois art" equates more or less with the middlebrow—art that is accorded some prestige and is not as mass produced as industrial art but not the sanctified "real" art of the top-left quadrant. "Bohemia," the bottom-left quadrant, has low economic capital, a small audience, and low symbolic capital—art made with few resources garnering little viewership or cultural recognition.

With his focus on older European forms of art and music and predating the ascendance of digital media, Bourdieu said little about mass media and did not account for its complexities. For one thing, the social stratification that he described as associated with cultural consumption often does not apply to television and film texts; many of these are being watched across the class spectrum.[58] In a related vein, the elements of large-scale and restricted production as Bourdieu defined them had become increasingly mixed in the late twentieth century, with many highly popular, expensively produced media also enjoying high symbolic capital—that is, critical acclaim is not simply accorded to indie-budgeted content attracting only small audiences.[59]

Still, Bourdieu's account remains valuable for its attention to how power differentially positions cultural agents and representing media production and texts as constructing a relational space, one where cultural agents and the work they produce constitute the field. His interest in producers also manifested in the concept of "habitus," or professional disposition. Although professional disposition is relatively stable, it is disruptable to some extent and continues its formation as an individual moves through a social trajectory.[60] In other words, cultural agents entering particular contexts of production bring to their work the professional dispositions they have formed up to that point, but in turn, the experiences of working within such contexts continue to shape their professional dispositions.

With a new cohort of LGBTQ workers becoming part of Bravo and Logo, a revised version of Bourdieu's model presented in this book provides a framework for capturing the complex changes to the cultural field, one that recognizes both long-standing inequalities of capital and power and the possibilities for new cultural agents to reshape as well as be shaped by the contexts of their work. Such a framework expands on scholarship about convergence culture, which, as noted earlier, addresses the ways that traditional boundaries have been breached in contemporary media, but my account more explicitly identifies the relational dimensions among cultural agents and the media they produce.

In theorizing the practices of Bravo's and Logo's producers, this book is also situated within media-focused production studies scholarship, which built on earlier accounts of Hollywood in the 1940s and 1950s[61] to examine other popular genres in print, radio, and television,[62] as well as documentary, news, art, and classical music.[63] Indebted as well to Bourdieu's concept of habitus, ethnographic research on media industry workers by Vicki Mayer, John Caldwell, and their colleagues address "how media producers make culture, and, in the process, make themselves into particular kinds of workers in modern, mediated societies."[64] Previous accounts of how cultural workers frame what they do (to both other industry workers and outsiders) and therein form their identities underscore the significance of what producers say about their work, and this book considers interview data through such an analytical lens.

Although acknowledging the importance of producers' social identities, much production studies scholarship does not examine sexuality and queerness in any detail. Alfred Martin has argued for a distinct queer production studies approach that includes examination of "the ways queers produce their own media both within and outside the 'mainstream' culture industries."[65] Earlier research in this vein revealed how the gay and lesbian identities of cultural producers informed their work when LGBTQ media was first being mainstreamed to a significant degree. With race (mostly white) and class (middle and upper-middle) identities intersecting with sexuality, key gatekeepers tended to hew to dominant norms around media representation and consumer culture. For example, as Katherine Sender discussed, media and marketing professionals shaped U.S. gay and lesbian publications when they evolved into a commercially viable market in the 1990s and 2000s.[66] While more radical queer activism had earlier asserted the importance of non-normative sexual expression and critiquing structural inequalities, staff at the then-newly national magazines such as *Out* downplayed or removed sexual content that might offend mainstream sensibilities, instead inviting readers to associate their gay/lesbian identities with forms of consumption that did not overtly reject dominant social and economic systems. The advocacy group GLAAD illustrated similar dynamics, as Vincent Doyle detailed: with the organization becoming increasingly staffed by those who worked within or alongside mainstream media, it successfully attracted corporate sponsorship that enabled it to rise to greater prominence but also moved away from the grassroots queer politics that had characterized GLAAD at its inception.[67]

At the same time, LGBTQ cultural agents in the mainstream can still challenge norms around sexual identity. This may happen through what Julia Himberg described as "under-the-radar" practices by industry professionals in U.S. contexts, such as behind-the-scenes work to help celebrities come out or executives quietly realizing their companies' diversity initiatives in politically significant ways.[68] In research on Irish media, Páraic Kerrigan and Anne O'Brien found that although a worker's queer identity was sometimes an impediment to their professional goals, it could also contribute to them getting and keeping jobs in the industry as well as contributing to successful activism for including more gays and lesbians in production work.[69] Thus, the industrial integration of LGBTQ workers does not simply involve the loss of meaningful queer agency but can also lead to changes to the conditions of production. Bravo and Logo, as this book details, demonstrated both the possibilities and limits of such changes.

Research Approaches

Because of the scope of this study, I made use of multiple research approaches that included both in-person methods such as interviews and visits to relevant events, and the examination of texts by or about Bravo and Logo. Each of the upcoming chapters integrates some mix of these forms of data alongside discussion of pertinent prior scholarship and the presentation of my analysis, in order to provide descriptive richness and theoretical grounding for the account.

The largest amount of data, and the most significant, derived from my interviews—the majority in person but also by phone and email—with people involved at various levels with Bravo and Logo, including executives and other staff working in multiplatform content, original programming, marketing, digital media, and operations, and editors, directors, and contributors of Bravo's and Logo's websites, as well as a few staff at other media companies and several independent queer artists.[70] Gaining access to network executives was the most challenging, but once one Logo executive responded to me, I was referred to his colleagues, which created a snowball sampling effect. I also attended industry events, including LGBTQ film festivals supported by Logo, industry conferences,[71] and a set visit for the Logo reality show *The A List: New York*, which gave me further opportunities to speak to cultural workers and to observe how industry professionals discussed key terms, including digital media, convergence, and LGBTQ content. In addition, I examined Bravo's and Logo's websites for their video content and forms of user interaction. Primary documents from Logo and Bravo were another important source; the ones from Logo were internal and made available to me by a senior executive there, while those from Bravo were publicly available, though targeted at industry insiders. Various secondary sources, including academic, trade, and newspaper articles about Bravo and Logo and published interviews with Bravo and Logo staff, were also relevant.

Although this book focuses on production and producers at Bravo and Logo, the genesis of my project lies in my investments as an entertainment fan who initially encountered two of the main websites as a user: Television Without Pity and AfterEllen. At the time of Bravo's and Logo's purchases, then, I felt the familiarity of an insider who discovered both these sites when they were still relatively unknown. The significance of media scholars having roles as both academics and fans or users of the same media has been discussed as part of the broader debate about conducting research as an "insider" versus an "outsider." Against positivist assumptions that researchers should maintain "objectivity," Jenkins argued that being a fan of the same media as his subjects provided him with a productive perspective for investigating fan texts and practices, coining the term *aca/fan* to describe himself and similarly positioned scholars,[72] and other researchers have agreed that the two roles can be fruitfully combined.[73] My own insider-outsider status shifted to some degree depending on who I was interviewing. With website editors and contributors, my history as an enthusiastic and longtime site user partially aligned me with them through our shared interests in the popular media they were writing about. However, otherwise, as a long-time academic with essentially no media production or corporate work experience, my unfamiliarity with such arenas distinguished me from most of the cultural workers I communicated with, particularly those working at the networks, as well as the independent artists I spoke to.

Research in the social sciences, particularly anthropology and sociology, has traditionally focused on groups who are more disempowered than the scholars studying them, leading to an exhortation by Laura Nader to "study up" instead in order to uncover how institutional and other structural power works.[74] To some extent, my research topic encompassing two major media networks, with their substantial financial resources and the proprietary cause and authority to deny me access to their physical spaces, had the characteristics of these circumstances. However, Sherry Ortner has suggested that it may be useful to conceptualize ethnographic research on the media industries as "studying sideways," given that "people who work on the creative side of the film industry are in many ways not that different from . . . highly educated academics, journalists, critics, and the like,"[75] although differences in economic and cultural capital may become apparent in particular contexts. Even though I was unable to access the creative spaces of the networks and a few highly positioned executives did not respond to me at all, my interviews with some network staff and most of the site editors and senior contributors often better fit the frame of studying sideways rather than up. Several interviewees had been to or completed graduate school. More importantly, in having shared investments in media analysis and LGBTQ community interests, my conversations with website workers frequently felt like ones between cultural agents who were equals, though we had our distinct professional qualifications and experiences. Such similarities tended to override other dimensions along which I was mostly different from my interviewees, particularly my nationality, race, and ethnicity (Australian, Asian, Chinese).[76]

Since I was studying LGBTQ media where numerous interviewees identified as lesbian, gay, or bisexual, another axis of possible identification was sexuality. Although I did not explicitly identify my sexuality in my initial emails or letters, in face-to-face interviews I was probably read (correctly) as lesbian, and in conversations with many interviewees, it was a commonality often assumed by both of us (though only occasionally referred to explicitly). I suspect this worked in my favor in terms of comfort and rapport during the interview and getting subsequent referrals to interviewees' colleagues. Similarly, Sender noted that the gay marketers she interviewed appeared to believe that they belonged together with her to "a gay collectivity," which probably also contributed positively to the interviewees' willingness to help, even though she did not necessarily share the political or philosophical positions that the interviewees held.[77]

Still, even when good rapport contributed to interviewees answering my questions readily, I did not assume that their responses were unedited. Network executives in particular are careful about how they represent their organizations, and the tone of their responses to me was notably upbeat. Website editors and freelance contributors more often voiced neutral or negative assessments about the circumstances of their work, while my interviews with independent artists not affiliated with major media organizations yielded the harshest assessments of commercial media. However, a queer filmmaker, for example, may be eager to stake their identity as an artist committed to quality over commerce and respond accordingly to a question about Bravo's or Logo's roles in LGBTQ representation. Thus, I was careful to interpret my data cognizant of each interviewee having their own investments that would inform their self-presentations.

Upcoming Chapters

The chapters ahead examine key developments for LGBTQ media at Bravo and Logo with respect to content and content producers, digital spaces for user engagement, and overall network programming strategies. Drawing from and expanding on theories of convergence culture, media production, queer media, digital culture, and the post-network television landscape, the analysis explains what was distinctive about the changes that took place, how they occurred within broader shifts in the status of LGBTQ expression and visibility in the United States, and their enduring impact for contemporary media use and production.

Chapter 1, "New Convergences in LGBTQ Media Production: Digital Pathways into Commercial Media," traces how the convergences of legacy and digital, and queer and mainstream media shaped the trajectories of Bravo's and Logo's website staffing. Initially, site originators found additional contributors from informal networks of shared fandoms, work on independent queer publications, and activist circles. The fact that several rose to gatekeeper positions, such as site editors and network executives, illustrated the possibilities of convergence to bring outsiders into commercial media production beyond just a single individual here and there. However, staffing of the sites was increasingly professionalized post purchase, so that positions were filled by people who were already working in the industry. Convergence, then, resulted in substantial changes in facilitating unprecedented pathways into commercial domains for queer cultural agents, even though these pathways were later curtailed.

Chapter 2, "The New Queer Digital Spaces," discusses the expression and interaction that Bravo's and Logo's websites facilitated, with the social mediafication of the sites' infrastructures cultivating practices of queer sociality that were precursors in both form and function to social networking platforms and mobile apps. Furthermore, the sites, particularly AfterEllen, also became important for the production of LGBTQ video for several years, before YouTube and other video-hosting services were as readily available and when almost all other sites offering original queer video content were by subscription. Thus, Bravo's and Logo's websites offered free-to-use spaces for queer engagement, more well known than alternative sites at the time and more centralized in contrast to the much more numerous and dispersed spaces in contemporary media. However, their trajectories—of establishment, growth, acquisition, expansion, and then decline—also underscore the precarity inherent when LGBTQ community forms in commercial spaces that may shutter due to financial considerations.

Chapter 3, "Dualcasting, Gaystreaming, and Changing Queer Alignments," discusses programming directions termed "dualcasting" by Sender for Bravo and "gaystreaming" by Logo executives for their network, aimed at attracting specific configurations of heterosexual and LGBTQ viewers. These strategies emerged due to a confluence of several factors, including industrial conditions favorable to producing reality series, the attitudes of networks' decision makers about sex and sexuality in media content, and a certain level of gay and lesbian integration into mainstream culture. The trend toward a narrower range of LGBTQ material on the channels was initially counterbalanced with greater content heterogeneity at the websites, but overall, network discourses accompanying the programming changes drew on "post-gay" discourses about acceptance and evolution, obscuring the intersections of gender, class, race, and nation with sexuality. Later on, the distinctiveness of Bravo's and Logo's programming diminished as similar shows became available elsewhere on cable and LGBTQ narratives appeared on an increasing number of scripted series as well. Some efforts in the last few years by other U.S. cable networks to capture a "diverse" audience segment have also faltered, while streaming services have continued to make inroads in attracting viewers seeking LGBTQ content, including Netflix's rebooting of what had been Bravo's signature show, *Queer Eye*.

Chapter 4, "Beyond Queer Niche: Remaking the Mainstream," begins by examining how executives, staff, and content contributors at Bravo and Logo framed their work of producing LGBTQ media within commercial contexts. Narratives of working to serve the LGBTQ community and of being "small" downplayed the corporate character of the networks and their websites. However, these discourses also revealed complex engagements across the mainstream-independent spectrum, which involved both the networks profiting from the economic and creative contributions of queer producers, as well as independent artists deriving the benefits of exposure that the networks could provide. The fact that LGBTQ content did not remain prominent in Bravo's and Logo's programming beyond a few years, however, was due to ensuing, broader shifts within mainstream U.S. media—spurred in part by Bravo and Logo themselves—namely, increases in both reality and scripted series with LGBTQ characters and narratives, which Logo especially was then unable to successfully compete with. The changes wrought by the trajectories of Bravo's and Logo's digital and linear programming are represented by a model of the cultural field significantly reworked from that of Bourdieu. This model captures the relational character among different forms of media production and texts and is able to account for the expansions of LGBTQ content into commercial media via a range of content distribution modes, including broadcast, cable, and digital platforms, that now comprise the "mainstream."

For the book as a whole, two general points stand out. First, the larger significance of the analysis arises from the fact that the media domain is also part of the culture at large, and thus, the discussion of "mainstreaming gays" in this book demonstrates how technological, economic, and sociopolitical factors are intertwined. For example, the use of LGBTQ content by cable networks to carve out brand distinction reflected conditions of the post-network era for television, and digital technologies for media production and circulation have become much more important in the last two decades, but Bravo's and Logo's use of LGBTQ-focused content also reflected and comprised changes in the social status of LGBTQ people in the United States. The incorporation of LGBTQ producers into commercial spaces as creators of LGBTQ content was the result of financially motivated strategies of specific media corporations, but a more general contributing factor was the broader mainstreaming of entertainment fan cultures. Second, the various developments that constituted "mainstreaming gays" tell a story about neither simple commercial co-optation of subcultural energies nor one of unproblematic integration and linear progress. Rather, the set of gains, losses, and mixed outcomes in terms of queer expression and agency presented here deconstructs monolithic notions of the "mainstream"[78] and unpacks the more complex dynamics of contemporary media cultures.

1

New Convergences in
LGBTQ Media Production

● ●

Digital Pathways into
Commercial Media

Digital Media and Remaking the Field
of LGBTQ Cultural Production

With the rapid spread of internet access in the 1990s, an increasing number of
online spaces emerged for engaging with popular media, including for viewers
invested in LGBTQ representation, like me. Due to our shared enthusiasm for
The X-Files (Fox, 1993–2002), a friend had introduced me to Television Without Pity (TWoP), where I enjoyed the detailed episode recaps as well as the queer-
friendly discussion forums for that show and a number of others, including
Buffy the Vampire Slayer (WB/UPN, 1997–2003). From the message boards, I
followed someone's link to an article on *Buffy* at AfterEllen, when this website
was still an independently run blog covering popular television and film with
appeal to lesbian and bisexual women,[1] and I soon became a regular visitor.
After TWoP and AfterEllen were acquired by the Bravo and Logo networks,
respectively, within a year of each other, my interest in the sites became not just
that of a user but also a media scholar. The scope of my study then broadened
out from the websites to include the networks that had purchased them, as I
realized that distinctive convergences were happening that involved digital and
legacy media, fan cultures, and LGBTQ content.

Because this book traces multiple developments at Bravo and Logo, anywhere I choose to begin is already amid intersecting stories: about the networks, their content, and the people involved. I start, in this chapter, with the websites and their staffing because they offer particularly clear illustrations of the promises of convergence culture in shaking up the cultural field. My conversations with cultural producers associated with Bravo's and Logo's programming across platforms reveal the ways that digital media provided significant new pathways for LGBTQ fans, bloggers, and independent producers to convert their labor and expertise into economic capital.[2] As it turned out, these developments were occurring just before legacy television was about to be challenged by streaming services, which would then in turn stake out their own spaces in part through prominent inclusions of queer characters and narratives. This media and its evolution will be examined in more detail in upcoming chapters. Here, the focus is on the cultural workers themselves.

Crucially, it was not simply that site users or contributors provided content for Bravo and Logo, but that some of them, via the websites, became regular staff members and executives within the network hierarchy. How did personal and professional networks bring the various editors, writers, and bloggers in as contributors to Bravo's and Logo's websites? Once there, what impact did they have on the networks, and conversely, what effects did the increasing professionalization of the websites have on who became the main content creators and gatekeepers at these sites? Convergence culture, as first proposed by Henry Jenkins, provides a framework to address these questions, since it theorizes how ordinary media users gained a greater degree of access to commercial producers and production.[3] Conversely, discussing the staffing of Bravo's and Logo's websites also provides vital data to consider elaborations and critiques of convergence culture, and how a convergence account can be productively woven in with theories of professionalization from the other major framework on media production from which this book draws, Pierre Bourdieu's field of cultural production.[4]

As the introduction chapter noted, intersectional disempowerments have often sidelined traditionally marginalized groups even as their white and/or male counterparts gain access through convergence. For example, Suzanne Scott detailed how the media industry's embrace of fans has been conditional, characterized by persistent gendered biases disadvantageous to fan practices and creative work most commonly associated with women, and valorizing identities like the "fanboy auteur" for men, while "fangirl" retains a set of negative connotations. She also identified concerns that fans who end up "functioning as gatekeepers" or "acting as intermediaries for other fans" may introduce unwelcome social hierarchies among fan communities in "moving from 'amateur' to 'professional' status," with their erstwhile "fannish peers" becoming "followers."[5] At the same time, she noted that the character of "a media landscape that has moved increasingly toward catering to niche demographics" has made the role of the "grassroots fantrepreneur"—a fan with no prior media industry connections who comments on or curates media content—a "hybrid fannish identity" more available to "female fans, queer fans, and fans of color" than the auteur position.[6] Although most of the cultural agents who became staff at Bravo's and Logo's websites were not entrepreneurs proper (a role best assigned to the site founders), many of them were women and/or LGBTQ identified, with a few also being people of color. This did not in itself, however, guarantee that the website content would accord with feminist or queer political perspectives.

The mapping between social identities and the kind of content produced is of course a complex one. Thus, examining how things played out at Bravo and Logo provides a significant case study on the outcome of having LGBTQ-identified staff in gatekeeper roles. As discussed in the introduction chapter, a key component of Bourdieu's account of cultural production is the habitus, or professional disposition, of producers. Central to the shaping of such dispositions are the professional contexts in which cultural agents work; in turn, their professional dispositions help shape the character of their work, which in this case, includes the media content they produce or facilitate the production of.

Katherine Sender identified an earlier cohort of gay and lesbian professionals who emerged as the commercialized gay and lesbian print market in the United States was being created in the 1990s. Gay marketers played a "pivotal role in shaping gay consumer culture" and "circulat[ing] ideas about gayness in the national imagination" alongside writers, editors, and advertisers.[7] The professional disposition of these cultural agents vis-à-vis LGBTQ content was crucially informed by their need to "construct their identities not only as members of the professional-managerial class but as openly GLBT-identified members of that class."[8] The classed dimensions of this endeavor both shaped and were reflected in the tenor of the then-newly national gay and lesbian magazines, such as *The Advocate*, *Curve*, and *Out*, which sought to distance themselves from earlier gay publications with respect to sex and sexuality. Shunning text and images of queer sexuality considered to be "sleazy," such as sex ads, in favor of "tasteful" content meant producing "a desexualized, class-respectable venue for national advertisers and, in turn, offered mainstream culture more broadly an image of a sexually discreet group of gay and lesbian readers and consumers."[9] At Bravo and Logo, as this chapter will discuss, the picture was more complex. Although some of the new LGBTQ website workers had similar professional dispositions to the gay marketers Sender discussed, there were also important differences: not all of the contributors felt obliged to embrace more safely mainstream representations of LGBTQ people nor to accept the legitimacy of academic feminism, particularly its positions critical of sexual objectification. Thus, while LGBTQ identity was entwined with class and cultural capital, as Sender had found, the specific valences and therefore outcomes for content were more mixed.

With respect to longer-term outcomes, the new digital pathways into mainstream media did not end up lasting at Bravo and Logo, as the increasing commercialization and professionalization of the websites ultimately closed off more informal or fan-based routes into the networks. For those who made it in, many moved into the general media industry or the corporate world more broadly, while some have remained active in producing LGBTQ media. Collectively, the professional trajectories for the contributors at Bravo's and Logo's LGBTQ and LGBTQ-friendly websites illustrated how convergence facilitated unprecedented pathways into commercial domains for some queer cultural agents, but these pathways were later curtailed.

Overview of the Sites

The two networks' development strategies in the mid-2000s, when Bravo had recently rebranded itself from a high-culture arts network to a pop culture one and Logo had just been established, were similar in their multipronged efforts to expand into digital spaces. Initially, before social media and mobile platforms became as dominant, online presence via websites was one obvious strategy, and at the height of this proliferation, Bravo had five sites with distinct URLs and Logo had nine. This book focuses on the LGBTQ-centric sites, but it is useful to see how they were situated alongside their network's digital properties overall, especially since some sites lasted only briefly while others persisted for years.

Bravo's Websites

Bravo's websites were a mix of network-originated sites, sites that derived from other properties of Bravo's parent company NBC Universal, and sites acquired by Bravo. First, besides the expected information about shows and schedules, the network site BravoTV.com had content designed to engage viewers more immersively or interactively, including blogs by Bravo personalities, message boards, show-related quizzes and games, and downloads for mobile devices. It also hosted a limited number of full episodes of Bravo shows. Since many of Bravo's show stars or contestants were gay or lesbian, some of this content was incidentally LGBTQ-friendly even when there was no specific queer narrative involved.

Three other websites came about due to the fact that NBC Universal became the owner of the Trio network in 2004, a couple of years after acquiring Bravo.[10] Administratively, the channels became closely associated when Lauren Zalaznick, president of Trio, was given the nod to also head up Bravo, and she infused Trio's "pop, culture, TV" spirit into Bravo as Bravo was rebranded, undergoing reconfigurations also aimed at encouraging consumers to engage beyond simply viewing channel content. When DirecTV stopped carrying Trio in early 2005, NBC Universal shifted some of Trio's programming to stream online at a dedicated site,[11] something that was discontinued at the end of 2008. "OutZone" was originally a Trio channel programming block, which included both new series and reruns with gay-friendly content, and OutZoneTV.com was launched as one of Bravo's websites in June 2006, with a mix of video and text content. Another one of Trio's original programs, "Brilliant But Canceled," dedicated to canceled television series that were critical and cult favorites, briefly had its own website to stream such shows but was then morphed into a link off Bravo's Television Without Pity (TWoP), which Bravo had acquired in 2007, a link that contained only text reviews and commentary.

TWoP had a couple of earlier incarnations, starting off in September 1998 as a site recapping only the teen drama *Dawson's Creek* (WB, 1998–2003), then a year later expanding its scope to fourteen shows, many also youth-oriented dramas, of particular interest to the site founders, Tara Ariano, Sarah Bunting, and David Cole.[12] The site became known as "Television Without Pity" in 2002 and was covering about thirty shows just before Bravo's acquisition. At that time, it was a largely text-based site with two major sections: (1) the lengthy (4,000–6,000 word) episode recaps and (2) an extensive message board, including full forums with multiple threads for recapped shows and single discussion threads for shows not being recapped. Ariano, Bunting, and Cole maintained a highly visible presence on the site, particularly through moderating and posting at the message boards.[13] Thus, TWoP was a prominent example of what extensive engagement around popular media texts looked like in a pre–social media era.

Like the Bravo network, TWoP was never focused exclusively on LGBTQ content, but its gay-friendly sensibility fit well into a larger context of Bravo's post-2003 rebranding. More specifically, it stood out from other fan entertainment sites at the time in routinely offering queer readings of textually straight characters, both by TWoP writers in their episode recaps and by posters at the message boards on which the term *HoYay* was coined from a truncated blend of "Homoeroticism? Yay!" For the subforums of some shows, entire threads were dedicated to HoYay discussion (sometimes alongside "HetYay" threads), usually characterized by a playful tone.[14]

After Bravo's purchase, TWoP's HoYay content lessened somewhat, partly because a larger number of shows without strong fan followings for queer readings were recapped, partly because moderation of the discussion boards became more stringent, resulting, for example, in the deletion of disagreements about how obvious or intentional homoerotic subtext on a show was.[15] Still, Jacob Clifton, TWoP's longtime and most popular recapper, commented three years after Bravo's acquisition that "TWoP harbors queer and queer-friendly audiences and readings." Yet Clifton, who identified himself as "super-gay," also criticized how gay male sexualities had become entertainment fodder for straight women, and he was therefore ambivalent about the queer sensibilities of TWoP. Indeed, some queer content was inserted primarily for humor by straight recappers. For example, Jeff Alexander (TWoP pseudonym M. Giant) acknowledged that he included HoYay commentary here and there in his recaps of Fox's action adventure series *24* because it was part of the stylistic repertoire of TWoP. Noting that he would "make fun of a couple of characters; you know, they'll have an argument, and I'll just say, 'Oh, just kiss already,'" Alexander gave the example of his recap of a season 8 episode (in which he calls Jack Bauer's character by actor Kiefer Sutherland's first name), where he wrote:

> They [Jack Bauer and another male character, Cole, played by Freddie Prinze Jr.] head across the street and into the alley at 8:08:23.... They break into a jog as soon as they're clear of the street, and **look nothing at all like a couple of dudes sneaking into an alley for a tryst**.
>
> . . .
>
> Cole stuffs [a female character] in the car.... Then he stomps over to Kiefer, yelling, "I can't do this!" and shoving Kiefer to the ground. Whoa! Nobody pushes Kiefer around. Maybe that's why when Kiefer sits up, he's got his gun leveled at Cole. They pant furiously at each other until Kiefer lowers the weapon, saying, "She's just trying to get inside your head." ... Furiously flexing every muscle in his entire head, Cole finally spits, "Yeah, okay." ... **There's going to be so much hate sex later, and I don't even know who's going to be having it.**
> —M. Giant, *24* S08E20 episode recap; highlighting mine

While snide content like this could function at some level as pointed commentary on the canonical heteronormativity of a largely homosocial genre, this was not Alexander's goal. Therefore, even as TWoP provided some distinctively queer-friendly space online centered on entertainment, most of its user base consisted of straight women. Although this aligned the site with what Bravo internally termed its "Will and Grace" strategy—programming content targeted to gay men and straight women, which chapter 3 will examine in more detail—it also meant that many queer viewers might be in search of content more explicitly targeted to them. Initially, OutZoneTV looked like it would fit the bill.

Network plans for OutZoneTV were quite ambitious, with Bravo's press release on the site's launch in June 2006 promising a dizzying array of subjects and genres:

> OutZoneTV.com is the first online broadband destination for entertaining, thought-provoking content about and for the LGBT audience. The site will feature a wide array of exclusive, seriously fun long and short-form video. Subjects will range from eye-opening historical examples of queer images in media to contemporary explorations of LGBT subjects, to content that is not overtly LGBT, but appeals to the audience. Genres will range from vintage films and television to contemporary documentaries and viral short subjects. The site will be updated daily with a wealth of blogs, features, news, photos, community and user-generated content.

The site did start off with some streaming video, though rather than current series, it was of programming that had previously aired on Bravo, including the reality series *Gay Weddings*; *Cooking's a Drag*, a short-lived cross-dressing food show; and the one-season reality series *Manhunt: The Search for America's Most Gorgeous Male Model*. There was some web-only content associated with the Bravo shows *Queer Eye*, *Kathy Griffin: My Life on the D-List*, and *Watch What Happens Live*, as well as a small selection of gay-themed movies and documentary series such as *My Husband Is Gay*, acquired from the United Kingdom. There were also occasional one-off collaborations, for example, with the Human Rights Campaign for the 2007 National Coming Out Day, when the site featured videos of Bravo's reality series stars.[16]

Some textual material was contributed by LGBTQ participants on Bravo's reality shows, such as blog posts by Daniel Vosovic from *Project Runway* and Josie Smith-Malave from *Top Chef*. However, the main producer for the site was Zac Hug, hired by Bravo as a senior writer, along with Dennis Hensley.[17] Hug was instrumental in curating third-party content, such as AP newswire stories presented "with an OUTzone spin," a fun Photo of the Day selected by site staff, and a "Gay of the Day" photo and information submitted by users. Site users could also engage at a community section with regular polls and a message board.

Hug recounted Bravo executives being enthusiastic supporters of the site for its importance to the LGBTQ community despite the fact that it was never particularly profitable. The network certainly provided the site with publicity; besides the initial press release, OutZoneTV was regularly mentioned in Bravo's *Affluencer* literature aimed at advertisers and it also benefited from on-air promotion. Still, OutZoneTV's early aspirations to include both entertainment and news content eventually fell by the wayside; as the site became less and less active, several of its offerings did not sustain their planned daily pace, and the community message board often did not have new posts for multiple days. OutZoneTV also experimented briefly with broadening its scope beyond popular media, with Hug recalling a moment when they considered getting college students to blog for the site, before determining that that "was weird and it didn't really work."[18]

OutZoneTV's lack of video content from currently airing shows distinguished it from rival network Logo's LogoONLINE (now LogoTV) site, which streamed full episodes of its channel programming. In addition, OutZoneTV was criticized by some other queer pop culture sites for the original video that it did have; for example, Queerty mocked Bravo's deal with William Sledd to stream his "Ask a Gay Man" webisodes, which had been enjoying some success on YouTube, as well as arguing that Sledd's failure to bring his YouTube audience over to OutZoneTV was partially attributable to the latter site being "yuck, corporate."[19] Thus, at least part of the intended audience for OutZoneTV was both unimpressed with the site's content and disdainful of its affiliation with Bravo.

Bravo's core audience included heterosexual women, so in theory, OutZoneTV might have targeted viewers particularly interested in LGBTQ stories and representations, with BravoTV casting a broader net via its focus on food, fashion, and style. However, once OutZoneTV's purpose was streamlined as essentially profiling the gay and lesbian contestants of Bravo's shows, its rationale for existing separately from BravoTV was weakened, as it also struggled to carve out a space distinct from other sites aimed at gay men. As Hug put it, "It wasn't that it was hard to keep it going. It was just . . . hard to figure out how to drive people to it. The joke that I always had was 'Why does Bravo have a gay site? Bravo *is* a gay site!'"

Logo's Websites

Logo launched as a cable channel one or two tiers above the most common package,[20] initially reaching only 17 million U.S. households in 2005, and although it was viewable in 46 million U.S. homes by 2010,[21] the inaccessibility of Logo the channel to a majority of the American television audience was a key consideration for the network's online strategy. At a time when the official websites of television networks mostly existed to advertise the channel,[22] Logo's main site, LogoONLINE, was intended to deliver a sizable amount of channel content from its inception. With a byline of "Gay, Lesbian, Bisexual & Transgender TV Shows & Specials" for several years,[23] LogoONLINE's front page provided links to full episodes of its most popular channel shows and a menu with sections for video content, which included movies, show and schedule information, links to Logo's other websites, and an online store for Logo products. The site also included "The Click List for Music" and "The Click List for Short Film," which allowed site visitors to vote for their favorite music videos and short films, with the most popular items making a weekly top ten list; for music, the list was described on the site as "Indie, pop, rock and hip-hop music videos (with gay leanings, of course!)."

In addition, Logo had two music video shows on its channel, NewNowNext Music and NewNowNext Pop Lab, featuring emerging artists, that began airing in 2005; the following year, Logo launched the NewNowNext website, with a broader scope than the shows, with the byline "Gay Pop Culture, News and Clues Served Fresh Daily."[24] A menu contained subsections such as "TV," "Music," "Movies," and "Celebs & Gossip," reorganized later into "Music," "TV and Movies," "Ask an Expert," "Style," and "Travel." Articles and videos were mainly posted by John Polly, who was also the editor of LogoONLINE;[25] site visitors could comment on posts but rarely did.

There were also a couple of short-lived websites dedicated to Logo shows. One, www.happiestgaycouple.com, was established in 2007 for the animated sitcom *Rick & Steve: The Happiest Gay Couple in the World*, which drew a larger and broader audience than Logo had expected. The site contained show information and episode recaps, video clips from the TV episodes, and "digisodes" (short web episodes). Launched in 2009, www.TripOutTravel.com/ www.TripOutGayTravel.com was the site for Logo's *Trip Out* show about gay and lesbian travel, and contained text and video posts about destinations for LGBTQ travelers, with regular contests for travel prizes. Southwest Airlines was a major sponsor, its advertising displayed prominently along the top of the page. Once the series concluded airing in 2011, the website soon became inactive. Another Logo site, VisibleVote08.com, covered the U.S. 2008 elections. Content was contributed by staff at Logo's other sites, primarily 365gay, and consisted of commentary on LGBTQ-specific topics as well as more general campaign news about candidates of interest. Visible Vote '08's most prominent achievement, co-organized with the Human Rights Campaign, was a forum about LGBTQ issues with six of the 2008 presidential candidates, which was televised on Logo in August 2007.[26] The site became inactive after the conclusion of the 2008 elections.

While developing its own websites, Logo also sought to acquire preexisting websites, with the goal of displacing rival Regent Media's Gay.com as the most popular online destination for LGBTQ content overall. In a period of under two years, Logo acquired the social networking site Downelink, the LGBTQ news site 365gay, and—with the most significant impact on the LGBTQ media landscape—the pop culture sites AfterEllen and AfterElton.

Downelink was founded in 2004 by Danny Nguyen, Michael Abraham, and Ronaldo Mabagos shortly after all three graduated from college and purchased by Logo in August 2007, reportedly for $4.8 million. Most recently described on the site as "a free social network and mobile app for lesbian, gay, bi and trans people online and on the go,"[27] it started out as more racially diverse than comparable sites and continued to draw queer people of color, although without explicitly targeting them, until it shut down in 2015. Site users could set up profile pages and then interact with other users in ways comparable to Facebook or sign up using their Facebook accounts.

In certain key respects, Downelink was an odd fit for Logo because it was solely for users to connect with each other and had no ties to LGBTQ entertainment, like AfterEllen/AfterElton, or news, like 365gay. Thus, while it continued to operate under the Logo umbrella for almost a decade, it was never as well integrated into Logo's brand and programming strategies. Unlike Logo's other websites, there were no links to any of the network's other sites, although beginning in 2010, a small box labeled "DowneTV Latest Videos" began featuring videos from Logo's other sites (e.g., NewNowNext) or from the channel, but other brand logos were for the various social and mobile platforms on which Downelink could be accessed.

365gay, one of the earliest online LGBTQ news sites, was founded in 1995 by Rob Sands in Toronto.[28] For several years, there were a large number of sections, including those on science and technology and gay history, entertainment-focused pages on movies, books, and music, as well as "lifestyle" categories such as food, health and fitness, a humor page, and an advice column. After Logo's acquisition in June 2006, Sands stayed onboard for a couple of years as a consultant before the site was completely overhauled in terms of both staffing and site design. Jay Vanasco served as editor in chief (and the site's only full-time staff member) from 2007 to the site's demise in 2013, assisted by James Withers, and with content also contributed from several regular freelancers. With a new tagline of "Gay, Lesbian, Bisexual & Transgender News & Free Video," 365gay published text and video news items of LGBTQ interest on which users could post comments, and there were regular mini-polls. Until May 2009, its content had an unusual relationship with Logo's channel programming through *365gay News*, billed as "the first-ever, multi-platform, on-air, online news hub for the LGBT audience." The program, produced by CBS News, aired both on Logo's channel and on 365gay, but it was the site that drew in more viewers, an early example of how video content helped bring traffic to the websites.[29]

AfterEllen was started in 2002 by Sarah Warn with a byline of "news, reviews & commentary on lesbian and bisexual women in entertainment and the media." Warn launched a brother site, AfterElton, with a matching byline of "news, reviews & commentary on gay and bisexual men in entertainment and the media," in 2005.[30] Both sites were originally part of Warn's Erosion Media company, which also included the websites The Big Gay Picture, a blog about gay and lesbian politics and culture; All Gay News, a news site; and Fake Gay News, which published spoof news items. Following Logo's acquisition of Erosion Media in June 2006, All Gay News was discontinued, unsurprising given Logo's acquisition of news site 365gay in the same year. Fake Gay News became essentially defunct shortly after due to a lack of staffing capabilities, although for a few years there were occasional "Fake Gay News" submissions by AfterEllen contributor Dara Nai posted at that site. The Big Gay Picture became inactive when Logo created its own Visible Vote site about the 2008 U.S. elections.

Mapping the Cultural Field

Although the websites described in the last section mostly started small, with just a handful of site runners or content contributors, they acquired additional staff as they grew, something particularly true of the initially independent sites after being bought by Bravo or Logo. Who these staff, together with the earlier site founders, were in terms of their professional backgrounds and dispositions and how they came to the sites are crucial to analyzing the cultural field. This section discusses the key cultural agents and maps out the relationships among them, thus delineating digital media production at Bravo and Logo as social spaces structured by executives, other staff, and interns at the networks involved with content production, marketing, and technical elements; website editors, writers, designers, and technical workers; and users who visited the sites.

As noted in previous scholarship, media industries have gatekeepers whose institutional power has significantly shaped which texts attained the greatest prestige, circulation, or both. Examining the canonization of U.S. fiction, Richard Ohmann identified the top gatekeepers as members of what Barbara Ehrenreich and John Ehrenreich called the "professional-managerial class"—editors at publishing houses, print reviewers at prestigious publications (*New York Times Book Review* and *New York Review of Books*)—who, with a certain commonality of life trajectories, tended to find the same types of narrative compelling.[31] Sender discussed a newer iteration of this in the U.S. publishing industry as writers, editors, and marketers who constructed new gay and lesbian markets played central roles in delineating desirable forms of gay media content and identities.[32]

To a certain extent, there were gatekeepers at the Bravo and Logo websites comparable to those discussed by Ohmann and Sender for print media. However, content production for sites like TWoP and AfterEllen involved cultural agents other than those with clear institutional affiliations, such as writers, bloggers, and other site users. In other words, cultural authority had become negotiated among more types of agents. While this in itself did not guarantee more diverse content, it means looking beyond the usual suspects, such as network executives and website editors, to understand how LGBTQ digital content at Bravo and Logo was produced.

Because there are multiple organizations and individuals involved, I first provide two summary figures. Figure 3 shows the timeline for the founding and network acquisitions of Bravo's sites and the trajectories of the key cultural agents involved; figure 4 shows the same for Logo's sites. For legibility, these diagrams illustrate only a portion of the dense networks of relationships between many LGBTQ workers that were central to the staffing of both the channels and the websites; the specifics are discussed in the upcoming sections.

For both figures, along the bottom is an axis with the years 2000–2011, during which key events—purchases of properties or staff joining particular networks or websites—occurred. Looking at figure 3 first, several larger media networks important to how the websites came to be staffed are represented as long rectangles closest to the horizontal axis; these are USA Networks, Vivendi Universal, NBC, and NBC Universal. The smaller media networks are represented with convex left edges; in figure 3, these are Trio and Bravo. For websites, figure 3 shows BravoTV.com at the top, then TWoP, as well as the three that ceased operating in 2008: OutZoneTV, Brilliant But Canceled, and GetTrio. The light blue lines from the Trio network indicate how its channel content became transformed into those three websites. Red arrows on the diagram indicate acquisitions, both for networks and websites; figure 3 thus indicates a series of acquisitions that brought a number of key staff to Bravo's digital properties. Finally, the pink lines indicate how specific people came to work at the networks or websites represented in the diagram.

In figure 4 for Logo, there is a single parent company represented—MTV Networks, on the top left—to which Comedy Central, from which several key staff came, also belongs. Logo the channel and Logo-originated websites are represented as two adjacent long rectangles at the top of the diagram. The four

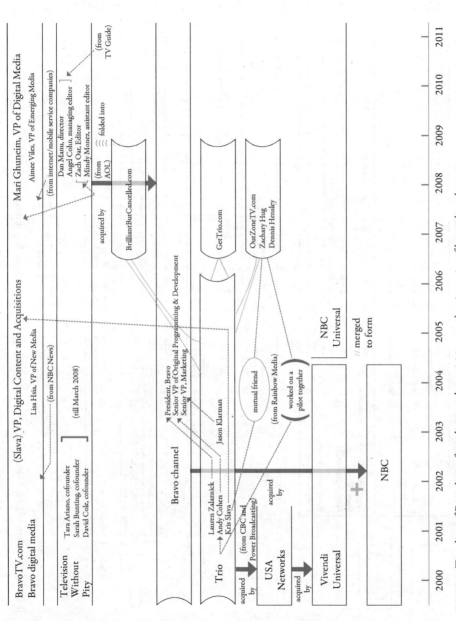

FIGURE 3 Timeline of Bravo's site foundings and acquisitions and trajectories of key cultural agents.

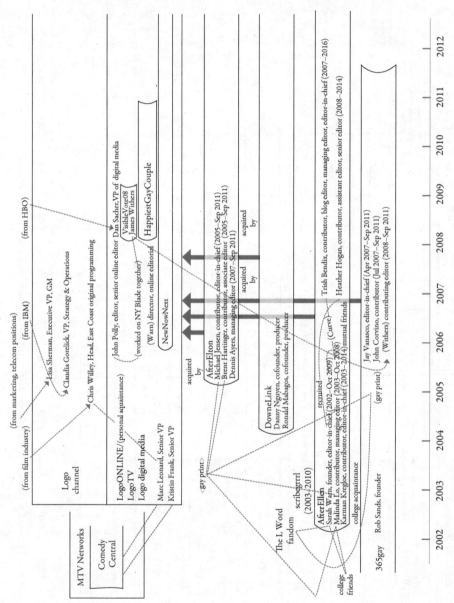

FIGURE 4 Timeline of Logo's site foundings and acquisitions and trajectories of key cultural agents.

websites acquired by Logo—AfterEllen, AfterElton, Downelink, and 365gay—
are represented in the bottom half of the diagram; with the exception of 365gay,
which was established before 2000, the time of their founding is represented
by where their concave left edges begin. Again, red arrows indicate acquisitions, while pink arrows indicate how specific people joined a network or
website as a staff member. Figure 4 also has one additional area not present in
figure 3, gay print (see below the Logo channel and website rectangles), since a
number of contributors to Logo's websites originated from working for LGBTQ
newspapers and magazines.

The section below begins with the genesis of the acquired websites and how
contributors joined the sites early on as fans connected by personal ties as well
as, in several cases, individuals with experience writing for the gay print media.
It examines the extent to which the sites arose as grassroots efforts and how their
agendas overlapped with those of LGBTQ politics and activism in other domains.
As subsequent sections discuss, several shifts occurred after the sites were purchased by Bravo and Logo, involving not just the injection of economic capital
into the sites but also the move of some fans and site users into positions as content producers and decision makers. With additional staff joining after the initial founding as well as post-purchase, processes of professionalization became
increasingly important, meaning not just the formalization of employment
arrangements but also the development of professional dispositions that informed
how queerness was (and was not) articulated in site content. This combination
of who these workers were and how they both shaped and were shaped by the
contexts of their work constitute central elements of the new field of LGBTQ
cultural production emergent at Bravo and Logo.

The Genesis of the Acquired Sites: Site Founders and Early Site Staff

Prior to the sites' acquisitions by Bravo and Logo, the trajectories of site founders
and other staff show that they were often started up by "just a few friends," and
personal contacts were particularly significant early on in adding staff. In this
way, social capital as Bourdieu defined it came into play—that is, resources linked
to a person's durable network of relationships of mutual acquaintance and recognition; thus, the import of social capital for the websites is not primarily about
friendship per se but that it can potentially be converted into other forms of capital, including economic. Although the websites did not start off as financially
lucrative, their eventual purchase by Bravo and Logo meant that the social connections through which early site staff were brought in by site founders became
valuable. Furthermore, for the Logo-acquired sites—AfterEllen, AfterElton,
365gay, and Downelink—the founders were all gay or lesbian, and this meant that
they were tapping their personal and then professional networks to draw in other
LGBTQ friends and colleagues to work for the sites.

Given the establishment of the websites in the 1990s or early 2000s, when
internet access was most readily available in higher education and commercial

settings, it is unsurprising that site founders were invariably college educated, and most had worked professionally for some time. Rob Sands graduated with a journalism degree and held journalism positions in Canada with CBC, CTV, and Rogers Broadcasting before starting 365gay in 1995 while based in Toronto. Prior to founding Downelink in 2003, Danny Nguyen, Ronald Mabagos, and Michael Abraham had met in college while majoring in computer science (Nguyen and Abraham) and graphic design (Mabagos) at California Polytechnic State University, and each then worked in their fields for a couple of years at different companies. Sarah Warn completed a degree in women's studies at Wellesley and then worked for online companies including Expedia and Amazon before starting up AfterEllen in 2002 and AfterElton three years later. Among TWoP cofounders, Tara Ariano completed bachelor's and master's degrees in English (at Brock University and the University of Toronto, respectively) and worked briefly for a print magazine; Sarah Bunting graduated from Princeton with a degree in creative writing and worked as a records clerk at Barnard College; and David Cole majored in history and geography at Brock University and was then involved with online marketing for a couple of companies.

In the earlier stages of the sites, a number of additional contributors came onboard as friends or colleagues of the site founders or other initial staff members. For example, at Bravo's sites, Daniel MacEachern ("Daniel" on the site) knew TWoP founders Tara Ariano and Sarah Bunting in the earliest stages of their entertainment sites and was asked by them to recap after they expanded their site beyond *Dawson's Creek*. Lauren Shotwell ("Lauren S") was close friends with two early recappers, and Bunting invited her to recap after following Shotwell's personal blog for a while.[33] Zac Hug started off as a freelancer at OutZoneTV through sharing a mutual friend with the site's creator and Bravo executive Kris Slava, while Dennis Hensley was hired after having worked previously with another Bravo executive, Andy Cohen, on an unaired Bravo pilot.

The early staff for AfterEllen and AfterElton were drawn from the personal contacts of founder Sarah Warn. Brent Hartinger, who became a staff writer at AfterElton, contacted Warn in 2003 about reviewing one of his novels (featuring a bisexual female character), and Hartinger and his partner, Michael Jensen, who along with Warn was instrumental in establishing AfterElton (and soon after started serving as its editor in chief), became friends with Warn after discovering they lived within driving distance of each other. AfterEllen staff writer Malinda Lo was a close friend of Warn's from college, and she was the first person Warn asked to help write articles for the site; she became managing editor after Logo's acquisition of the site until she left in 2009 to pursue her fiction writing. Another key player, Scribegrrrl, came to Warn's attention through her *L Word* recaps at a Yahoo! community group and, after agreeing to contribute more detailed recaps for AfterEllen, became blog editor. Additionally, Warn became acquainted with Karman Kregloe, who started as a freelance writer and eventually succeeded Warn as editor in chief in October 2009, through a mutual friend. Trish Bendix was also one step removed from Warn when she started; she had known Malinda Lo when both worked at lesbian magazine *Curve*, and Lo brought her to the site as a freelancer (Bendix then became blog editor after the Logo acquisition and then managing editor until she was fired in 2016 after Evolve Media acquired AfterEllen). Ryan Haynes, cocreator and copresenter for the video blog *Gay in the UK*, recounted that the show ended up associated with AfterElton because he knew an executive producer at Logo and, through that contact, communicated with editor in chief Michael Jensen about his ideas for the vlog.

At 365gay, Jennifer Vanasco and Sarah Warn had been college acquaintances at Wellesley, although Warn stressed that Vanasco went through the same interview process for the position of editor in chief as several other candidates. John Corvino had written for the Independent Gay Forum as well as *Between the Lines*, a Michigan LGBTQ paper, and joined 365gay as a regular opinion columnist after Vanasco, who was familiar with his contributions in the gay print media, invited him to submit his work. James Withers knew John Polly, the editor in chief of LogoTV and NewNowNext, when both wrote for the same company (Withers for the *NY Blade* and Polly for *Genre* magazine, both gay publications). When Logo-originated website VisibleVote08 was active, Logo sought a political writer, and Polly put Withers in touch with Vanasco. Withers eventually moved from freelancing for 365gay to becoming a contributing editor.

Another path to a staff position at the sites was starting off as a reader and fan and then either submitting one's work to the editors or coming to their attention. The phenomenon of fans becoming producers within industrial production existed before digital media, such as romance novel authors who had started out as readers,[34] the recruitment of gaming modders by games companies,[35] as well as, occasionally, fan fiction writers who are hired to write scripts.[36] At Bravo and Logo, however, certain cohorts of fan writers—particularly recappers for TWoP and a number of AfterEllen columnists and bloggers—became employees of the sites or networks. They thus moved out of the ranks of media users whose unpaid labor has provided a substantial amount of content for the industrial owners of those media.

For those who did not have any previous connections to site runners, another way in was sending their work unsolicited. Both Jeff Alexander and Jacob Clifton sought out positions as TWoP recappers by submitting their writing to the site runners fairly persistently. As Clifton noted, the informality of his path to recapping—with respect to both the channel and the tenor of his requests—was only possible in the early days of the site, occurring at a time that Sarah Bunting and Tara Ariano were working from their homes, paying recappers a rather low stipend:[37]

I wrote to both Sars and Wing, offering madly to recap "Mists of Avalon." . . .
Wing wrote back immediately and very professionally, as is the Canadian way,

telling me it wasn't happening. But something in Sarah's parallel dismissal caught at my nerves, and I wrote back a very powerful, very obnoxious, very funny concession speech, thinking it was my last goodbye. Of course, this was in the very narrow window where that kind of acting-out might work—TWoP was itself entirely contained in a Park Slope brownstone and the cellar of a Toronto rental house—but the sheer mania and determined aping of the house style won me a reprieve. . . . I mean, none of this would have played two years later, much less after the acquisition, but it was the perfect storm. And six years later it's been a pretty great job.

At AfterEllen, Heather Hogan and thelinster were invited to try out as bloggers after their comments on posts at the site caught the attention of Scribegrrrl and Sarah Warn, respectively. Thelinster detailed a path to AfterEllen through multiple fandoms around lesbian representations on television:

I met Scribegrrrl, who was blog editor at the time [2007], online at the *All My Children* email group that discussed Bianca's gay story line. When Scribe started recapping *The L Word*, I became a devoted fan and followed the recap—and her—to AfterEllen.com. I just commented now and then, but that's about it. Then she posted that AE needed bloggers and asked for "test blogs" as submissions. I sent one and she responded that she had been wanting to ask if I was interested in blogging but just hadn't gotten around to it (a huge compliment!). Apparently, the editors thought my "audition" was acceptable. At the time, we had a month trial before officially being hired. I guess I passed.:)

At AfterElton, Anthony Langford had a similar experience after posting comments for a while about gay storylines on soap operas. When his knowledge about the shows drew the attention of editor in chief Michael Jensen, he was asked to submit a sample column, which then became his weekly regular contribution about daytime soaps. There were, however, not as many instances of site users becoming regular contributors at AfterElton as at AfterEllen, because there are substantially more sites aimed at gay men, whereas at the time, AfterEllen was the clear go-to site for lesbians interested in speaking to an online audience. As Michael Jensen noted, most AfterElton contributors were solicited by the site after Jensen came across their work or were referred to them by sources at Logo.

Other Site Contributors and Network Staff

Looking more generally at the cultural agents involved with Bravo's and Logo's websites, some—but by no means the majority—of the site contributors had a background in LGBTQ journalism, writing, or activism. More common were a range of trajectories from general corporate professions such as advertising, marketing, and accounting as well as from media production, including television and film production or publishing.

Network executives at Logo generally came from another position in the media industry. Marc Leonard had been at Comedy Central, another MTV network. Chris Willey had worked for some time in film production and was looking to get into television; he joined Logo through his connection to Leonard. Kristin Frank was working in media marketing and distribution and at the time of Logo's inception, was the head of distribution for what she fondly recalled was nicknamed "the funny gay music group," which included Comedy Central, the set of MTV and VH1 channels, and Logo.[38] Claudia Gorelick had previously worked in marketing and advertising for general publishers, including Routledge, as well as companies such as IBM.

A few site contributors had also worked in television or radio production or as entertainers prior to coming to the sites. Jeff Alexander had spent a year as a staff writer for the NPR program *A Prairie Home Companion* when he was hired as a TWoP recapper in 2004, with a corporate "day job" of proposal writing. Ryan Haynes, cocreator and copresenter for the vlog *Gay in the UK*, had a long background in radio production. Dara Nai, who has contributed both text and video content for AfterEllen, was working in production management for sports programming on television. Those who had been working as performers professionally (if not full time) include Jennie McNulty, a comedian whose vlog *Walking Funny with Jen McNulty* was hosted on AfterEllen; Tim Macavoy, Haynes's copresenter on *Gay in the UK*, who "still work[s] as an actor . . . and teach[es] Shakespeare and slapstick and stage fighting in London"; and Dalila Ali Rajah and her copresenters on the lesbian talk show *Cherry Bomb*.

Some site staff and contributors had worked in general publishing or media domains. As I mentioned earlier, Sarah Warn had been employed in online marketing positions for several years. Danny Nguyen had worked at Yahoo! and a couple of other online media companies at the time that he established Downelink. AfterEllen blogger thelinster was a freelance advertising copywriter. However, most contributors, the vast majority of whom had regular employment elsewhere, did not have experience in the entertainment industry. At TWoP, the freelance recappers Daniel MacEachern and Lauren Shotwell were probably typical: MacEachern was a newspaper journalist, while Shotwell did legal work. Only Jacob Clifton, the most well-known recapper, noted that he was able to sustain himself by his writing (for TWoP as well as elsewhere), although when he first started, he did a patchwork of "admin and other temp or half-time work."

AfterEllen founder Sarah Warn had majored in women's studies at college, and the staffing of that site early on reflected her political sensibilities around gender and media representation. Malinda Lo, Karman Kregloe, and Trish Bendix also had familiarity with critical academic fields: Lo was in graduate school for anthropology and Kregloe for American studies, while Bendix had taken several women's studies classes as an undergraduate student. Bendix had also started Queer Fest Midwest in 2007 as a more radical alternative to the Chicago Pride celebrations. At AfterElton, editor in chief Michael Jensen had fought for domestic partner rights when he was working as a flight attendant, and Brent Hartinger had been involved with LGBTQ youth organizations.

365gay, being a news site, was primarily staffed by people engaged in writing or activism around LGBTQ social, cultural, and political issues. Editor in chief Jay Vanasco had had a long history of writing primarily in gay print journalism, first with Chicago's LGBTQ paper *Windy City Times* and then freelancing for *The Advocate* as well as "a *lot* of gay publications, and some mainstream publications," even when she had a "real job" with the University of Chicago (which she quit after being hired at 365gay). John Corvino had also written for gay newspapers prior to his work for 365gay (although his full-time position is philosophy professor). Other contributors included Pauline Park, an activist for transgender rights; Jenna Lowenstein, who has worked for the Stonewall Democrats, which aims to connect LGBTQ Democratic activists; and James Withers, who had been a reporter for the *New York Blade*, a gay print newspaper, and freelanced for other LGBTQ publications.

Several other staff and contributors at Logo's sites had backgrounds in LGBTQ print media. John Polly, editor in chief of LogoTV.com, noted that he had "had, like, supergay jobs forever!" working for multiple gay newspapers and magazines for over a decade as well as some general publications:

> In 1994, I started working for a gay men's magazine called *Genre*, out in LA. And I worked there . . . for a few years, and then I left and was doing freelance stuff. . . . And then I moved away and did a lot more travel kind of writing, but I was writing for gay travel publications. And then I moved to New York, I was doing freelancing for a lot of gay magazine stuff, and then I became editor of a gay nightlife magazine here for three and a half years. Then I ended up working at *Genre* magazine *again*, when I was just switching jobs, because they were then based here for a year. And then I took a job at Logo.

Others who had been involved with gay publications at some point include AfterElton's associate editor Brent Hartinger (also a novelist of gay fiction) and Malinda Lo at AfterEllen, who had written for *Curve*. Michael Jensen, editor in chief of AfterElton, had published two gay-themed novels when he started at the site, although his primary source of income was from working as a flight attendant.

Some site staff had been writing without remuneration for LGBTQ readers online. Grace Chu and Dorothy Snarker[39] maintained blogs about lesbian culture and entertainment prior to writing for AfterEllen, which Snarker continues to do so.[40] Trish Bendix had started and been running *CHILL*,[41] an online magazine targeted toward lesbian readers in the Chicago area, when she began freelancing at AfterEllen. All three had full-time jobs elsewhere; Chu worked as a lawyer, while Bendix was working as a research editor at the media company CISION, a position she quit after she joined AfterEllen as blog editor.[42]

Site Staffing Post-acquisition and the Processes of Professionalization

Network acquisition of 365gay, AfterEllen/AfterElton, Downelink, and TWoP, as well as the development of OutZoneTV under Bravo resulted in increased professionalization of staffing at the sites, a process that proceeded in stages with distinct characteristics. In addition, the ways that Bravo and Logo workers talked about their work both staked claims about positive contributions to LGBTQ viewers and communities and were indicative of changes in the significance of grassroots LGBTQ and feminist political positions that had characterized the independent gay print press.

At websites that had originally been started and run by media fans, professionalization of staffing occurred in two senses: (1) individuals who had been running the sites on the side became paid full-time or part-time employees of the networks, and (2) some of the sites—TWoP, AfterEllen, and AfterElton—expanded their staff by hiring, in part, from the ranks of freelance writers and media workers, some of whom then moved up the ranks to become regular employees. The most prominent cases of the first situation were Sarah Warn of AfterEllen/AfterElton, Downelink cofounders Danny Nguyen and Ronald Mabagos, and the cofounders of TWoP, Tara Ariano, Sarah Bunting, and David Cole.[43] Other senior staff who had started out as freelance contributors include Karman Kregloe, who became editor in chief at AfterEllen, and Brent Hartinger, associate editor at AfterElton.

In the case of freelancers becoming regularly paid employees, some additional contributors were specifically solicited after senior site staff had come across their writing, such as Grace Chu and Dorothy Snarker for AfterEllen. Thus, after noticing Snarker's own blog, which was a lesbian take on popular media, AfterEllen's blog editor Scribegrrrl had emailed her. Shortly after, Snarker emailed Sarah Warn to suggest a topic AfterEllen might consider covering, and Warn, who was also familiar with Snarker's blog, asked if Snarker would consider writing for AfterEllen.

In the early days of AfterEllen, Trish Bendix, another blog editor (later managing editor), would draw from a pool of writers she knew from the lesbian magazine *CHILL*, or other prior writing. Bendix noted a shift from recruiting via personal contacts in the past to a broader set of possibilities, including referrals from other people, partly in order to fulfill a site mandate to be as representative as possible of queer women and ensuring that "we have a group of women of color, we have a couple of older [contributors] . . . and also just from all around the world," and during this time, AfterEllen and AfterElton did have a number of staff and contributors of color.[44]

At AfterEllen, several contributors joined the site after responding to an open call for additional text and video bloggers. Senior writer Dara Nai, who was working in television production for sports programming, submitted her work without having any personal connections to AfterEllen staff at the time: "They posted something on AfterEllen that said they were looking for writers for Fake-GayNews, and if you think you're funny, send us something; if we like it, we'll post it. So I thought, 'I can do that.' . . . So I wrote something in about half an hour . . . and I sent it. . . . [Then] I got an email, what seemed to me to be out of the blue, from someone [editor in chief Karman Kregloe], saying that they loved my submission, could they put it up on FakeGayNews, but also did I want to write for them." A competition for vloggers in 2008 attracted professional and aspiring entertainers, including Jennie McNulty, a working comedian who ended up with a regular vlog called *Walking Funny with Jen McNulty* where she interviewed a guest as they take a walk, and the presenters for *Cherry Bomb*, a talk show whose five cohosts Dalila Ali Rajah, Gloria Bigelow, Nikki Caster, Tatum De Roeck, and Bethany Landing were trained or interested in performance.[45] (Chapter 2 discusses the importance of the video blogs to AfterEllen in more detail.)

The situation for Bravo's sites was mixed. At OutZoneTV, Zac Hug was a prominent example of how Bravo's embrace of digital media facilitated his trajectory "from a freelancer to an executive" in just six years. Hug commented that this would have been an unusual path in a segment of the industry outside of online media; his day job prior to OutZone had been managing a café. However, staffing at TWoP followed different patterns. First, TWoP's freelance recapper pool grew substantially after being purchased, as the site came to recap about twice as many shows as previously, and a couple of freelance contributors did become regular employees as site moderators. But most prominently, after the departures of TWoP's founders Tara Ariano, Sara Bunting, and David Cole in March 2008, Bravo brought in several staff from mainstream media companies who had no connection to the TWoP community, including hiring Dan Manu from *TV Guide* as the director of the site.[46]

In exemplifying pathways to industry insider status besides the more conventional ones, such professionalization of site staff illustrated a key characteristic of media convergences as described by Jenkins: a less rigid boundary between fan and industrial media workers.[47] It was not only that fans were able to attain network staff positions but that they joined Bravo and Logo as a small group of such previous outsiders who now had an unprecedented potential to shape mainstream LGBTQ media. And yet, what became clear with respect to professionalization was that relatively soon, site contributors were no longer sought via general appeals to users but through industry contacts and recommendations. Thus, writers like Grace Chu and Dara Nai at AfterEllen, Anthony Langford at AfterElton, and Jacob Clifton at TWoP, who had either pitched their work to site runners or had site runners notice their writing online, would probably not have been hired even just a couple of years after the purchases. The influx of professional freelancers into AfterEllen and AfterElton did not have an immediate effect on the sites because Sarah Warn was still the director of online editorial for Logo. However, at TWoP, the increase in coverage of mainstream media diluted its previous cult feel and gay-friendly sensibilities, even though a couple of recappers such as Jacob Clifton continued to infuse their recaps with overt homoeroticism, and there remained a number of HoYay[48] discussions for non-canonical same-sex couples on various shows.

Changes to site content are discussed in more detail in the following two chapters, but the general point is that professionalization both placed former industry outsiders into important gatekeeper roles *and* ended up largely shutting out the fans and consumer content creators who had provided the initial lifeblood of the sites that Bravo and Logo acquired. This did not mean that websites and cultural agents originally located outside of mainstream media were simply absorbed by the networks post-purchase. However, being an LGBTQ-identified content creator (or LGBTQ-focused website) per se became less definitively associated with some specific position in the cultural field. Indeed, as the next section discusses, there were disagreements among the new site workers about the content they were producing that were tied to the forms of cultural capital they wielded.

The New Cohort of LGBTQ Content Creators

Even before the site purchases, there were prominent gay and lesbian executives working at both Bravo and Logo. There was a consensus among my interviewees that a sizable proportion of male staff at Logo were gay, including Marc Leonard as senior vice president of multiplatform programming and Chris Willey as a development executive,[49] while most of the female staff were straight. Notably, though, at the time of the site purchases there were two lesbians in senior positions: Lisa Sherman as Logo's head and Kristin Frank as an executive in charge of online media.[50] In comparison, at Bravo there were also several gay male executives—most prominently, Andy Cohen as the executive vice-president of original programming and development—but no prominent queer women. These executives enjoyed the professional advantages (and economic capital) of significant prior experience in the media industry, seemingly set apart by their senior gatekeeping roles. Still, as earlier sections in this chapter detail, some of the founders and initial staff of the websites shared similar backgrounds with such network executives, although the websites had been started in more grassroots fashion. Thus, their preexisting professional dispositions, bound up with the classed dimensions of education and cultural capital more generally, shaped the LGBTQ content they produced.

LGBTQ Identity and Cultural Capital

LGBTQ people have been present in the media industries long before the internet, but the influx of queer cultural agents to Bravo and Logo through their websites meant a new cohort working as producers and gatekeepers of LGBTQ content. The changing status of gayness vis-à-vis mainstream culture compared to an earlier generation meant that being queer was no longer as definitive a marker of subcultural identity. Still, as a minority historically underrepresented in popular media, being LGBTQ-identified conferred a certain legitimacy in the eyes of audiences and other cultural producers with respect to creating LGBTQ content, even if was not an absolute necessity. As Chris Willey at Logo commented, a talented non-gay producer "might make a more interesting gay show or observation than *I* could as a gay person," but generally, those who sought to address LGBTQ viewers benefited from knowing their audience "in the most intimate way" from a shared identity. Indeed, the vast majority of the editors and contributors of Logo's sites were LGBTQ-identified, as was also the case at Out-ZoneTV, while at TWoP, there was a minority of gay writers, such as Jacob Clifton, who identified as "super gay," and Jeff Alexander noted that "we probably do have a fairly sizable gay readership, not to mention a writing staff that represents that population." But how actually did LGBTQ identity figure in the work of site staff in terms of changes to commercial LGBTQ media? Commentary from interviews revealed that cultural capital was significant in two ways. One was the extent to which the new workers were similar to executives already at the networks. The other had to do with contestations among site editors and contributors around what constituted the best kind of LGBTQ representation.

The logos for AfterEllen and AfterElton were originally "Because Visibility Matters,"[51] and other staff articulated similar positions, including Heather Hogan, senior editor at AfterEllen, and Anthony Langford, a soap opera columnist at AfterElton. However, there was no consensus on what constituted "good" or positive LGBTQ representation, even among content creators for the same site, and the divergences reveal important shifts in how closely tied (or not) LGBTQ media workers were to earlier feminist perspectives on gender, sexuality, and representation. First, this was evident in how AfterEllen staff and contributors spoke about their responsibilities, which were expressed in terms that were both overtly and more subtly classed, with reference to education and the acceptability of evaluating women on the basis of physical attributes. Founder Sarah Warn discussed her conscious promotion of diversity at AfterEllen and AfterElton, attributing it to four years of "women's studies boot camp" education at Wellesley that stressed the intersections of race, class, and gender, and saw it as an obligation to use her racial privilege to improve the visibility and rights of minorities. And in discussing how she recruited contributors in her capacity as blog editor, Trish Bendix commented about the importance of having some familiarity with feminist theory. Although she backtracked somewhat about the preferability of formal education, her response reveals a partially class-based evaluation of queer women who do not share this background:

> I took a lot of women's studies classes when I was in college. . . . I haven't asked everyone that does write for me or that I do read if they do have that background. But I tend to find that the writers that *I* admire the most and that *I* like to read the most do have that, just because it allows you to think a little

bit more critically when you're analyzing things. And I do have some writers that will fall into the category of, you know, "This is really offensive, but it's OK, because, like, she's really hot and I don't really care that she's straight or something like that, because I still like her," you know, sort of thing. And I think that maybe if you had that education and you realize what overall that does do for feminism, for queer women, and for homophobia at large, you might have a better sense of what that is and what it is doing. . . . But on the other hand, I think that you can be a really great writer and a great thinker without having gone to college. . . . As long as you have an interest in finding out other ideas about queers in history, queers in contemporary culture, queers in society, that you're always going to have an edge on the people that just relate lesbianism to being women that love other women for the sake of it.

On the other hand, Grace Chu, a lawyer who was a contributing writer at AfterEllen, was critical of academic feminism, which she noted that she had never had any interest in studying, although she recognized that "Sarah [Warn] and Malinda [Lo] often wrote from that perspective and kind of expected that AE's writers would." Blasting "radical politics and esoteric queer-only university courses" as "only practiced by a tiny minority of lesbians," yet dominating a lot of the discourse in a problematically judgmental fashion, Chu contrasted those practices with lesbian culture arising from and comprising everyday spaces whose down-market character marked its authenticity: "REAL lesbian culture comes from the mainstream and from the streets, not from the ivory tower and not from the underground. Lesbian culture, as practiced and perceived by the overwhelming majority of lesbians, is mainstream, with a twist: *The L Word*, Ellen/Portia, Buffy, *The Dinah*, etc. Lesbians are fierce, fun, sexy and very much a part of mainstream culture."

Dara Nai, another contributing writer, recounted a conflict arising from her comments about the physical appearance of a lesbian on a VH1 reality show, *Tool Academy III*. In noting that she also ridiculed aspects of the male contestants' bodies, she pointed to and then dismissed the standard feminist analysis that women are subjected to narrower standards of attractiveness than men and that evaluations of a woman's appearance tap problematic gender norms emphasizing what women look like over what they do:

My reason for saying something about [the lesbian contestant's] body is because, on the show, she goes out of her way, *over* and *over*, to say how hot she is. . . . And if you're going to proclaim how f-ckin' awesome you are, how hot you are, I'm going to call you on it, because you're not. . . . Because there is this thing where we can make fun of men, but we can't make fun of women, and I don't think that's right. . . . [One male contestant] thinks he's awesome, he's about five foot six, so I practically called him a dwarf; nobody cared about that. And then it was, "Well, that's not the same thing." If you called a woman fat, it *is* the same thing as calling a guy short because within the genders, those are two things that they really care about: women are concerned about their weight, men really are concerned about their height and their hair loss, that's their thing.

Another AfterEllen contributing writer, Dorothy Snarker, has discussed the challenges of offering images depicting racial and body diversity when she draws from a pool of mainstream entertainers. Yet more often, her posts on her own blog unabashedly admired the conventional beauty of female entertainers. Occasionally, she explicitly (if acerbically) acknowledged the tension between being a lesbian—glossed as a woman interested in attractive female representations—and being a feminist, as in the following post about a photo gallery of female tennis players:

> The New York Times, the staid national paper of record, ran an exhaustive special package on the women of professional tennis this week . . . [which] included . . . a slo-mo video gallery of the incredibly fit, incredibly toned, incredibly strong women of tennis hitting balls really, really hard. . . . This is porn, porn for muscles.
>
> Now, I could get into a long-winded discussion about whether an article about the present state of women's tennis really needs a blow-out multi-media package featuring some of the game's biggest and most comely stars in flowing, spangly outfits and immaculate, full makeup hitting tennis balls. Objectification, glamorization, etc. etc., blah blah. But this is not the time or place for that.

Thus, amid discourses of accountability and responsibility to LGBTQ communities, these examples also illustrated a loosening of the link between a certain form of second-wave feminist critique on the one hand and lesbian media on the other. The cultural capital of formal education and familiarity with academic feminism was relatively low in the esteem of some AfterEllen contributors, and overall, there was a shift toward imagining a queer female audience as less uptight, more down to earth than feminist scholars and, therefore, happy to indulge in guiltless enjoyment of normative standards of female attractiveness.

Another thread in comments from Bravo's and Logo's site workers about their contributions to LGBTQ viewers was a downplaying of overt queer sexuality: even though there was no sense of shame or apology, a gentility around sex was a recurring theme. Such distancing of their work from websites with explicit sexual content or overtly geared toward sexual encounters illustrated a newer professional disposition: those more explicit sites had emerged after struggles for them in earlier decades by activists seeking to make non-normative sexual expression expressly visible as a key part of LGBTQ community and empowerment, both in person (such as at Pride parades) and online.[52] This accorded with what

Sender had found for the "professional homosexuals" instrumental in producing glossy commercial gay and lesbian magazines in the United States, which involved a clear demarcation from the gay and lesbian newsprint weeklies that had constituted the bulk of LGBTQ media in earlier decades.

In 365gay's earlier days, for example, when it was run by founder Rob Sands in Toronto, it was also a space of community sexual engagement online. Sender discussed how gay and lesbian magazines "cleaned up their act" as they became advertising-supported national publications by decreasing explicit sexual material, and 365gay underwent a similar makeover after Logo's purchase that was not simply imposed by network executives but backed by the site's editor in chief, Jay Vanasco. Vanasco was keenly aware that in shifting 365gay's focus to covering mainstream gay rights, those who were even "more marginalized in the community" through belonging to sexual subcultures, for example, "might feel like they have no place to go." At the same time, she also asserted the improperness of having queer sexual expression being visible at 365gay, noting that "forums that had a lot of sex chat in them," which the site had previously, were not appropriate for a news and politics outlet, and that while "the gay community used to be a lot more focused on sex than it is now, I think it's a lot more focused on political rights."

The aversion to content deemed too sexually explicit was shared by Sarah Warn, whom Trish Bendix, the managing editor of AfterEllen, recalled vetoing an ad for KY lubricant for being too sexually suggestive, even though Bendix herself thought it was fine and preferable to "those ads for things that you know only gay men really care about . . . like *Mamma Mia* on DVD!"[53] Warn herself recalled that she had nixed video blogs from contributors about sex toys and was pleased to note that there was "very little racy content" on AfterEllen. She remarked that her standards were more stringent than those of executives at Logo as well as Michael Jensen, editor in chief of AfterElton, with whom she sometimes had rather divergent opinions on what counted as "over the line" in terms of sexual content, with occasions where she had mandated, "Get the half-naked guy off the home page!" Jensen, in turn, distinguished AfterElton from Perez Hilton's site,[54] sharply rebuking Hilton as a "low-level, scumbucket, bottom-feeder" who trucked in "salacious" content, particularly in one instance when he published explicit photos of a gay entertainment figure having sex. However, the differences between Warn and Jensen were relatively minor in comparison to the large extent to which they agreed on what was beyond the pale.

Bravo's OutZoneTV was the most ready of the sites to both post sexy images to attract readers and play up the entertainment angle of stories with sexual content. Zac Hug described the scandal involving Republican U.S. senator Larry Craig, who was arrested in 2007 for "lewd conduct" in a men's bathroom, as "OutZone gold," given Craig's hilariously weak defenses of saying, as Hug put it, "'I wasn't soliciting anything; I was just sort of scooting over on the toilet,' and to me, it was like the weirdest, funniest story *ever*." At the same time, he also pointed to the example of a gay male contestant on Bravo's *Project Runway* discussing coming out of the closet,[55] stressing that profiles of such people on OutZoneTV were important particularly to young queer viewers to provide alternative representation to the sexualized images common at hookup sites where there were inevitably topless men and "a lot of nipples."

Still, taken together with the divergent stances among some of the AfterEllen contributors discussed above, the picture at the sites was complex. On the one hand, there was movement away from only foregrounding sexually discreet gays or representations that deemphasized gender-queer and other nonconforming sexual expression; on the other hand, the classic feminist critique of women (and increasingly, men) being oversexualized in the media was by no means the dominant discourse at AfterEllen or any of the sites. Both these trends were probably due in part to younger contributors influenced by third-wave feminist perspectives on the media as a rich site for empowered self-representation rather than primarily a domain of misrepresentation. Partly generational and partly due to the production contexts, then, this newer spectrum of political positions epitomized how both more specific changes and broader cultural shifts about queerness, media, and culture played out in the spaces of Bravo's and Logo's websites.

Taking Stock: The Outcomes of Convergence

Within studies of LGBTQ media, there has been a strand of critique that mass culture threatens the integrity of queer communities, often based on an oversimplified construction of a once-pure LGBTQ subculture.[56] A more general assumption is that the absorption of one-time outsiders into commercial organizations results in the incorporated individuals conforming to the interests and practices of the (larger, more powerful) organization. Against that line of argumentation, Jenkins's theory of media convergence proposed that unprecedented exchanges between industry producers and ordinary media users facilitated by new media technologies were fundamentally reconfiguring the cultural field. This chapter and the book overall present examples of these processes, while remaining mindful that unequal positionalities can limit the potential of sustained user empowerment.

The beginning of this chapter traced the development of staffing at Logo's and Bravo's acquired websites, moving from their geneses to the shifts that occurred after being purchased. The narratives of site founders and other early staff illustrated the significance of both social and professional intersections among them—by dint of friendship, sharing a mutual acquaintance, attending the same college, meeting through fandom spaces online, writing for the same print publication or publisher, making a television pilot together. Trading in social capital has, of course, always been part of media industries, but there had never been the formation of such networks of LGBTQ workers producing LGBTQ media in commercial domains. Subsequently, convergences of legacy and digital, and mainstream and independent media brought new cultural workers to the field of commercial media, including into key gatekeeper positions, from areas that they had for the most part previously not come from: fandom and independent queer media. Such processes resulted in a complex network of workers wrought from both personal and professional relationships, with a range of expertise, dispositions, and practices around LGBTQ media that shaped and were shaped by the contexts of production at Bravo and Logo.

With this expansion, there was for a time a noticeable heterogeneity among site contributors in terms of professional disposition—what Bourdieu also called habitus—and how it figured in shaping website content. Site staff shared a general consensus about the importance of visibility, a discourse that echoed that of the mainstream gay rights movement represented by organizations such as GLAAD. Yet there were differences in editorial decisions around posting sexually appealing images for readers and in how site contributors should or should not express their own desires, as well as about the importance of academic gender studies for defining feminism and for feminism to shape queer expression. Thus, the disagreements among AfterEllen contributors, as well as comments by Danny Nguyen and Zac Hug that distanced Downelink and OutZoneTV, respectively, from the goal of (simply) providing sexual gratification were telling: they suggest that even as LGBTQ content was becoming a more regular component of mainstream media, there remained tensions around overtly appealing to queer desire versus either a more analytical stance or providing other kinds of community connection and validation of LGBTQ identity.

Although the number of staff at Bravo's and Logo's sites grew post-purchase, the multiple pathways to becoming paid contributors did not end up lasting. Indeed, the paradox of professionalization—which had initially led some contributors working for little or no pay to becoming hired as regular employees— was that it ended up normalizing having industry media experience. When the websites were first purchased, agents with queer cultural capital who joined the networks benefited financially, and in their editorship positions, Sarah Warn and Trish Bendix at AfterEllen, Michael Jensen at AfterElton, and Jay Vanasco at 365gay also sought to increase the number of other LGBTQ contributors with an eye to both racial and sexual diversity. Yet as professionalization played out further, it ultimately excluded most industry outsiders—those who had been just site readers and fans or others who encountered the sites or their key gatekeepers in various ways: as friends, commenters who caught an editor's eye, or entrants to competitions for new contributors. As upcoming chapters further explain, this was both an outcome of and a contributing factor to overall changes at the sites: a stronger focus on attracting a regular number of viewers, having a more predictable slate of content, and more coordination of the sites with the channel regarding content and tone.

Given that all of the acquired sites, with the exception of AfterEllen, as well as Bravo's OutZoneTV eventually shut down, what were the longer term outcomes of convergence bringing new cultural workers to Bravo and Logo, both for the professional trajectories of these workers and for the field of LGBTQ production more generally? Looking at where the key figures are now provides an answer at one level. Many of them have ended up in employment unrelated to LGBTQ-specific media. Sarah Warn freelanced for a variety of businesses after stepping away from AfterEllen and her executive position at Logo, then became employed at general media companies, in some ways reprising her pre-AfterEllen days working for Expedia. At AfterElton, Michael Jensen and Brent Hartinger returned to freelance writing after leaving the site in 2011, when it was renamed TheBacklot and underwent major reconfiguration. 365gay editor in chief Jay Vanasco is now an editor and theater critic at WNYC, a New York public radio station. Downelink cofounder Danny Nguyen moved to a position dealing with online content at the Gap when his site shuttered in 2015, and fellow cofounder Ronaldo Mabagos worked for a decade at Landmark Label, another non-media company, before becoming a nurse practitioner. From OutZoneTV, Zac Hug moved on to a number of non-LGBTQ-related executive, directing, writing, and producing positions, including at ABC Daytime and ABC Family (now Freeform), and is currently freelancing, while contributor Dennis Hensley has also held a variety of general entertainment-related positions.[57]

On the other hand, former AfterEllen editor in chief Karman Kregloe became vice president of strategy at Tello Films (www .tellofilms.com), which produces and hosts web series and films about queer women, and Trish Bendix held an editorship position at INTO, an online outlet for the gay dating app company Grindr, until 2018. In 2014, Heather Hogan moved from a senior contributor position at AfterEllen to a similar one at Autostraddle, now the leading independently run pop culture and news website targeting queer women. And John Polly transitioned from editor of Logo's NewNowNext website to a producer role for *RuPaul's Drag Race* parent company World of Wonder.

These multiple kinds of moves, from outside to inside mainstream media networks and to different positions within commercial media, are not uncommon for queer producers, a phenomenon that Lisa Henderson theorized as "queer relay," versus the disparaging characterization of "selling out" when independent media makers seek and attain mainstream commercial success.[58] Thus, the fact that not all of the LGBTQ contributors to the websites remained as producers of LGBTQ media does not detract from the significance of their work during the time that the sites were most active, illustrating in more nuanced ways how the cultural field for producing LGBTQ media was restructured. Indeed, this cohort predated by a few years the rise of more prominent LGBTQ producers of television series with substantial LGBTQ content, such as Ryan Murphy with *Glee* (Fox, 2009–2015), *American Horror Story* (AMC, 2011–present), and *Pose* (FX, 2018–2021), I. Marlene King, producer of *Pretty Little Liars* (ABC Family/Freeform, 2010–2016), and Joey Soloway, with *Transparent* (Amazon, 2014–2019).[59] As such, it comprised an important transition period in commercial media that both signaled and augmented more general, though conditional, social and political integrations of LGBTQ subjects in the United States.[60] Furthermore, with these developments occurring just prior to the rapid rise of streaming services (subscription video on demand [SVOD]) and social networking platforms, Bravo's and Logo's websites were key in contributing to moves of independently produced queer content into mainstream media, as well as providing new sites of queer social networking, changes to queer digital spaces that the next chapter examines.

2

The New Queer
Digital Spaces

● ●

Creating New Queer Spaces

In 2002, I was at a little dinner party of six people or something. And I was
rattling off all sorts of random factoids about entertainment, like how few TV
characters were lesbian or gay. . . . Back then, it was really pretty rare, except on
a few shows that had continual characters like *Buffy* or something, it was really
hard to find out about lesbian characters or storylines until *after* they had
already happened. And they didn't have TiVo back then. And so basically, if
you missed it, you missed it. And everyone was missing it, unless it happened to
be on a show you watched. So I think I was talking about that. And someone
just said, "You should do a website about that." So I started thinking about it
on the ride home, and I thought, "That's a good idea!" And I mentioned it to
my partner, Lori, and she said, "Yeah, why don't you?" And I literally created it
in five hours and launched it that weekend.

—Sarah Warn, founder of AfterEllen

In March 2008, British newspaper *The Observer* named Logo's AfterEllen website one of the fifty most powerful "blogs"[1] in the world, placing it in the company of The Huffington Post, Gawker, Dooce, PerezHilton, and Jezebel. Launched
before MySpace (August 2003), Facebook (February 2004), YouTube (February 2005), Twitter (July 2006), or Tumblr (January 2007) became significant
social media presences, its rise to such prominence was notable for an LGBTQ

outlet that began, as AfterEllen contributor Dara Nai put it, "in [founder Sarah Warn's] bedroom."

The last chapter discussed how convergence culture, as originally proposed by Henry Jenkins, brought new cultural workers into LGBTQ media production. This chapter looks at the effects of convergence on the content and interactional characteristics of Bravo's and Logo's websites, when major media corporations were home to digital LGBTQ spaces for the first time. The trajectories of sites like AfterEllen as well as Bravo's OutZoneTV illustrate specific intersecting historical moments: how legacy media got into digital, how independent queer production became entwined with mainstream media, and how popular culture became a queer water cooler, the crux of new digital spaces for LGBTQ interactivity.

In terms of LGBTQ content, an obvious early attraction of online platforms for commercial networks was the ability to serve different niche audiences, delivering a larger range of programming without taking up valuable telecast airtime. A secondary consideration was that online material might travel under the political radar: although conservative media watchdogs in the early 2000s would reliably campaign against, for example, ABC/Disney allowing kissing between teenage girls (on its prime-time 1999–2002 drama *Once and Again*), they were less likely to protest the ownership of OutZoneTV by NBC Universal, Bravo's parent company. However, rapid technological developments and changes in the habits of media users soon weakened the divide between content types (e.g., television vs. computer vs. mobile), so the industry shifted to multiplatform programming.

Both Bravo and Logo pursued strategies to increase viewer engagement by integrating digital platforms. Beyond promoting the programming of their parent companies, Bravo's and Logo's websites also cultivated the development of new LGBTQ content. In particular, Logo's acquisitions of queer short films and music videos for its channel and LogoONLINE (later LogoTV) website, as well as AfterEllen and AfterElton hosting original web series, provided a significant source of support for independent queer production. Digital technologies had made both the production and dissemination of media content much more accessible, something of particular import to marginalized sexual, racial, and class communities that had traditionally been poorly or underrepresented when television and film were the only forms of mass video, but what remained a persistent issue was publicity and distribution. Sites such as YouTube had become available to host video content for free but did not solve the problem of how to reach potential viewers. As Amanda Lotz noted regarding the era of peak TV, "Just as the deluge of content among legacy services drowned even the most distinctive series, the vast ocean of YouTube content made it difficult for innovative content to find an audience."[2] For queer video, then, websites associated with Bravo and Logo, which were already known for LGBTQ programming on their channels and could drive traffic to their online properties, emerged as key digital spaces for hosting and promoting independent queer video, with AfterEllen being especially illustrative of these dynamics.

The participatory modes of convergence culture, facilitated by digital technologies, have encouraged nonprofessional media users to share the content that they produce with other fans, usually within fan-specific spaces but in some cases, at officially sanctioned websites.[3] In the latter case, there have been concerns, as the introduction chapter noted, that such fan content is subject to restrictions that diminish their ability to challenge gender and sexual norms, instead corralling fan producers to create "affirmational" content that validates the main narrative underpinnings of the canonical text.[4] Furthermore, fan production serves to benefit the media industry financially, as it expands the amount of paratextual content generating interest in the source texts, while the fan producers typically remain uncompensated,[5] although other fans also benefit from this fan labor.[6] However, the AfterEllen and AfterElton web series that I will discuss were mostly original content not linked to Logo's channel programming. Thus, they were not the kind of nonprofessional production typically being considered in critiques about the economics and politics of convergence culture. In their formal characteristics, many of these web series shared similarities to those being independently produced but differed in streaming on websites belonging to a major media corporation.

Even though AfterEllen's model of hosting original queer video was not ultimately sustainable for either the content producers or the site, the different streaming video experiments at Bravo's and Logo's sites were an important development presaging the two main subsequent directions for LGBTQ video content: independent web series and commercial streaming sites. Thus, the convergences of legacy and digital media, and independent and commercial production at Logo in particular resulted in LGBTQ media being solicited and distributed in ways distinct both from what had previously been possible and what has subsequently become available.

Bravo's and Logo's websites also developed features for fostering engagement among users or with site staff—first, message boards and then user accounts and the ability to provide feedback on other people's posts in ways similar to social networking sites—which resulted in new spaces for queer user engagement. A range of other websites were also undergoing processes of what I label "social mediafication," including the fan fiction archive Fanfiction.net, travel sites like Trip Advisor, and even sites now known as social media platforms like YouTube, which was transitioning from simply hosting video to enabling visitors to leave feedback and interact. However, such websites were not LGBTQ-focused. Of course, there were numerous spaces online where queer people interacted for the purposes of dating and hookups, such as Gay.com, which around the time of Bravo and Logo launching or purchasing their LGBTQ-focused websites was the most visited site for queer users.[7] In contrast, with the exception of the social networking site Downelink, which Logo had acquired, none of Bravo's or

Logo's sites were primarily centered on facilitating sexual encounters,[8] but instead intended to appeal to users with common interests around popular culture or news and politics.

Again, an important question centers on the commercialization of queer digital spaces: what would be the gains and losses? Since the earliest days of online technologies, users had been gathering in queer and queer-friendly spaces on the basis of shared interests in LGBTQ representation, including a range of fandom-specific message boards to interact and share creative works. In the late 1990s and early 2000s, there had been shifts toward more centralized and sometimes commercialized websites for fans more generally, such as Fanfiction.net, where readers could leave reviews, and the LiveJournal platform for fan blogging. Again, however, none of these sites were LGBTQ-centric. In contrast, AfterEllen and AfterElton, which began as fan sites posting commentary and analysis of popular media, developed into substantial spaces for LGBTQ communities, first as independently owned websites and then as part of Logo's digital holdings. Furthermore, as Logo did not require website visitors to subscribe, the sites were freely available to users with internet access. Bravo's less visited site OutZoneTV served a similar function.

It is true that the corporate owners of the sites benefited from user engagement, including, as many have pointed out, the unpaid affective and organizational labor that produce and sustain these myriad subcommunities.[9] In this respect, Bravo and Logo were no better or worse than owners of other sites. The difference, however, is the historical precarity of LGBTQ-centered spaces within the mainstream. When queer media outlets were community based, they were frequently sustained for many years—indeed, decades—with modest financial resources.[10] With commercialization, Alfred Martin has argued that industry media often practice "queer dispersal," interested in appealing to LGBTQ audiences but then "just as quickly discard[ing] them in the hunt for more profitable 'mainstream' consumers, while maintaining nods to queerness."[11] The issue for commercially run sites for LGBTQ interaction, then, is what users would be left with if sites shut down for financial reasons. After all, even digital spaces for community engagement cannot be instantly re-created despite the availability of several free message board options, and such user-run sites do not have the same level of infrastructure. As it turned out, the rise of social media platforms both helped precipitate the closures of Bravo's and Logo's websites and provided much more numerous, dispersed networks for queer social interaction. However, as I will discuss, these newer spaces have generally failed to replicate the character of sites like AfterEllen as queer digital water coolers.

In the upcoming sections, a discussion focused on AfterEllen illustrates how both of the key dimensions identified here—the hosting of video content and the cultivation of user engagement—were central developments for LGBTQ digital media more generally. In these respects, the years when Bravo's and Logo's LGBTQ-centric websites were at their most popular constitute an important bridge period for contemporary conditions of queer media production and queer sociality.

LGBTQ Digital Video

LGBTQ video on Bravo's and Logo's websites included both content that was coordinated with channel programming and content that was distinct from it. The first kind was an example of multiplatform programming, similar to endeavors that numerous other television networks were exploring. The second, particularly as it applied to AfterEllen and AfterElton, illustrated both the possibilities and limits of convergence for bringing independent queer media into the commercial domain. Examining AfterEllen as a case study demonstrates mixed legacies for contemporary forms of queer media online, on the one hand involving a growth of outlets, both independent and commercial, and on the other, once most of Logo's sites shut down, a loss of free-to-user content centrally located on a website known for LGBTQ content, rather than dispersed through general sites like YouTube.

Establishing Multiplatform Programming

With digital media allowing legacy television to deliver content beyond the channel, the 2000s saw commercial media explore different modes of multiplatform content, with the overall goal of cultivating users in more immersive consumption compared to conventional audiences: a viewer who did not simply watch a show on the linear channel but also went online to find webisodes, interact with other viewers at message boards, or look up associated products was more attractive to advertisers. The drama *Lost* (ABC, 2004–2010) was an early television-based franchise that encompassed not just the network episode airings but also officially produced books, web comics and other website content, and mobile and video games;[12] numerous film-originated franchises, of course, such as *The Matrix* and *Star Wars*, have built even more expansive transmedia presence.[13] In more modest fashion, Bravo and Logo also sought to connect up their channel and digital programming in order to direct viewers from one platform to another.

CBS News on Logo/365gay.com and the AfterEllen/AfterElton Hot 100 are two different examples of how this played out. Originally, Logo had partnered with CBS to produce a weekly news segment called "CBS News on Logo," given that at the time of the channel's launch, it was little known, so as programming executive Marc Leonard noted, "to be able to have CBS News in the title established the validity of them as a legitimate news bureau." After Logo acquired 365gay in 2006, the CBS News segment was renamed *365gay News*. Billed as "the first-ever, multiplatform, on-air, online news hub for the LGBT audience," the program drew in more viewers at 365gay than on Logo's channel. Furthermore, the show as aired on the channel did not direct viewers to LogoONLINE, as Logo's other shows would, but to 365gay.com, with what Leonard called "one news brand" rooted in the identity of an online property rather than the channel.

AfterEllen and AfterElton began a "Hot 100" list in 2007, determined by site user votes for those women and men in the entertainment industry or other public figures that they considered the "hottest."[14] In 2009, Logo produced a cross-platform event, where the channel aired content—television shows, movies, and documentaries—featuring the people on the lists, and drove viewers from the channel to the websites; in turn, AfterEllen and AfterElton also directed visitors to the channel, though more selectively (e.g., AfterEllen announcing a Logo-sponsored competition to win a trip to meet Melissa Etheridge).

One persistent tension in coordinating content between AfterEllen/AfterElton and the channel had to do with the degree of sexual explicitness. Whereas Logo the channel was able to schedule uncut films at 1:00 A.M. on Saturdays, the websites could not vary access to their content in the same way. Sarah Warn commented that she had always wanted AfterEllen to be "PG13," counter to a history of lesbians and gays being oversexualized in mainstream depictions. At AfterElton, editor in chief Michael Jensen noted that although "sex sells" and the site used photos of people that readers were likely to find physically appealing, he would not go for the lowest common denominator even if that would undoubtedly increase readership. Such positions sometimes put the sites at odds with Logo staff who would have preferred more sexually explicit content to be posted.[15]

Logo also acquired some independent queer content to develop for channel programming, but it was a short-lived experiment. An illustrative example is the show *Jeffery & Cole Casserole*; comedians Jeffery Self and Cole Escola had posted sketch comedy episodes as "VGL (Very Good Looking) Gay Boys" on YouTube, and Logo picked up the show for development as a Logo television series, two seasons of which aired 2008–2010. Development executive Chris Willey noted that the episodes were deliberately designed to mimic the grainier look of online video—rendered by filming with an actual webcam—in order to preserve "the gritty, authentic feel . . . versus a really glossy, beautiful production that obviously would cost more money." However, overall, the channel focused on long-form, high-production-values content, leaving it to its websites, particularly AfterEllen, to find and host short-form web series and other cheaper formats of programming.

AfterEllen: The Rise and Fall of Its Video Blogs

At its outset, as a one-woman operation, new posts appeared at AfterEllen just once or twice a month, consisting of text and minimal graphics that required relatively little bandwidth. Warn recruited a few part-time writers—initially, Malinda Lo, Karman Kregloe, and Scribegrrrl, who would go on to become regular contributors[16]—and as AfterEllen expanded, posts became more frequent and varied. From having occasional articles, frequently analytical in nature, and later its first regular column, "Best Lesbianish Week Ever," which began in October 2005,[17] by 2010 there were two daily columns Monday through Friday, "Morning Brew" and "Afternoon Delight," covering the same ground as "Best Lesbianish Week Ever" had in terms of entertainment content of interest to queer women, as well as posts of show recaps, interviews, critical analysis, humor, and lifestyle.[18]

Before Logo's purchase, the single most important development contributing to the site's growth were Scribegrrrl's recaps of *The L Word* (*TLW*), which was the first program on mainstream American media to feature a group of predominantly queer female characters. AfterEllen began posting about the series when it was still in preproduction (with a working title of *Earthlings*), and once Sarah Warn successfully recruited the most popular *TLW* recapper at the time, the recaps "became this monster hit, more than either [Scribegrrl] or I ever imagined would happen. In some ways, *The L Word* really helped put AfterEllen on the map, but by the same token, we were the only ones writing about *The L Word*, for about a year before anyone else touched it." AfterEllen added more recaps of television series with queer women or close female friendships, which were also popular, including *Glee*, *Grey's Anatomy*, *Lip Service*, *Lost Girl*, *Pretty Little Liars*, *Rizzoli & Isles*, and *The Real L Word*, along with recaps of particular episodes when there were storylines of interest on shows such as *Boardwalk Empire*, *The Good Wife*, and *Modern Family*. These earlier text posts built AfterEllen's initial community, but it was video content that helped grow the site even more substantially, particularly younger users who, as the next section discusses, were also more interested in interacting online.[19] At the same time, AfterEllen did not move to an all-video model, such as rival site Tello Films, since many older users preferred text to video, so, as Warn noted, "having a mix of video and written editorial [made] the most sense."

Video blogs and series at AfterEllen were an amalgam of content with different origins, site hosting arrangements, and financial considerations, illustrating not just how Logo was exploring ways to deliver content via digital platforms but also how queer producers along a range of the independent-to-commercial spectrum found new digital spaces for their work. For a couple of key years, AfterEllen offered a crucial pathway for LGBTQ video to expand substantially into major commercial media. The site maintained its "street cred" as the first lesbian-oriented entertainment website, with Warn at the helm even after Logo's purchase, while having the increased resources that its ownership by Logo made possible.

The first video blog at AfterEllen was *She Said What?*, a weekly talk show featuring four lesbian/bisexual women, including site founder Sarah Warn,[20] informally discussing pop culture and entertainment news; nineteen episodes were posted from January 2006 to May 2007. Shortly after Logo's purchase, AfterEllen gained additional capabilities for streaming video, and began a period of hosting video produced by both its own staff and new freelance contributors.

While other sites were also starting to include video, AfterEllen's status at the time as the most visited entertainment website targeted to queer women made this development particularly significant.[21]

The first wave of new video blogs launched at AfterEllen in late 2007 to early 2008, and as managing editor Malinda Lo recalled, they were "wildly successful." In particular, several vlogs with talk show/commentary formats—*Brunch with Bridget* hosted by Bridget McManus (weekly-biweekly, January 2008–December 2009), *Gay Girls Who Game* hosted by Tracy and Angela (weekly-biweekly, December 2007–March 2011), *She Got Me Pregnant* hosted by Dana Rudolph and Helen Maynard (mostly weekly, October 2007–April 2011), and *What's Your Problem?* hosted by Cathy Buono (weekly-biweekly, January–May 2008)—gained loyal audiences and enjoyed relative longevity as various other vlogs ceased production. Also notable were *This Just Out with Liz Feldman* (weekly, May 2008–March 2009)[22] and five episodes of *The Big Gay Vlog* (February–April 2008), featuring Kate McKinnon and Julie Goldman discussing the Logo sketch comedy series on which they were regulars, *The Big Gay Sketch Show*. Feldman moved into mainstream television production in creating a comedy for NBC, *One Big Happy*, produced by Ellen DeGeneres (2015) and later, *Dead to Me* for Netflix (2019–2022); McKinnon went on to become a regular on *Saturday Night Live* (NBC, 1975–) in 2012.

In early 2008, AfterEllen solicited additional web series via a competition announced at the site. According to blog editor Trish Bendix,[23] who helped bring some contributors on board, the goal was to have content from a range of perspectives, both to appeal to a broad swathe of viewers, from both lighter and humorous to "serious and critical" content, and to fulfill Sarah Warn's mandate of diversity at the site, including women of color, older women, lesbian mothers, and so on. Although AfterEllen had been hoping to get scripted series, several vlogs came to AfterEllen via that competition. For example, *Walking Funny with Jennie McNulty* involved the host interviewing a guest while they both took an outdoors walk somewhere in the Los Angeles area. McNulty is a comedian who already had professional-grade audiovisual gear when she saw the contest announcement and thought she was well set up to produce something suitable. AfterEllen told her that her submission was "not at all what we're looking for, but we still like it," and she ended up producing a number of episodes for the site.

Cherry Bomb ended up at AfterEllen by way of the same contest. Like *Walking Funny*, *Cherry Bomb* did not place in the top three, but Sarah Warn liked it so much that she asked show creator Dalila Ali Rajah to produce as many episodes for the site as possible. An unabashedly lesbian version of ABC's *The View*, the cohosts sat in front of an actual audience and discussed topics particularly pertinent to queer women. Rajah noted that it was fortuitous timing that *What's Your Problem*, an AfterEllen vlog with a similar format, was in the process of moving over to fellow lesbian entertainment website SheWired (where it ran till

2010), so "they had an empty spot exactly where that was, where the audience would be into watching women talk about topics over wine."

AfterEllen also played an important role in hosting and promoting web shows that were produced and sometimes hosted independently elsewhere. Two prominent examples were the scripted dramas *Anyone but Me* and *Venice: The Series*. *Anyone but Me*, produced, written, and directed by Susan Miller and Tina Cesa Ward in New York City, featured a relationship between two teenage girls, along with several supporting characters, in webisodes about five to fifteen minutes long. Its first season initially streamed in 2008 on Strike TV, a website for independent productions, and then became available on a variety of other sites, including the show's own site (www.anyonebutmeseries.com), YouTube, Hulu, as well as having all of its episodes posted at AfterEllen. There were no financial transactions between the involved parties;[24] what *Anyone but Me* gained was the exposure that AfterEllen provided, while *Anyone but Me* brought traffic to AfterEllen.

Venice had a somewhat similar history, with the additional element that the executive producer and star of the show was Crystal Chappell, who played one half of the enormously popular Olivia Spencer/Natalia Rivera ("Otalia") pairing on the long-running CBS daytime soap *Guiding Light*, a relationship that AfterEllen covered quite extensively as one of the few lesbian romances on American television at the time. When *Guiding Light* finished airing in 2009, Chappell announced that she was coproducing a web series that would include Chappell's former *Guiding Light* costar Jessica Leccia and that both she and Leccia would play lesbian characters. AfterEllen gave the development and launch of *Venice* prominent coverage, although unlike *Anyone but Me*, the show was not directly streamed at AfterEllen.

After that, a few other scripted web series were linked at AfterEllen, including *Girl/Girl Scene* (2010–2011), *The Slope* (2011–2012), and *Webseries the Series* (2010). For a few months in 2010, AfterEllen also posted weekly retro airings of *South of Nowhere*, a drama in which the relationship between two teenage girls was the central focus and which had originally aired on The N (later TeenNick), another MTV Networks channel.

However, after peaking in 2009, the amount of video content began to decline over the next couple of years. One major reason was insufficient compensation for the video producers: whereas text bloggers were paid, the cost of streaming video meant that video contributors generally were not, and even those who were received only a small stipend that did not come close to covering production costs. At the end of 2009, issues around vloggers wishing to solicit and acknowledge external sponsorship on their shows—something Logo began to disallow— resulted in several video blogs leaving the site. Although AfterEllen treated its video producers no worse than they would have been at most other digital outlets and vloggers did benefit from exposure and the opportunity to redirect viewers to their own websites, the acquisition of most of this content without paying the creators underscored how AfterEllen conformed to the commercial norms of digital media.

Another factor in the decline of video at AfterEllen was the rebranding that Logo began implementing in 2010, discussed in more detail in chapter 3. Much of the content that had been more diverse in both content and contributors did not survive, with an overhaul of AfterEllen and AfterElton in the second half of 2011 eliminating almost all of the video blogs, most of which were low-budget programs in commentary or talk show format such as *Brunch with Bridget* on AfterEllen and *Two Gay Guys* on AfterElton, as well as *She Got Me Pregnant*, about lesbian motherhood, and *The Gay Agenda*, about LGBTQ politics, on AfterEllen. These shifts did not just affect Logo's acquired websites. In 2009, Logo executive Marc Leonard described the network's music programming as "predominantly made up of independent LGBT artists," and affirmed Logo's commitment to such shows even when this would not be the most profitable decision because while "there's something about a music video on an MTV-owned channel" and so "we'll find room for it on the schedule because this matters." Yet less than two years later, Logo eliminated both *The Click List: Top 10 Videos* (for music videos) and *The Click List: Best in Short Film* from LogoONLINE, demonstrating their eventual dispensability as well.

Contemporary Legacies: New Bifurcations of Independent and Commercial Production

Although Bravo's and Logo's websites did not endure long term, their emergence and existence had multiple impacts on the subsequent production and distribution of LGBTQ media. They demonstrated the range of content that audiences were interested in as well as modeling ways that it could—or could not be—financially viable at different levels of investment, from independent producers making a single web series to large streaming services hosting LGBTQ content as part of a large library, as well as endeavors in between these two ends of the scale.

In terms of their demise, the struggles that Bravo's and Logo's websites experienced even after some prominence and financial success were not unique for LGBTQ sites. Discussing the 1995–2009 rise and fall of PlanetOut, the clear rival to Logo's digital properties, Ben Aslinger argued that a site that had "promoted itself initially as the alternative to old media representations of queerness" suffered the outcomes both of the fact that LGBTQ content had become increasingly available in mainstream media, and thus advertisers seeking queer audiences had more options, and that its own processes of mainstreaming and conglomeration "risked nullifying its own existence for being—its status as a new way to address queer audiences."[25] These factors were in play to some extent for Bravo and Logo, but the reasons that the networks' strategies for their websites did not end up being sustainable were also due to a range of different reasons. OutZoneTV's primary issue was that it had little original video content that differentiated it from what was available on the BravoTV website, so Out-ZoneTV did not attract enough traffic. Bravo also shuttered TWoP in 2014 for financial reasons. For 365gay, the capacities of the internet to rapidly circulate content, which had initially been key to the appeal of its *365gay News* segments, also contributed to its declining ability to draw viewers. For three years, the *Week in Review* show aired on the Logo channel was divided into shorter clips and uploaded to 365gay, where it was initially very popular, but this was discontinued in 2009 since, as 365gay editor in chief Jay Vanasco commented, "it's kind of silly . . . because there's nothing new at that point; everybody's seen it."

AfterEllen and AfterElton had a more complex legacy. Unlike OutZoneTV, the two sites had a large amount of original video content that drew, especially for AfterEllen, a significant amount of traffic. Yet even as the most popular lesbian entertainment website, AfterEllen's numbers were not considered lucrative enough for Logo, which eventually sold the site to a non-LGBTQ-focused digital media company, Evolve Media, in 2014. AfterElton was rebranded as The-Backlot for a couple of years before being folded into Logo's NewNowNext site in 2015. However, AfterEllen in particular helped both demonstrate and generate the demand for original LGBTQ video made by both major commercial media providers and independent producers, through a series of overlaps between what it streamed and promoted at its site as part of Logo and a broader subfield of queer independent production.

As the previous chapter outlined, some site staff moved to other positions within commercial media, and in that sense, websites such as AfterEllen, AfterElton, 365gay, and OutZoneTV ended up functioning as bridges between fan or independent spaces and other contexts of media production. Yet beyond these more concrete outcomes, the sites also contributed to subtler changes in normalizing the production and streaming of LGBTQ video. Bravo and Logo had first begun doing so by making episodes or clips of their own shows available on their main websites—including *Queer Eye* on BravoTV and *RuPaul's Drag Race* on LogoONLINE. However, Logo's acquired websites, especially AfterEllen with its success in soliciting and hosting original queer video, demonstrated the demand for original LGBTQ digital content, especially scripted shows. This was important for the emergence of such content on streaming platforms, or what the industry calls "streamers."

Facilitated by a confluence of streaming and viewing technologies,[26] streamers rose rapidly to prominence at the end of the 2000s: Netflix added streaming content to its DVD delivery service in 2010, while the two other earliest such services, Hulu, which started streaming in 2008, began producing original programming in 2011, and Amazon launched Prime Video in 2011. In the last few years, these have been joined by an influx of network- or studio-specific services such as (HBO) Max, Paramount+, Disney Plus, and Peacock, as well as "over-the-top" multichannel providers such as Sling TV that allow consumers to choose specific channels for their package. None of the major services are LGBTQ-focused, but because they have such large inventories, just a minority of series or films on these sites having queer content means that they constitute a significant part of the LGBTQ media landscape. Furthermore, the first major streamer, Netflix, made its mark early on with several acclaimed shows featuring queer protagonists.[27]

As for independent production, in the last decade and a half, as Aymar Jean Christian has discussed, a number of platforms with goals, practices, and scales of production distinct from both legacy television and major streaming services have emerged, drawing producers and viewers invested in narratives rooted in queerly specific lived experience. Most of those focused on queer content developed after the most successful years for Logo's websites, including No More Down Low for Black gay news in 2010; GLO, The Arthouse, and SLAY TV for series about queer people of color in 2010, 2015, and 2016, respectively; and Between Women TV with content about queer women in 2015.[28] However, many of these websites have not survived more than a few years, facing constant challenges of securing sufficient funding for production if they are also involved in content creation, as well as reaching viewers in a dense streaming landscape. Besides the largest streaming services, consumers can search for free LGBTQ content on general video hosting sites such as YouTube, which is home to numerous queer bloggers and LGBTQ web series.[29] As a concrete pushback to the dominance of such commercial services, Christian, a media producer as well as scholar based at Northwestern University, founded the Open TV platform (https://www.weareo.tv) in 2015 with funding from various noncommercial sources, which supports and hosts "intersectional pilots and web series" made by Chicago artists. Although its content is not exclusively queer, Open TV is home to several series centered on queer characters of color, with *Brown Girls* (Fatimah Asghar and Sam Bailey, 2017) attaining some mainstream prominence in being nominated for an Emmy for Outstanding Short-Form Comedy or Drama Series and attracting interest from HBO.[30]

Occupying a middle ground between Open TV and the largest streamers are several commercial sites dedicated to LGBTQ films and series. One of the earliest is Tello Films, its trajectory another legacy from the era of Bravo's and Logo's websites. With only content featuring queer women, it was founded in 2007 in the wake of AfterEllen's success, although it did not have any text-only content. Also unlike AfterEllen, it soon went to a subscriber model, as it could not be sustained by advertising revenue; subscription fees were initially $3.99 per month and are currently $6.99 per month, still less than Netflix's cheapest $9.99-per-month option. Its content has primarily been a mix of series specifically supported by fan contributions, such as the lesbian detective series *Nikki and Nora* (2013), funds for which came primarily from an Indiegogo campaign, and other modestly budgeted web series. In 2013, Tello Films merged with the One More Lesbian (OML) website (OML.com), with Tello producing the content and OML hosting it, promising to deliver a "lesbian Netflix" with the joint resources of the two companies.[31] This arrangement lasted several years before

Tello returned to streaming its content at its own site, while OML now primarily aggregates freely available content hosted at other sites.[32] In 2018, Tello also began streaming acquired content, including the BBC-produced series *Lip Service*, and independent lesbian-themed films such as *Beyond Love* (Silvio Nacucchi, 2015), *Fear of Water* (Kate Lane, 2014), and *S & M Sally* (Michelle Ehlen, 2015). However, Tello does not have exclusive screening rights to such films (all of the aforementioned were available for purchase on Amazon Prime as well), and in the last few years, Tello has begun making its own films, which it had earlier forgone in favor of web series for budget reasons. Its Christmas romantic comedy *Season of Love*, made available to subscribers in December 2019, garnered some positive attention in the LGBTQ and mainstream press.

A newer example is Revry (revry.tv), which was established in the United States in 2016 but aims for a more globally oriented service that has included acquiring non-English-language content and subtitling it. As Julia Himberg noted, the platform explicitly positions itself as distinct from mainstream LGBTQ media, with Revry's website describing its programming as "unapologetically . . . queer and made for the queer community,"[33] featuring the kinds of queers— including Canadian Indigenous women, gender nonconforming people, and trans people of color—"often omitted from television."[34] Its strategy of making "short-form digital content—including digital series, music videos, pure audio music, and podcasts—the backbone of our service"[35] also distinguishes it from the major streamers and makes Revry more like smaller platforms such as Open TV, though with a 2022 annual revenue estimated as around $8.8 million,[36] Revry is still substantially larger. Supported through a mix of advertising revenue and subscriptions, Revry is able to offer its ad-supported options free to users,[37] although much of its original content is marked "Premium," available only for subscribers.

Other subscription streaming services with only LGBTQ content that have started up in the last few years include the Taiwan-based GagaOOLala (www.gagaoolala.com) in 2016,[38] South Africa's Pride TV (www.pridetv.co.za), which was in operation 2016–2020, and in the United States, Dekkoo (www.dekkoo.com) in 2017. These services, some of which are available as add-on apps to platforms such as Amazon and Apple TV,[39] provide a mix of content that has already aired or streamed elsewhere, independent films or series that the sites acquire, and for some sites, a limited amount of programming that they produce themselves. In addition, WOW Presents Plus was launched by *RuPaul's Drag Race*'s production company, World of Wonder, in 2018 and primarily streams the various global versions of *Drag Race*.

There are, however, no longer any major commercial LGBTQ-centric websites like AfterEllen and AfterElton, where full access to free original video was not dependent on paying subscription fees. As such, those sites constituted a distinct period in the emergence and development of queer digital content, one involving the convergence of independent and network producers and resources within commercial media. They also provided spaces for engagement between queer producers and their fans that was often crucial to publicizing the series to other potential viewers. The character of these digital affordances facilitated user interactions more generally, which the next section examines first at Bravo's and Logo's websites, and then how queer interactions around LGBTQ media expanded beyond those sites.

Digital Engagement and Social Mediafication

As the last section discussed, websites such as OutZoneTV, AfterEllen, and AfterElton emerged as new digital spaces centered on LGBTQ media, including original video content. Another characteristic of these developments was crucial: they occurred just when online spaces were cementing their status as the primary ways for viewers to engage with each other (and with producers) *and* when both LGBTQ content and popular media fandoms more generally were becoming more central in mainstream culture. The interactivity that the sites facilitated was, of course, attractive to the network owners as well as the content producers, factors that informed how the sites were developed. Interactivity also meant that the websites comprised new spaces for LGBTQ users to engage with each other through an initial meeting point of pop cultural interests, something that had been happening in smaller fan spaces online but not, until this moment, in the domain of major commercial media.

User interactions were also sometimes in service of romantic/sexual connection, which was to some extent an unintended by-product of the social mediafication of especially Logo's websites.[40] Given the range of LGBTQ interactions online geared to sexual encounters, there has been a substantial body of research examining issues such as anonymity and self-presentation, the formation of sexual identities online, and intersections of sexuality with other axes of identity.[41] Here, however, my primary focus is how spaces for LGBTQ interaction emerged within commercial media, before social media and mobile platforms became widely available for digital interaction more broadly. Jenkins and other fan studies scholars have discussed the ways that popular culture provides spaces for expression and connection for traditionally disempowered groups, but they were typically talking about either sites that are not part of major media networks or studios, or about officially sanctioned websites soliciting fan content for particular media texts/franchises such as *Star Wars*. The distinctiveness of Bravo's and Logo's websites was that they were neither of these; instead, established as sites centered on popular media, they belonged (after acquisition, for some of the sites) to a major commercial media network and were freely accessible for users to engage with each other through public and private interactions online.

Network and Producer Uses of Digital Media

Bravo and Logo were at the vanguard of television networks that began using digital media to both promote their on-air content, particularly on Facebook and

Twitter, and as new content platforms. For example, for Logo's most popular show, *RuPaul's Drag Race*, the network sometimes showed users' tweets about the show scrolling across the bottom of the screen during the episode airings. Similarly, Bravo fostered user engagement by giving fans the opportunity to interact with each other as well as with stars of particular Bravo shows on Facebook, Twitter, and mobile chat, during scheduled events such as "viewing parties" or when a show was on air.

Another emergent strategy was to have reality stars maintain a social media presence even when their show was not airing. For example, numerous judges and contestants on Bravo's reality shows and all the stars of Logo's *The A List* had Twitter accounts to routinely interact with fans. And as detailed by Jacquelyn Arcy, although the stars of Bravo's *Real Housewives* series were not contractually required to post on social media, the network created strong financial incentives to devote considerable labor to doing so, particularly in performing the kinds of dramatic personalities and conflicts that drew viewers to the show episodes.[42] For scripted programming, characters also started appearing on Twitter soon after the platform became available. This first gained prominence when fans of AMC's *Mad Men* created accounts for each of the main characters. AMC forced Twitter to shut these down briefly for reasons of proprietary content but then had a change of heart and allowed the accounts to be reinstated.[43] Fan-run Twitter character accounts popped up for other popular shows, including HBO's *True Blood*, SyFy's *Battlestar Galactica*, and TNT's *Rizzoli & Isles*, and even shows that were already off the air, such as *Twin Peaks* and *The West Wing*.[44] Unsurprisingly, networks began initiating such accounts for some of their shows as well. For example, David Gale, executive vice president of new media at MTV (Logo's parent company), described a "sitcom-type show" in production where the actors were contracted to enact their characters on Twitter and Facebook, with the rationale being that viewers "fall in love with the characters" even though "you know they're not real, but that doesn't mean you don't want to watch their comings and goings if you could, like if you didn't have to wait a whole week to engage with them."

As for LGBTQ content producers, the ability of online media to reach audiences in a way that had been far more limited in a pre-digital era had both positive and negative aspects. For some producers, digital outlets meant that they could now partially support themselves from their work. At AfterElton, Brent Hartinger commented that it was "easy to idealize the old gay press," but when he was working in print gay journalism in the 1990s, he could barely make a living, in comparison to being on the editorial staff of AfterElton after Logo's purchase. Dalila Ali Rajah noted that social media sites were what had enabled the success of her talk show *Cherry Bomb* without the aid of any major sponsors or media networks. GD, a queer musician whose work was featured in a film screened at the Logo-sponsored NewFest LGBTQ film festival in 2010, saw You-Tube as "an amazing tool," particularly as she recalled trying to distribute and publicize her music earlier in her career. And Sekiya Dorsett, a queer filmmaker who was working as a producer at NBC Universal at the time, pointed to You-Tube enabling a queer Black vlogger, B. Scott,[45] to gain hundreds of thousands of followers, so much so that he had made it onto mainstream radar.[46]

Yet the ways that digital media circulate also entail producers knowing far less about who is likely to engage with their texts versus the earlier, more insular circuits of print. In some cases, this led to losses for queer media in terms of content diversity and sociopolitically significant challenges to the status quo of both mainstream and LGBTQ communities. Thus, 365gay editor in chief Jay Vanasco commented on the downside for LGBTQ news being so easily searchable and circulated online; if she ventured onto particularly hot-button topics, homophobic commentators could seize on parts of her articles and suggest that she was advocating for what they saw as outrageous positions, counter to Vanasco's intentions to promote informed debate. Whereas for the print publications she had previously worked for, Vanasco could assume that she was writing "just for a gay audience," she began noticing that with online columns, "stuff that I used to be able to say about . . . things that were edgy even for us" sometimes ended up on a conservative website that had quoted her out of context to further demonize the LGBTQ community. This led Vanasco feeling more and more pressed to do "advocacy journalism" on less controversial topics such as marriage equality or employment rights, rather than offering in-depth consideration of topics such as polyamory, intergenerational relationships, or the gay bear subculture.

Arguably even more transformative was how digital media changed the ways that users interacted, and in these respects, Bravo's and Logo's websites offered clear new possibilities. The addition of social media–like characteristics at these sites both reflected the rising prominence of social media platforms proper and comprised a key part of the landscape of queer interactions arising from popular media. In crucial ways, these developments at Bravo's and Logo's sites were positive for the growth of LGBTQ community, with the increased user traffic helping to pay for site expenses through the advertising revenue generated, although this did not prove sufficient in the longer term.

The New Queer Digital Water Coolers

As Jenkins noted when viewer discussions of popular media began flourishing online, "television provides fodder for so-called water cooler conversations. And, for a growing number of people, the water cooler has gone digital," with fans interacting at numerous online spaces "to share their knowledge and opinions."[47] For LGBTQ media more specifically, Bravo's and Logo's websites emerged around the same time as the major social media platforms, constituting important bridges to contemporary conditions of user interaction at a moment before the dominance of Facebook, Instagram, and Twitter, as well as a plethora of mobile dating apps. While there were already various other online dating spaces, particularly for queer men,[48] sites like AfterEllen and AfterElton in particular as well as OutZoneTV were not explicitly for dating—though in some cases they facilitated its occurrence under the radar—but primarily served as queer digital water coolers centered on pop culture and available free of charge.

Maria San Filippo discussed AfterEllen serving as the "new lesbian bar on the cyberscene," and constituting a queer counterpublic through media commentary that linked it to a longer history of feminist cultural criticism.[49] She also noted the rising proportion of user-generated content versus staff posts; indeed, this was symptomatic of the site's turn toward expanding user engagement more generally. A discussion of how AfterEllen underwent processes of *social mediafication* illustrates how it facilitated a greater amount and more kinds of interaction among the site's users, though there were also drawbacks to these changes. In addition, by no means did all efforts by media corporations to capitalize on queer interest for digital engagement succeed, and examining the failure of Our-Chart, a prominent lesbian social networking site arising from the Showtime series *TLW*, underscores the distinct relative longevity of Logo's websites.

Shortly after Warn launched AfterEllen, commenting on articles was enabled, and a message board was introduced where users were able to begin threads on any topics of interest. The message boards quickly became very active; managing editor Malinda Lo recalled one thread about Swedish athletes that grew to dozens of pages long, which meant thousands of posts. However, what substantially increased site traffic was the introduction of features originating at social media sites: member profiles with a number of Facebook-like options. Warn spearheaded these initiatives to attract younger users and increase the size of the sites' communities. The goal was not to compete with Facebook and MySpace but to incorporate some of their popular features into AfterEllen and AfterElton: the ability for users to register accounts, associate photos with them, and update their statuses, as well as add friends to a "buddy list" and see when they were online, comment on other people's profiles, and communicate via email-like messaging.

Soon after these features were introduced, AfterEllen in particular experienced a large surge in page views, driven significantly by the roughly 20 percent of users who had registered for a profile. Users could now interact publicly on the message boards or on comment threads associated with various AfterEllen official posts (written articles or videos), semipublicly through posts on their own profile pages or those of their friends, as well as privately by direct-messaging other users. The most active users could signal their recognition of each other across different comment threads, which sometimes occurred not just between site users but between the site contributors and users, thus strengthening the feel of the site as a community.

Sites like AfterEllen, AfterElton, and OutZoneTV did not simply facilitate pleasurable social interaction; they were also crucial lifelines for queer users for whom digital spaces were the only ones where they could read about and engage with other queer people. Zac Hug noted OutZoneTV's significance in providing a less highly sexualized space than gay men's dating sites for LGBTQ youth to visit and see that "there are more people like me out there who are funny and who are living a productive life," and the website also linked to resources such as the Trevor Project. AfterEllen staff spoke about receiving comments or messages from users, especially older lesbians outside the United States, saying that the only queer women they knew were those on the site.[50]

Furthermore, although it was not intended to function in this way, a number of AfterEllen visitors used it as an unofficial lesbian dating site: the social networking features meant that users could see photos of other users and interact with them without immediately and obviously signaling romantic interest. AfterEllen happened to be highly suitable for the reticence of many queer women with respect to dating, with Warn remarking that they "would rather actually meet other women just by liking the same things and getting into each other slowly over time," and AfterEllen was ideal since "it allows you to indirectly, passively look for dating options without looking like that's what you're doing!" Indeed, Warn and other AfterEllen contributors commented about knowing multiple women who had gotten together and even married after meeting on AfterEllen.

At the same time, some of the increased interaction resulted in tensions among commenters. Not surprisingly, 365gay's news and politics posts could attract strong disagreement on topics such as same-sex marriage, but even on AfterEllen and AfterElton, users often argued heatedly about entertainment topics, particularly when the sites published ranked lists such as "best couples."[51] The less positive outcomes went beyond simply differences of opinion but comprised a broader shift in online discourses wrought by norms of increasing speed of exchanges, leaving less time for fact-checking and greater possibilities of emotional/less-well-considered posts. Scribegrrrl explained on her personal blog why she left AfterEllen in 2010 after being one of its earliest regular contributors, harkening back to earlier online fan sites where "there was no opportunity for readers to fire off unedited gut reactions, or use an article as a soapbox, or otherwise spray impulsive, irrelevant, destructive digital graffiti on my wall of carefully tended words. When they started doing that, even just occasionally, it started to seem like all my late-night searches for the perfect phrase just weren't worth it." Sarah Warn had stepped down from AfterEllen (and all her Logo editorial responsibilities) the previous year partly from feeling burnt-out from similar incidents, such as users wrongly accusing the site of missing coverage of significant instances of lesbian representation,[52] or discounting valid critiques of queer representation because they did not properly understand the analytical premises.

Warn saw a fault line by age, with many older site visitors frustrated by younger counterparts who made assertions without having all the facts, including on topics such as the history of lesbian representation which the older users often knew better. Queer media buffs who had initially gathered at these new digital water coolers, interested in digging deeper into particular show episodes or analytical topics, were being crowded out by a newer generation of users more comfortable with the emerging norms of online interaction that prioritized speed over deliberation. This predated the ways that social media platforms, especially those allowing only short posts such as Twitter, have been examined more recently for working against considered debate,[53] although the intense polarization of positions now commonly observed was not characteristic of Bravo's and Logo's websites.

With both positive and problematic characteristics, then, for several years, AfterEllen, AfterElton, and 365gay were prominent commercial media outlets where many LGBTQ users interacted.[54] The significance of this is made clearer from a comparison with other efforts by media corporations to create sites for queer interaction. After Logo's multiple acquisitions, its main rival, Here Media, with *The Advocate* and *Out* magazines and Gay.com already under its belt, snapped up a host of URLs, including those intended for LGBTQ seniors, gays in rural areas, and various LGBTQ communities of color, sites for social networking and dating, and sites with news, entertainment, business, employment, sports, and travel information.[55] However, almost all of these soon became defunct; the exception was LesbiaNation.com, later renamed SheWired.com, which was similar to AfterEllen in focusing on queer women in entertainment and news, but did not attain as much traffic and in 2016 was folded into Here Media's Pride.com site,[56] now home to its *Out* and *The Advocate* magazine online outlets.

Also illuminating for considering the creation and maintenance of commercial queer digital spaces is a comparison with the lesbian social networking site OurChart. Launched at the beginning of 2007, OurChart was founded by *TLW* creator Ilene Chaiken and several of the show's actors[57] in the wake of that series' success. The site name echoed the complicated "chart" featured on the show that mapped out sexual liaisons and relationships among the characters, and its byline was "The official social network of *The L Word*." Clicking on "The Chart"/"Profiles" tab allowed users to search for other users by gender identity, relationship status, and geographic location; there was also a discussion forum for a range of *TLW* and entertainment-related topics, text posts by OurChart staff, and a list of links to other feminist and queer blog sites. Cross-promotion on the series included numerous scenes of *TLW* characters with OurChart open on their computer screens or even explicitly enumerating the site's features. In addition, OurChart partnered with the commercial FanLib website, which had an association with Showtime, to hold contests for fans to write for the show.[58]

Although OurChart was an obvious competitor to AfterEllen, the two sites had a brief association, during which a graphic link to AfterEllen was prominently displayed on the main page. According to Sarah Warn, the bulk of OurChart's financial resources was devoted to making the site visually attractive and easy to use, as well as to marketing it to potential users, while little attention was directed toward securing advertising or other revenue sources that could support OurChart long term. This unfortunately compounded the problem that AfterEllen was also familiar with: an enduring stereotype of lesbians as anti-consumerist ecofeminists who, as Warn summed up, "make their own clothes, make their own food, and are all vegan."[59] Furthermore, advertisers at the time were also wary of social networking sites since the content of user pages was unpredictable and companies feared that their ads might end up next to sexually explicit or other problematic content. Thus, OurChart had two strikes against it in terms of becoming financially viable.

Although OurChart's visitors could not miss its official ties to *TLW* and Showtime, regardless of who officially owns a website, many queer users have sought to inhabit spaces of interaction that felt like they belonged, in a sense, to the communities that patronized them,[60] dynamics that applied particularly strongly to sites like AfterEllen and OurChart. The fallout from OurChart's sudden collapse, when financial stresses reached a crisis point in November 2008,[61] was exacerbated by a lack of transparency from the site's management team, including Ilene Chaiken, to both its staff and its registered users. OurChart staff were informed just hours beforehand about being laid off, while on the website, users were confused for several days about the lack of new content or any information about what had happened to all the staff. Even though eventually, an anonymous "OC Editor" posted a brief message about the site's closure, there was no explanation about the reasons or what would happen to user accounts. Many site members posted angry messages, including some holding Chaiken responsible or noting that they would cancel their Showtime subscriptions.

OurChart's corporate origins and downfall made it an easy target for criticism, particularly since Ilene Chaiken had never enjoyed unequivocal support among lesbian media fans.[62] AfterEllen, on the other hand, successfully cultivated its authenticity for several years after Logo's purchase. Sarah Warn continued to highlight AfterEllen's similarities to its roots as a smaller, independent site, responding to users disappointed about content the site failed to write about by saying, "Look, we've got three people on staff! We can't cover everything." She also presented herself to site users as simply the founder and editor in chief of AfterEllen even when she was a Logo executive, and there were conscious strategies to keep users unaware of the extent to which Warn and AfterEllen were tied to Logo.[63] Jay Vanasco made similar observations about her editorship of 365gay.[64]

It is unsurprising that Warn and Vanasco encouraged perceptions of their sites as retaining the character of grassroots LGBTQ media; after all, this appeal was part of what drew continued user engagement even under conditions of corporate ownership. Relatedly, the success of the websites as digital water coolers depended on users feeling a sense of community. The social mediafication features enhanced this potential but did not guarantee it. Thus, strategies to present site editors and other staff as "one of our own," as Warn put it, along the lines of both fan affiliations and being LGBTQ identified, were also important. This unique digital environment—one home to social media–like interactions for queer users but at a centralized website where site staff and users interacted regularly—was not to last, as social media platforms proper rose to the fore.

Social Media Platforms and Dispersed Discourses

Even though the incorporation of social media–like features on Bravo's and Logo's websites increased user traffic and engagement, they were still modest compared to what was available on platforms such as Facebook, Twitter, and Tumblr for digital social networking. Along with issues of financial sustainability to do with original content, as discussed earlier in the chapter, such limitations helped usher in the end of these network websites. Before shutting down in mid-2022, Logo's NewNowNext had lasted the longest under the same ownership as it started with, drawing an estimated 20,000 unique visitors daily,[65] but it had never been a site of much social interaction via comment threads and had no social networking features. AfterEllen remains active, though no longer under the Logo brand. For a couple of years after being sold in 2014 to a non-LGBTQ media company (Evolve Media), the site continued to garner high traffic, despite some notable missteps which infuriated many users, particularly its pre-airing promotion of the 2016 episode of *The 100* (CW, 2014–2020) in which a fan-favorite lesbian character was controversially killed off, and to a lesser extent, for providing a sympathetic platform for the showrunner of the CBS series *Person of Interest* (CBS, 2011–2016) after the death of another queer female character.[66] The most significant change to the site occurred when editor in chief Trish Bendix was fired in September 2016, with Evolve seeking to rein in costs despite the fact that Bendix had become the sole full-time employee—down from a peak of four full-time staff after Logo's purchase of the site. A post from an Evolve executive suggested that AfterEllen would remain up and maintained by content from freelance contributors,[67] but most observers thought it would effectively shut down without any regular editorial staff, lamenting this as an irreplaceable loss to queer women.[68] In fact, AfterEllen did continue posting some content from freelancers, eventually hiring a new editor in chief, Memoree Joelle, in December 2016; she ended up purchasing AfterEllen from Evolve Media in March 2019. However, the site now has much lower traffic,[69] in part because the frankly transphobic tenor established by Joelle has alienated many queer women.[70]

At one level, this reflects one fault line of the fracturing of queer communities online, with a landscape of much more dispersed interaction. The digital cohort that AfterEllen, AfterElton, OutZoneTV, and 365gay constituted—websites belonging to major commercial networks that facilitated queer user engagement around popular entertainment and news—has been succeeded by a slate of other kinds of websites, each with their own set of differences from Bravo's and Logo's sites. There are commercial LGBTQ sites such as Out, Pride, and Curve (originating from print publications) that include some news and entertainment coverage, but their scope is broader, and they lack features that produce a community of users who engage regularly around the site posts. A range of major commercial blog and commentary sites aimed at a general audience—for example, Medium and The Huffington Post (rebranded as Huff-Post after its 2020 acquisition by Buzzfeed)—host content mostly from free-lance contributors, which sometimes include pieces pertaining to LGBTQ media. Similar such sites specific to entertainment and fandom include Hypable and The Mary Sue, and some of the posts here do attract long comment threads. However, since these sites are not LGBTQ specific, they do not draw a large group of queer users who regularly encounter each other; furthermore, the comments on pieces of LGBTQ interest may include multiple posts expressing hostility to queer readings.[71]

There are also a large number of LGBTQ news and commentary sites, although some of these have little if any original editorial content, instead putting up posts based on newswire reports or stories first published at other outlets.[72] Still, three sites primarily oriented to gay men—LGBTQ Nation and Queerty, belonging to the independently owned Q.Digital,[73] and Towleroad, started up by Andy Towle in 2003—were established around the same time as the Bravo and Logo websites and have continued to attract visitors, with some threads having dozens of comments from registered users, but the sites do not have the social media features that AfterEllen, AfterElton, and 365gay did.[74]

One site that combines the characteristics of a blog and a social networking site is the independently owned site Autostraddle. When it was founded in 2009, it was similar to AfterEllen in targeting lesbians and bisexual women and focusing primarily on popular media, with its two founders, Riese Bernard and Laneia, having been involved in *TLW* fandom at the same time.[75] In more recent years, it has sought to also serve trans and nonbinary users and broadened its coverage of news and politics, sex and dating, and lifestyle areas such as food. Still independently owned, it is now the most visited entertainment and news site for queer women,[76] and registered users can not only comment but also customize their profile with pictures and text, "like" posts, add friends, and private message other users. Thus, in various ways, it has taken over the digital space occupied by AfterEllen for many years.

However, in the last decade, queer interaction around popular media—along with a huge amount of online interaction overall—has increasingly shifted to social media platforms. Even websites that still attract a significant number of regular visitors also post links to their content on their social media accounts, particularly Facebook and Twitter, and user discussions often take place in greater numbers there. Yet, unlike a single website, such interaction is much more diffuse, both because it is spread across multiple platforms and because on any one platform, such as Twitter, there will be multiple threads associated with a particular website, perhaps even with a single post. Although users might choose to follow a website's hashtag and therefore see many of the posts about the site's content, there is still a less cohesive set of interactions than when all commenting took place on the website.

A related development has been how a large number of media fandoms, primarily English-language ones, became clustered on another social media platform, Tumblr. As Lori Morimoto and Louisa Ellen Stein discussed, the migration of fans to Tumblr and away from digital spaces that had been popular earlier—such as Yahoo! Groups and LiveJournal, as well as other websites dedicated to single fandoms—resulted in major changes to how fans communicated, particularly in terms of decentralization, with the way that Tumblr posts are reblogged characterized by "rhizomatic spread and limited authorial control."[77] For queer fandoms, then, this has been another cause of the dispersal of user interaction.

Many posts on social media platforms, including Tumblr as well as Twitter and Instagram, are highly visual, with still images or gifs. Although these can also convey complex messages, such as a countless array of memes on multiple topics,[78] they are less conducive to the kinds of dialogic communication that a single text-based comment thread facilitates. Still, as Lori Morimoto and Louisa Ellen Stein point out, the visuality of these affordances has "lowered linguistic/textual barriers to entry within heretofore predominantly English-language online fandoms," while the relative lack of borders segmenting the discourses of individual users has facilitated "fandom cross-fertilization" and increased the "visibility of peripheral fans and fan communities as they bring their own perspectives to what may originally have been intended as in-group utterances."[79]

Primarily text-based message boards for fandom discussion have also persisted, including subreddits on the main Reddit forum about specific media texts,[80] as well as larger message board systems such as the Primetimer forum, which is, in a sense, the descendant of Television Without Pity in both lineage and form.[81] There are also message boards (or subsections of message boards) more specifically geared to queer fans. For example, DataLounge, up since 1995, is aimed at gay men interested in popular media and celebrity gossip, while The L Chat, established in 2009 as one of the subforums of the Zetaboards forums system but now shifted to new sites, covers the same territory for lesbians.[82] However, unlike many other message boards, both these sites allow for anonymous posting and such posts constitute the majority of the content, which leaves threads vulnerable to trolling despite some degree of moderation. Non-English-language queer fandoms have also proliferated in a variety of spaces, with global circulation of popular LGBTQ series aided by fan subtitling efforts.[83]

In sum, then, the landscape of a few major digital water coolers about LGBTQ entertainment that emerged during the peak of user activity at Bravo's and Logo's websites has yielded to a much greater number of interactional spaces, including blog-based websites, message boards, and social media platforms, and quite dispersed within each affordance type, not to mention the explosive growth of phone-based apps for sex and dating, which has also drawn much queer engagement. Although such contemporary conditions are not direct legacies of Bravo's and Logo's digital strategies, the website cohort of AfterEllen/AfterElton, OutZoneTV, 365gay, and Downelink constituted a distinct and significant portion of these developments.

Convergence Outcomes: New Spaces of LGBTQ Content and Interaction—for a Time

As chapter 1 considered for a new cohort of LGBTQ cultural agents who became staff at Bravo and Logo's websites, one of the key issues concerning convergence culture is how meaningfully it empowers those who were previously industry outsiders. This chapter continued to address this question with respect to content creators and site users engaging with websites that operated under the umbrella of a media corporation. I focused on AfterEllen to describe developments that emerged from the site's purchase by Logo, which increased the budget for supporting streaming content and adding user features on the site. Collectively, Bravo's and Logo's websites illustrated two trends that have been important for LGBTQ media more generally: the emergence of queer video, which proved important for many producers who previously would not have had their content distributed on commercial media outlets, and the social mediafication of the sites, creating new spaces for user interaction distinct from the various dating sites that were also burgeoning online.

However, a persistent issue for users of commercially owned sites is that they are vulnerable to decisions made on the basis of financial viability, not community interests. OurChart was a clear, dramatic example, but Bravo's and Logo's websites, in more drawn-out ways, also lost their networks' backing for financial reasons. The site shutdowns or shifts in content strategies meant the loss of outlets previously available to independent queer producers for distributing their content or LGBTQ users for social engagement. Although other digital spaces have emerged, by and large they do not offer the same water cooler experience that AfterEllen and AfterElton did. If, as mentioned earlier, AfterEllen had been *the* digital "lesbian bar" to hang out at for queer women, its loss of this status as well as the demise of OutZoneTV at Bravo and of Logo's other sites in some ways paralleled the closures of bricks-and-mortar gay and lesbian bars that, somewhat ironically, the rise of websites like AfterEllen and subsequently social media platforms and mobile apps may have helped precipitate.[84]

Even when the outcome is not as drastic as site closings, users of commercial sites have limited power over site policies. For example, in early 2017, a number of YouTubers who posted about LGBTQ issues noticed that at least some of their videos were being blocked (and demonetized) by the site's "Restricted Mode" feature, intended to filter out "mature content." Although YouTube announced that it had instigated fixes a few months later, some vloggers reported in 2019 that their experiments with labeling videos that they uploaded to YouTube demonstrated that the site's algorithms were still biased against LGBTQ-themed content.[85] On a different platform, the infamous 2018 Tumblr ban on "adult content," intended to prevent the sharing of child pornography but written and enforced so broadly that it prohibited many kinds of sexual content, hit the queer communities that had patronized and thus supported the platform particularly hard. As commentator Steven Thrasher argued, such users helped produce "massive capital benefit for Silicon Valley and Wall Street," and yet "the people who generate that wealth have no influence over the digital commons where it resides and no recourse if they're evicted from it."[86] Earlier media fandoms had experienced various kinds of site censorships and shutdowns,[87] leading fan activists and scholars to establish the nonprofit Organization for Transformative Works in 2008, which includes running the queer-friendly Archive of Our Own site for fan fiction free for authors and readers,[88] but Archive of Our Own does not host audio or video content.

At another level, the significance of Bravo's and Logo's websites goes beyond what they offered while they were active and what was immediately lost when they became defunct. As this chapter also traced, the trajectories of the sites comprised an important transitional period leading to two major characteristics of contemporary media for LGBTQ users: the availability of LGBTQ content on streaming services and the crucial role of social media platforms to queer user interactions. For both content and interaction, there is now a more dispersed landscape of user engagement, with many of the most popular spaces belonging to major media corporations, although a number of independent sites remain. How to theorize and represent these developments in relation to the traditional mainstream-independent distinction vis-à-vis LGBTQ media will be taken up further in chapter 4.

Also central to such changes were shifts in Bravo's and Logo's linear programming, comprising content strategies that were initiated even as the cachet of queerness in popular culture seemed at a peak. The next chapter examines how rebranding strategies at both networks changed the trajectories of LGBTQ content at the channels as well as at the websites. As the fate of both legacy and digital LGBTQ programming at Bravo and Logo demonstrates, broader industrial trends for U.S. television also reshaped where and what kind of LGBTQ media was most successfully produced and distributed.

3

Gaystreaming, Dualcasting, and Changing Queer Alignments

• •

"Too Gay Niche": Channel Rebranding and Programming Strategies

> Just like in any type of storytelling, your first twenty minutes or whatever of the movie is a lot of exposition, like, "this is the world we're living in, these are the characters." And a lot of what Logo did when it first launched was "Here's a documentary about gay rodeo, because you don't know that it exists, but it does"; there was a lot of just sheer presentation and exposition.
>
> —Chris Willey, Logo development executive

> It's almost like the extremes of the balance of who we are are between two points: *Queer Eye for the Straight Guy* on one side and the *Real Housewives* on the other.... How does this group of women, these real housewives, whether they are characters in our series or if they're part of our audience, how do they translate that message that originally came from *Queer Eye* and how it was disseminated into current programming? That's what we are right now; we're in the middle of that area.
>
> —Bernard Grenier, Bravo development executive

When Logo began airing as a new cable channel in July 2005, its first moments on air were a rapidly intercut collage of gays and lesbians on U.S. television, followed by a thirty-minute documentary called *The Evolution Will Be Televised*. A riff on soul artist Gil Scott-Heron's 1971 political protest song "The Revolution Will Not Be Televised," the program located Logo's launch as a high point for LGBTQ media representation. In keeping with the tone set by *Evolution*, Logo produced or acquired a number of documentaries spotlighting different queer communities in its first year, along with airing films and series with lesbian and gay main characters. Five years later, the network's programming was headlined by *The A List*, a show following a group of well-off gay men in New York City that was one of several new reality series filling Logo's fall 2010 slate, though one of the few with a predominantly gay cast. Ratings-wise, the show was successful enough for Logo to both renew it and produce *The A List: Dallas* for 2011, although the more enduring success for Logo was *RuPaul's Drag Race*, which began airing in 2009.

Two years earlier, Bravo had begun a network rebranding that foreshadowed Logo's makeover. Through different ownerships since 1980, Bravo had largely aired independent and other critically well-received films, along with theatrical and orchestral performances. Its most prominent original programming at the time was *Inside the Actors Studio* in which host James Lipton held conversational interviews with household-name performers. As Bernard Grenier, who worked for the Bravo content development division, recalled, many of the network's older viewers were watching arts programming on what they saw as "a very *sensible* network." Another former development executive, Rachel Smith, noted that as an arts and entertainment network, Bravo had always had a sizable minority of "urban, gay" viewers, but in 2002, Bravo began to program shows that would more explicitly appeal to that audience, in the then-relatively new genre of reality programming. *Gay Weddings* and *Boy Meets Boy* were produced for Bravo just as NBC Universal purchased the network, and *Queer Eye for the Straight Guy* (later titled just *Queer Eye*) premiered shortly afterward.

During this period, comparisons of Logo and Bravo yielded clear differences in their strategies, content, and appeal. In a 2006 *New York Times* review of the premiere of Bravo's fitness reality series *Work Out*, Alessandra Stanley described the network as having "a gay identity and a strong following that reaches beyond gay audiences," with shows that provided "an arena where gays and straights interact, sometimes in harmony and sometimes in conflict, but almost always with flair and a sense of humor," leading her to declare that Bravo was "the premier gay network, even though it is not labeled as such."[1] In this vein, research by marketing firm Prime Access and the PlanetOut website found that in 2008, the Bravo brand was recognized by over half of gay consumers, and Bravo was also the company ranked most "gay-friendly" by these consumers (and also by a significant proportion of straight consumers).[2] In contrast, Stanley called Logo "an earnest, didactic celebration of sexual self-determination in even its most marginal manifestations: gay Republicans, biker lesbians and many gender-defying groups" that was "worthy, but too narrowly cast to draw a broad spectrum of viewers." As Katherine Sender put it, Logo was at this point engaged in "gay narrowcasting," which raised the question of whether it would "offer sufficiently diverse programming to appeal to a large enough audience to be profitable, and thus whether it can afford to provide a sustained television environment committed primarily to GLBT audiences."[3]

Preceding Bravo's and Logo's programming in the 2000s is a longer history of mainstream media including gay and lesbian content not primarily aimed at LGBTQ audiences, alongside shifts within and beyond the media domain. Much mainstream media has both hypersexualized and desexualized LGBTQ characters;[4] hypersexualization focuses inordinately on the *sexual* identities and practices of queers, particularly when non-normative sexuality is tied to criminal and/or psychological deviancy, yet actual sexual expression by otherwise "normal" LGBTQ characters has often been absent or downplayed, in case it is found to be too confronting to a heterosexual majority.[5] Ron Becker examined the proliferation of gay and lesbian narrative elements on many of the most watched U.S. network series in the 1990s, such as *Roseanne, Friends, Frasier,* and *NYPD Blue*, contextualizing these developments within cultural and economic trends in the United States, particularly processes of urban renewal that drew in cohorts of well-off, predominantly white, and politically progressive residents who were attractive targets for commercial media, whom Becker labeled "slumpies" (socially liberal urban-minded professionals).[6] Major corporations also became more willing to place their commercials in LGBTQ-themed programming or on LGBTQ websites; *New York Times* advertising columnist Stuart Elliott noted that during tough economic times, such as the 1990s U.S. recession, many companies sought out consumer segments they had previously steered away from in order to mine any untapped earning potential.[7] Still, making gayness palatable to mainstream audiences at that time relied heavily on desexualized representations, with gay and lesbian characters serving primarily as dramatic or comedic fodder for the heterosexual characters. Concomitantly sidelined were queer identities and practices that would seriously challenge existing sociopolitical norms.[8]

In the 2000s, scripted series such as *Glee* (Fox, 2009–2015), *Grey's Anatomy* (ABC, 2005–present), and *Modern Family* (ABC, 2009–2020) on the major networks and a slew of others on basic cable featured LGBTQ regulars whose sexuality was depicted in more nuanced ways, allowing viewers to see LGBTQ characters on popular shows with high production values; LGBTQ participants also became frequent on reality shows, such as *America's Next Top Model* (UPN/CW/VHS, 2003–2018), *Big Brother* (CBS, 2000–present), *Survivor* (CBS, 2000–present), and *The Amazing Race* (CBS, 2001–present). However, these shows continued to be aimed at "mainstream" audiences—that is, those assumed to be heterosexual.

Three important elements distinguished Bravo's and Logo's programming strategies from these earlier kinds of content. First, both Bravo and Logo had websites that figured into the networks' overall strategies, not just as spaces to promote channel programming but also as sites of original content. This meant that there could potentially be greater content differentiation, with the websites targeting specific audiences that the channel did not, as chapter 2 discussed, particularly through short-form web series and vlogs. At the same time, industry advice for web series creators was often to keep their series "promotable"— that is, no profane language, no nudity, and no overly explicit sex[9]—which was quite similar to the norms of legacy advertiser-supported television. Although there was some variation across the sites in terms of language,[10] such parameters were by and large followed by Logo's websites in particular, with the motivations not simply financial but also brand related. Logo executives were aware that they were competing against existing websites, particularly Gay.com, which drew considerable and profitable traffic from providing spaces for online dating. Logo was after a piece of the digital pie that was clearly distinct from websites that foregrounded sex and included sexually explicit user-generated content,[11] and thus, with the exception of Downelink, acquired or developed sites focused on entertainment (AfterEllen, AfterElton), leisure (TripOutTravel), and news (365gay, VisibleVote2008).

Second, both Bravo and Logo intentionally targeted queer viewers, though only particular segments and not exclusively. Indeed, several network executives drew on discourses of progress and evolution in tying programming developments to the increasing integration of LGBTQ people within mainstream society, indirectly referencing processes of decriminalization, depathologization, and destigmatization pertinent to their legal, medical, and political status, and argued that there was less and less reason to program so specifically to LGBTQ viewers.

Logo marketing executive Claudia Gorelick commented that "the need for niche is shrinking," a key consideration spurring Logo's rebranding strategies, and when asked about Gorelick's comment, multiplatform programming executive Marc Leonard stated that "all the people who were in our niche before are still in our niche, but we've just made some room for everyone else to come visit." Kristin Frank, a senior marketing and distribution executive with whom Leonard worked closely for several years at Logo, likened the growth of commercial LGBTQ media to the development of hip-hop's popularity; where hip-hop used to be "an incredibly niched" entertainment genre, it had broadened enough to garner the interest of a much larger spectrum of people. The rhetoric and realities of what Frank referred to as a broader "tent" had obvious appeal from both commercial and cultural perspectives, yet also raised the question of how this shift in the relations of the center to the margins would impact both LGBTQ and mainstream media.

The period examined in this chapter considers the programming directions for Bravo in the wake of its high-profile success with *Queer Eye* and for Logo a few years after its launch, which overlapped this period. Bravo's strategies, aptly termed "dualcasting" by Sender,[12] and Logo's, which network executives called "gaystreaming," both involved integrations of LGBTQ content designed to appeal to a mix of straight and queer viewers, and constituted the emergence of a new gay center in commercial media that—once again after flirting with greater diversity—catered most strongly to white men.

The pairing of gay men with straight women—in lived realities, media representation, and industry rhetoric—figured prominently in the discourses and practices of dualcasting and gaystreaming. A shared sympathy for strong emotional expression has often been attributed to these two groups, particularly in the form of being "drama queens." Film studies scholars have discussed the gay male identifications with women on screen, particularly larger-than-life characters in genres such as the classical Hollywood "woman's film," musicals, and horror,[13] and this thread informs how Bravo's and then Logo's reality programming targeted viewers. In addition, the appeal of gay male relationships to many straight women has been chronicled in fan studies[14] and may have been part of the reason why some straight women were drawn to Logo's programming about gay men's relationships.

A trend of depicting gay men and straight women as friends had already emerged in scripted programming in the 1990s—for example, the titular characters of *Will and Grace* (NBC, 1998–2006) or Carrie Bradshaw and Stanley Blatch on *Sex and the City* (HBO, 1998–2004)[15]—partly reflecting conditions where straight women, especially those who are well-off, interact with gay men who provide service as hair stylists, decorators, wedding planners, and so forth, or enjoy friendships around shared interests in beauty and fashion, design, and popular culture around which reality series centered on style and "living the good life" revolve. In such ways, the straight woman–gay man affinity hinges on a trope of taking pleasure in consumption, with the media and advertising industries having long seen heterosexual women as important and influential consumers,[16] while the construction of a gay market in the United States drew on and reinscribed assumptions that gay men rather than lesbians would be substantial spenders.[17]

Furthermore, as Elisa Cohen chronicled, in post–World War II America, activities in the realm of consumption became articulated as a primary form of public participation, tying consumerism to gendered, raced, and classed identities in discourses around patriotism and nation building.[18] Ben Aslinger noted that at the time of its launch, Logo reinscribed stereotypes of gays as affluent and brand-loyal consumers,[19] and this was true several years later as well, with Logo executive Kristin Frank's comments to me that the network's audience "indexes higher in income, indexes higher in education, indexes higher in discretionary spending, indexes higher in loyalty" typical of other interviewees. Thus, the ways that gaystreaming reinforced the trope of the good gay (especially male) consumer also enmeshed such imagined subjects more closely with dominant forms of national identity.

Third, LGBTQ cultural workers played key roles at Bravo and Logo, including as both new content producers and gatekeepers. I discussed these workers in chapter 1, including the origins for some of them outside of industrial media, from fandom, the gay print press, and independent queer production. as well as how, collectively, the particular identifications and professional dispositions of the majority—white and middle class—shaped their networks' programming.[20] Queer cultural agents marginalized by other inequalities, such as race, ethnicity, and gender nonconformity, found access to these new spaces of commercial LGBTQ production more limited, and dualcasting and gaystreaming exacerbated these inequities overall. Dualcasting and gaystreaming were characterized by "homonormativity," Lisa Duggan's term for the embrace of dominant heteronormative practices and institutions, such as marriage and the military, by a depoliticized gay culture oriented toward consumption and private home life.[21] As such, these programming strategies fed into narratives of progressiveness on LGBTQ rights that failed to interrogate Western complicity in the production and subjugation of abject sexual identities elsewhere, a phenomenon that Jasbir Puar has discussed with particular reference to the United States.[22]

Ultimately, neither Bravo nor Logo maintained any LGBTQ-centric shows; Bravo remained largely the same in terms of its reality programming sans *Queer Eye*, but Logo abandoned all original programming after 2017. This illustrated the phenomenon, mentioned in the previous chapter, that Alfred Martin has labeled "queer dispersal," with commercial media quick to program to queer audiences when it proves profitable but readily shedding such content when more lucrative options emerge.[23] Even though Logo did persist with different iterations of LGBTQ programming for over a decade, one of the main reasons for its eventual decline was that it could no longer use such content to brand itself with sufficiently appealing distinction. Thus, the chapter ends by highlighting how similar kinds of content to Bravo's dualcasting and Logo's gaystream programming have become more broadly available, pointing to questions these developments raise for television studies accounts of niche strategies, particularly for LGBTQ media in an era of "peak TV."

The Evolution of LGBTQ Content at Bravo

> When we do shows about beauty, fashion, pop culture, food, and design, you are attracting a certain type of person. There happen to be fields with a lot of gay people in them. . . . It's not enough to be a gay character in a show; that's not enough, that doesn't cut it. But that you're a gay character with a lot of personality and a lot of talent, *yes*, that is perfect for our audience, that's *exactly* what our audience wants.
>
> —Bernard Grenier, July 2009

Rebranding after NBC Universal's Purchase

Unlike Logo, Bravo did not begin as a channel primarily targeting LGBTQ viewers. Besides *Inside the Actors Studio*, its documentary series *Page to Screen*

(2002), which examined how novels were adapted into films, was another example of Bravo's more highbrow programming just before its official rebranding, when its ownership shifted in 2002 from Cablevision to NBC Universal. Still, even before this, former Bravo development executive Rachel Smith recalled that the network was "already moving into a much more pop-culture, less rarefied-arts programming before NBC came in," and developing for its urban, gay viewership, aware that there was little television content targeted specifically to these viewers.[24] *Fire Island* (1999), from British writer and producer Stephen Fry, was a four-episode reality series about two queer summer-share households at the resort island popular with gay and lesbian vacationers.[25] *The Gay Riviera* (2001), promoted as a "reality-based soap" featuring gay and lesbian individuals in New York City and Miami, aired over four nights in June 2001 as part of Bravo's gay pride programming that month, which also included the films *The Wedding Banquet* (Ang Lee, 1993), *The Opposite of Sex* (Don Roos, 1998), and *Love! Valour! Compassion!* (Joe Mantello, 1997).[26]

Although NBC Universal's purchase was not the initial catalyst in Bravo's rebranding, under NBC president Jeff Gaspin, Bravo accelerated the development of programming that strategically deployed LGBTQ content, particularly *Gay Weddings* (2002), an eight-episode series that followed two lesbian and two gay male couples as they planned their nuptials, and then *Boy Meets Boy* (2003), which set up its gay male star on dates with men. Doug Ross, head of the company that produced both shows, noted that *Boy Meets Boy* was the brainchild of Gaspin, who, in the wake of ABC's hit with *The Bachelor*, had asked Ross to develop a gay dating show in lieu of a second season of *Gay Weddings*.[27] While *Gay Weddings* had clear hallmarks of the reality genre in devoting some screen time to interpersonal drama and tensions, it also included more serious documentary-style elements, providing insights into the challenges of homophobic families and other aspects of what was then still a process largely unfamiliar to a mainstream audience. *Boy Meets Boy*, on the other hand, hewed much more to the reality show mold, with its secrets and twists: revealed to the audience but unbeknownst to any of the show's participants until the penultimate episode, some of the men seeking to be chosen as the date were actually straight.

The mark left by both these shows was soon eclipsed by *Queer Eye*, in which a heterosexual man was made over each episode by five gay men, cast as experts in the areas of (1) food, alcohol, and beverages ("Food and Wine Connoisseur" Ted Allen), (2) personal grooming ("Grooming Guru" Kyan Douglas), (3) interior design and home organization ("Design Doctor" Thom Filicia), (4) clothing and personal styling ("Fashion Savant" Carson Kressley), and (5) popular culture, relationships, and social interaction ("Culture Vulture" Jai Rodriguez). Aired on a prime-time Tuesday night slot for five seasons 2003–2007, *Queer Eye* was not simply a huge ratings success for the network but also became an exemplar of mainstream culture's enthusiasm for a particular kind of gay presentation, giving rise also to over a dozen *Queer Eye* shows outside of the United States.[28]

As many commentators noted, not only did *Queer Eye* feature multiple gay men front and center every episode, but it also seemed to reorder old hierarchies of sexual orientation in having gay men schooling straight men. And yet, the "queer" identity attributed to the experts was largely desexualized, reduced to jokey innuendos when depicted at all, and more generally depoliticized, divorced from addressing structural inequality and injustice and instead explicitly tied to consumption, particularly in the domains of lifestyle and beauty, all in service of improving the straight men's heterosexual appeal and relationships.[29] By comparison, *Boy Meets Boy* was better at presenting gay men as sexual agents for themselves, which, according to producer Doug Ross, worked against its renewal. Having aired its first season, like *Queer Eye*, the summer of 2003, *Boy Meets Boy* was about to proceed with a second season when NBC and Bravo canceled it, since although the show was "very G-rated"—it never depicted any sex—"just because the specter of gay sex was there, it was very scary for potential advertisers. And so our show stopped and *Queer Eye for the Straight Guy* went on to great success."[30] Still, Josh Gamson argued that *Boy Meets Boy* also failed to significantly challenge the status quo, particularly around gender expression and class, presenting gay men as gender-normative, middle class, and in pursuit of monogamous romance and domesticity.[31]

In any case, the successes of *Boy Meets Boy* and then especially *Queer Eye* led to about 70 percent of the network's unsolicited pitches being gay themed, according to Bravo development executive Bernard Grenier, who reviewed these. Yet network executives were explicit that Bravo was not aiming to become "the gay channel," with Jeff Gaspin pointedly noting that the largest audience of a program like *Queer Eye* would be (heterosexual) women. Indeed, Bravo's market research had found that 80 percent of its audience could be placed into two groups that it labeled: (1) "Wills and Graces"—that is, urban gay men and single female professionals—and (2) "PTA trendsetters," women who were married with children, living in a metropolitan suburb, but "still want[ed] to eat at the new hot restaurant in the city and show up at preschool pickup with a Marc Jacobs bag."[32] Furthermore, even *Boy Meets Boy* could appeal to straight female viewers through the presence of a straight woman as the main participant's confidante, and because some of the contestants were actually straight men.[33] As Sender put it, Bravo was "dualcasting"—seeking the more lucrative market of straight women drawn to content featuring attractive men who were experts in traditionally "feminine" areas of beauty, fashion, and design, while also targeting a select segment of the gay market that commercial media had first started identifying and constructing for advertisers in the 1990s.[34] In a 2010 interview, Andy Cohen commented that he preferred to call Bravo "bi" rather than "gay friendly."[35]

As Bravo expanded its reality programming, it was not just gay men who were featured but also lesbians. Alongside fashion gurus Tim Gunn and Michael Kors on *Project Runway*, designers Jeff Lewis on *Flipping Out*, Dean and Dan Caten on *Launch My Line*, and Todd Oldham on *Top Design*, were hairstylist Tabatha Coffey, first a contestant on *Shear Genius* and later the host of *Tabatha's Salon Takeover/Tabatha Takes Over*, and trainer Jackie Warner on *Work Out*, not to mention a continuous stream of LGBTQ contestants and guest judges. Discussing *Work Out* as well as Showtime's *The L Word*, Julia Himberg argued that inclusions of lesbian content reflected network strategies of "multicasting" to appeal to an even broader mix of audiences than the straight women–plus–gay men combination that dualcasting sought.[36]

In 2005, Bravo changed its byline from "The arts and entertainment network" to "Watch what happens,"[37] a phrase that was a nod to its slate of reality programming and also suggested a more contemporary, cutting-edge character. More generally, Bernard Grenier noted, Bravo's primary goal was drawing in a more lucrative demographic, some of whom would be gay but most of whom would not be; the aim was to lower the audience's median age from fifty-two prior to rebranding to thirty-five, and attract an affluent, urban, well-educated audience that was exceptionally savvy in its media consumption and would revel in repeated instances of what Bravo executives Lauren Zalaznick and Andy Cohen termed the "Bravo wink." Part of this had to do with a reflexivity about how commercial media works, including not-so-subtle product placement; as Zalaznick put it, this was a wry acknowledgment that "hey, you're watching commercials, and we know that you know that we know you're watching commercials. . . . Here are some more commercials."[38] Most relevantly here, the Bravo wink has involved provoking in viewers a mix of self-recognition and ironic distancing regarding the stars of the network's various reality shows, people whose lifestyles of wealth and consumption are to some extent presented as enviable and to be emulated, yet at the same time their frequent failures to live up to gendered and classed standards[39] are highlighted in humorous ways to invite viewer judgment of people not entirely different from the audience.[40]

From *Queer Eye* to *The Real Housewives*

Soon after *Queer Eye*, Bravo's biggest successes were competitive reality shows such as *Project Runway* (2004–) and *Top Chef* (2006–) in which advancement or victories depended at least in part on demonstrating some set of stylistic or culinary skills. The discourse of a desirable audience was associated by Bravo staff with its content being "quality" rather than, say, "trashy," the latter often attributed by commentators to at least *non*competitive reality shows thought to consist of contestants whose sole claim to fame is deplorable behavior. As Bravo executive Aimee Viles commented to me, "there's a higher sheen, a value in that association that products get from Bravo shows, because it's the quality of the shows that we put on air," and viewers are aware that Bravo would not just include "anybody" who was willing to pay for product placement.

Around the same time, Bravo also developed *The Real Housewives of Orange County* (2006–present), a candid reality series about a group of well-off women in Orange County, California produced by Evolution Production, which had previously made *Gay Weddings* and *Boy Meets Boy* for Bravo. Spawning many additional U.S. *Housewives* series and spin-offs for Bravo, as well as a number of international franchise series,[41] *Orange County* was a moderate success, but it was the *New Jersey* series, premiering in 2009, that became the breakthrough ratings winner and made the *Housewives* franchise the programming through which Bravo's future programming development was filtered. While on the face of it, such shows about almost exclusively straight women[42] would seem to be diametrically opposed to *Queer Eye* with respect to gay content, Bernard Grenier pointed out that wealthy women typically have relationships with gay men as friends or high-end service providers, asserting that "there is not one of those women, in any of those series, in any of those cities, who does not have one or several close gay male friends, not one who does not have a hairdresser, a designer—an interior designer, a chef, a manny."

Besides seeking viewers in particular class backgrounds, Bravo also had racial demographics in mind. Although Cohen, Zalaznick, or other network executives did not publicly comment on their network's strategies in regard to viewers' race, it is clear from other data that Bravo sought to appeal primarily to a white audience. For example, the cover of Bravo's 2008–2009 *Affluencer* publication, presenting Bravo's show and audiences for its potential advertisers, showed a white man and a white woman, both sharply dressed and on the go, the man with a cell phone and a messenger bag, the woman a purse and several shopping bags. A few pages into the brochure, a page explaining that "affluencers" are "the most affluent, most influential, most engaged audience in cable" showed two white men, two white women, and a racially ambiguous man and woman who might be read as Asian, Latina, or bi-/multiracial. More tellingly, Bernard Grenier recalled that when *Being Bobby Brown* (2005) was first pitched to Bravo, development executives were on the fence about it since "even though it was Whitney Houston, and it was Bobby Brown, and we did somehow deal with pop culture, it just didn't seem a perfect fit for us." He identified that show and *The Real Housewives of Atlanta*, which had a majority African American cast, as the exceptions that would draw in significant numbers of African American viewers in contrast to Bravo's other programming.

In terms of its websites, the trajectory of Bravo-originated OutZoneTV is also illustrative of the move toward "lifestyle" content. As the previous chapter discussed, the 2006 press release for the site's launch highlighted its focus on "entertaining, thought-provoking content about and for the LGBTQ audience," including both older and contemporary LGBTQ media. The year after its launch, OutZoneTV partnered with the Human Rights Campaign during National Coming Out Day to have prominent gay and lesbian entertainers film short videos about being out, and the two years that the site was active closed out the peak of Bravo's efforts to draw gay male viewers, following the successes of its television series. Still, site writer Zac Hug recalled that OutZoneTV's primary raison d'être evolved to be "because [Bravo] had gay characters on reality shows and people wanted to know more about them," such as access to photos and videos providing additional snippets of their daily lives. With OutZoneTV's shuttering at the end of 2008, Bravo no longer had any content explicitly directed just to LGBTQ viewers.

Bravo's purchased website, Television Without Pity (TWoP), fit its dualcasting strategy much better from the start, and thus it is no surprise that it endured for several years beyond OutZoneTV. As chapter 2 mentioned, TWoP had prominent gay writers, but it was more its hip sensibility around popular media that attracted Bravo, part of which was constituted by the "Ho(moeroticism) Yay" threads of its discussion boards. The fact that TWoP moved into Bravo's folds was both sign and symptom of the changed status of LGBTQ content. With mainstream media now often featuring at least humorous play with queer narratives, the HoYay discussions per se no longer marked the oppositional stance that some observers had attributed to TWoP's recaps and forums several years prior to Bravo's purchase;[43] rather, it was comparable to the presence of LGBTQ contestants on Bravo's reality shows, functioning as entertainment for site users who were mostly straight women, alongside a minority of LGBTQ visitors.[44] Although queer users could still find the HoYay discourses and the queer friendliness of TWoP meaningful, the site's overall tenor continued to shift toward a broader audience after OutZoneTV's demise. For example, Bravo set up a partnership with Yahoo! TV that resulted in advertising for a range of mainstream content that further diluted its earlier gay sensibility.

Gaystreaming at Logo

We're not living in a walled garden anymore. I mean, gay people are moving out of cities and back to suburbs, next to straight people, and raising kids.
—Marc Leonard, Logo executive

The Development of Gaystreaming

In its earliest years, Logo's programming was a relatively eclectic mix. News coverage was provided in *365gay News* (2005–2009) and *The Advocate Newsmagazine* (2006); as chapter 2 noted, *365gay News*, first begun as *CBS News on Logo*, shared content with the 365gay website that Logo purchased in 2006. *Real Momentum* (2005–2007) featured a range of documentaries that Logo produced, acquired, or coproduced, from acquisitions of better known films such as *Paris Is Burning* (1990) and *The Celluloid Closet* (1995) to items such as *Gidyup! On the Rodeo Circuit* (2005), which profiled competitors in the International Gay Rodeo Association, as well as independently produced documentary shorts. One of the *Real Momentum* documentaries, *Curl Girls* (2006), on lesbian surfers, gave rise to a season of the *Curl Girls* (2007) reality series, which spent more time on the women's personal relationships. Other documentary and reality series showcased coming out and transgender identity in *Coming Out Stories* (2006) and *TransGeneration* (2005); an AIDS awareness bike ride in *The Ride: Seven Days to End AIDS* (2006) and a gay men's basketball team in *Shirts & Skins* (2008); the efforts to open a gay bar in *Open Bar* (2005) and a lesbian nightclub in *Gimme Sugar* (2008–2009), or to make it in the music industry in *Jacob and Joshua: Nemesis Rising* (2006); LGBTQ travel in *Round Trip Ticket* (2005) and *U.S. of ANT* (2006); and a dating show featuring a transgender woman as the person choosing among potential suitors in *Transamerican Love Story* (2008). While few of these series went beyond a single season, collectively they reflected an ambition to reflect a spectrum of LGBTQ experience.

Logo executive Marc Leonard, who had previously worked at Comedy Central, jokingly labeled Logo the "Tragedy Channel" in its earliest days for its coverage of topics such as homophobia, coming out, and AIDS, and even before gaystreaming was more solidified as a programming strategy the network sought to include lighter content, especially comedy. *Wisecrack* (2005) showcased performances of LGBTQ stand-up comedians, and *The Big Gay Sketch Show* (2007–2010), which aired for three seasons, featured LGBTQ-themed sketch comedy, including a then-relatively unknown Kate McKinnon as one of its regulars. However, it was *Noah's Arc* (2005–2006), a comedy-drama centered on a group of gay Black men, and the animated comedy series *Rick & Steve: The Happiest Gay Couple in All the World* (2007–2009), about two gay male couples and one lesbian couple, including three characters of color,[45] which were the surprise hits; Logo's internal numbers showed that both shows attracted heterosexual women as well as gay viewers.[46] *Noah's Arc*, distinct from other LGBTQ shows where most of the characters were white, such as *Queer as Folk* on Showtime, had the highest ratings out of all Logo's original series, and its fans were disappointed when it was canceled after only two seasons; a wrap-up movie was later produced by Logo and released theatrically in 2008. As chapter 2 noted, the popularity of *Rick & Steve* led Logo to set up a dedicated website that provided additional content; in 2008, the series won Best Television Series of the Year at Cartoons on the Bay, a small international animation festival,[47] and was aired in several other countries.

Less successful ratings-wise was *Exes and Ohs* (2007, 2011), a drama revolving around several white lesbian friends, but it stood out as the only television series other than Showtime's *The L Word* with multiple lesbian lead characters. AfterEllen recapped the episodes after they aired and in 2013, after the show had been canceled, streamed both seasons for free. Another original series, *Sordid Lives: The Series* (2008), was a sitcom with one major gay character that also featured the music of one of its stars, established singer Olivia Newton-John, as well as starring Rue McClanahan, one of the leads of *The Golden Girls* sitcom that had been popular with many gay men;[48] however, it lasted only a single season. One series that Logo acquired early on was the British women's prison drama *Bad Girls* (ITV, 1999–2006), which featured a central lesbian relationship and several other queer female characters; in the United States, three seasons of the show were shown on BBC America, and Logo eventually aired all eight seasons beginning in 2007.

Logo also programmed LGBTQ short films, in *Alien Boot Camp* (2007–2009) and *The Click List: Best in Short Film* (2006–2010). The second of these aired the short films that had garnered the most viewer votes online, a format shared by two other shows: *The Click List: 50 Greatest Films* (2007), narrowed down from a list of 250, and *The Click List: Top 10 Videos* (2007–2010), which featured music videos by LGBTQ performers. Like most cable networks at the time, Logo's feature film airings were of existing content rather than originally produced for the network, but with its short film programming, it provided an avenue for queer filmmakers to have their work aired on television.

Logo's initial programming, which as mentioned earlier had been seen as too earnest and narrowly targeted, was also subject to critique for "reinscrib[ing] class, race, and national hierarchies in queer cultures" even as Logo made commitments to inclusiveness, as Ben Aslinger argued. Aslinger examined the network's content and promotional discourses, particularly around *Noah's Arc*, for their problematic representations of Black masculinity, and *Roundtrip Ticket*, a travel show that was sometimes transphobic and situated "English-speaking elites in global cities to define queer cultures."[49] With gaystreaming, the network's goals moved even further away from presenting critical perspectives on these inequalities. As Logo development executive Chris Willey commented, just as depictions of Black experience on commercial television do not focus primarily on racism, gaystreaming aimed to increase the amount of lighter fare versus narratives about coming out and homophobia. It was in 2008, its third year on air, that Logo began discussing gaystreaming as a new direction for the network, when, Marc Leonard recalled, "it became apparent that ratings were necessary for us to scale as a business." Planning and development continued through 2009 with the intention of a January 1, 2010 launch, coinciding with the date Nielsen began to collect ratings data on the channel, although some series that began airing in 2009 were already in line with the shift in programming strategy. For the websites, a key meeting occurred in March 2010, involving an unusual face-to-face gathering at Logo's New York offices that included online editorial (i.e., all the website editors), the technical online production team, the programming department, and Logo brand staff who would be charged with, as Leonard put it, "explaining Logo's new brand position and shift in broader audience direction."

Logo's concept of gaystreaming, developed internally and unused as a "consumer-facing term," was devoid of negative connotation, encapsulating a range of related but distinct meanings to do with going beyond what "gay content" has traditionally connoted with respect to people or characters, storylines, and entire genres of entertainment. However, the notion of gaystreaming or the "gaystream" is not a singular one and did not originate with Logo, although Logo's formulation both drew on some of gaystream's earlier senses and imparted it with distinct connotations.[50] In the early 2000s, "gaystream" resurfaced in a range of commentary critical of assimilationist directions in LGBTQ political movements, often counterposed to genuinely "queer" politics.[51]

The disparity between Logo's sense of gaystreaming and those for whom the concept of gay mainstreaming is problematic highlights Logo's distancing from agendas critical of dominant commercial culture. The fact that the term incorporated the word *gay*—but not *lesbian, bisexual, transgender*, or *queer*—was also partly indicative of which of the "LGBTQ" identities would be most central, but gaystreaming was intended to reflect and encourage a move away from explicit categories of gender or sexual identity. Even before rebranding, an early internal working slogan for Logo was "See yourself; be yourself," which eschewed the terms *gay, lesbian, bisexual, transgender*, or *queer*. Appealing to discourses of individual choice and freedom unconstrained by structural considerations, Marc Leonard explained Logo's logic for rejecting the terms and images most clearly associated with gay identity, noting that they had avoided "the traditionally gay symbols, the rainbow flags, the pink triangles and everything. . . . Ultimately, [Logo] is a brand that's about identity, and your identity can be whatever you want it to be."

Internal discussions generated a long list of categories for channel and website content, which were refined and then redefined as four major categories. Table 1 shows the gaystream categories and subcategories, categories that were identified as *not* gaystream, and examples of each as identified in Logo's internal documents. The gaystream subcategories, along with the non-gaystream categories, were named in one document ("Gaystream or Not?") and the four major gaystream categories in another one ("Organizing Principles"). I have listed the gaystream subcategories under the major categories, with a few subcategories that did not fit into a major category listed separately. Passages in quotation marks are from the original Logo documents; the other descriptions are my paraphrases of the information in the document.

Although the documents do not describe it explicitly this way, in various respects the four major gaystream categories all have to do with being "outside the box" in some fashion, even as some of these contrasts to the mainstream are familiar. Discovery/Next Big Thing has to do with what is not yet well known; OMFG/JAW DROPPING describes material sufficiently outrageous or spectacular to inspire the titled reaction, even if such reactions are expected by the particular genre, such as comedy; Unconventional/Innovative references people or programs that challenge conventional norms, especially around gender; and Beat the Odds/Underdog includes female characters who defy the traditional expectations of their gender to "kick ass," as well as the category of "Outsiders." Marc Leonard remarked that in not being straight, a person is "outside of the structure that everybody else around you is in," which "forces you to examine things differently, to think differently,' which might help explain "the perception that

Table 1
Logo's gaystream categories and subcategories

Major Category	Subcategory	Examples
Discovery/Next Big Thing "Programming that keeps you in the loop about the next big artist, film, film maker, travel destination, and anything in pop culture that matters. So you can impress your friends." (Includes content associated with the NewNowNext brand, the Click List for music videos and short films, and travel-themed content such as TripOutGayTravel.com.)	Fashion	*Project Runway*
OMFG/JAW DROPPING "The litmus test is simple, if our jaws drop at least once every seven minutes the show passes muster. We'll also accept continuous exclamations of 'Oh no, no, no they didn't,' and watching through your fingers with your chin on your knees." (Includes depictions of outrageous behavior, explicitly sexual content such as "NSFD" (unedited filthy stand-up and racy movies)," and material showcasing non-normative relationships such as *Rules of Attraction* (2002).)	Outrageous Camp Spectacle	Joan Rivers, *Real Housewives* *Showgirls, Starship Troopers* *Moulin Rouge*, Sacha Baron Cohen
Unconventional/Innovative "In a perfect world everybody would be this interesting. Meet the innovators, the magic makers, and the oddballs who make life interesting for the rest of us. We wish we were them but since we're not we have to settle for watching every minute of these shows." (Includes larger-than-life personalities on *RuPaul's Drag Race* and *The A List*; movies that air on the weekly Graveyard Shift slot, billed as "from gay B&B slashers to killer condom attacks"; films such as *Quinceañera* (2006), a Mexican drama featuring unconventional familial relationships; *Internet Uprising*, an online video show about "what's hot in pop culture from a lesbian perspective.")	Celebration of the Individual Sensitive Guys People Who Seem like Drag Queens Even Though They're Not Social Studies	Adam Lambert Paul Rudd, *Noah's Arc* Grace Jones, Janice Dickinson *Mad Men*

(continued)

Table 1

Logo's gaystream categories and subcategories (continued)

Major Category	Subcategory	Examples
Beat the Odds/Underdog	Girls Who Kick Ass	*Buffy*, the *Alien* movies
"Even the most fabulous of us have a profound respect for the outsider, and the less of a chance they have the more we love 'em."	Outsiders	*Edward Scissorhands*, X-Men
(Includes *Beautiful People*, a British series about two effeminate teenage boys who dream of making it to London; *Real Momentum* documentaries; *Gimme Sugar*, a Logo reality show about queer women trying to launch a ladies club night in Los Angeles; and movies with offbeat characters.)		
Additional Subcategories	Mean Girls	*Popular, Heathers*
	Divas	Whitney Houston, Lady Gaga
	Guys Confident in Their Sexuality	Brad Pitt, Jake Gyllenhaal
	Sexy	*Spartacus* (Starz series)
	Smart Stuff	*Arrested Development, The Daily Show with John Stewart*
Not Gaystream	Hypermasculine/Violent Sports	football, wrestling
	Super-Broad Comedy	Jay Leno, *Two and a Half Men*
	Down Home	country music, *Touched by an Angel*
	Objectified Women	hip-hop videos, *Maxim*
	Jingoism/Hypernationalism	*Walker: Texas Ranger*, Sarah Palin
	Too Gay Niche	*The Big Gay Sketch Show* season 1, *Coming Out Stories*

ᵃ NSFD = not safe for daytime.

gay people are more creative, or more innovative, or have a better sense of what's stylish or what's cool."

These gaystream categories demonstrated the production of a desired viewership that is urbane and educated, akin to Bravo's "affluencers," and contrasted with a list that—with the exception of "Too Gay Niche"—are conventionally associated with straight males, particularly those in lower socioeconomic classes with conservative political positions. The Objectified Women category drew on another characteristic attributed to working-class men as more likely to hold sexist attitudes or be intolerant of difference, with the latter also a common thread between Down Home and Jingoism/Hypernationalism. Thus, these tapped a trope in mainstream American culture of white working-class males being unintelligent and culturally unsophisticated or, as Richard Butsch called the depictions of such characters on situation comedies, "buffoons."[52] Sender also discussed advertisers making a bifurcation between "sitcom-watching blue-collar drinkers and PBS-watching, affluent, educated gay drinkers," thus leaving out consumers who were "both blue-collar and gay."[53]

Although Logo had earlier produced or aired programs with working-class characters such as the drama *Sordid Lives* or documentary programs on *Real Momentum* about rural gays and lesbians, the language and implementation of gaystreaming worked to collapse rural and working-class spaces into a hinterland of conservatism, sexism, homophobia, and racism, particularly in the larger context of how denigrated sexuality and class subjectivities often stand for each other in popular televisual depictions.[54] Thus, straight working-class men, who are both valorized and denigrated in mainstream discourses of ideal masculinity, were the counterpoint to the urban, gay viewership that both Logo and Bravo sought.

Gaystreaming Implemented

> No matter what, we're always going to have that sort of gaystream part of us . . . but it just so happens that we're probably doing it the opposite of Logo, where Logo started doing all gay and then now they're incorporating this. But *we* have always been gaystream, but now because there's more actual lesbian content, we can kind of actually make it look bigger!
>
> —Trish Bendix, AfterEllen editor

The implementation of gaystreaming was first evident in decisions about acquired content. Gaystream strategy informed the acquisition of rights to air *Buffy the Vampire Slayer*, which had previously been in syndication on the FX cable network (after first runs on the WB and UPN networks), and *Reno 911!* and *The Sarah Silverman Program*, after their first airings on MTV Network's Comedy Central. *Buffy* had one lesbian main character, Willow, while *Reno 911!*, a parody of police reality shows such as Fox's *COPS*, and *The Sarah Silverman Program*, a comedy series, both had one main gay male character (Lt. Dangle and

Brian Spukowski, respectively). These three programs began their airings on Logo and the LogoTV website in fall 2009, and Logo experienced an immediate ratings bump, with *Buffy* in particular attracting the younger viewers that Logo was seeking. However, none of these were "gay" or "lesbian" shows like *Queer as Folk* or *The L Word*. As Marc Leonard explained, "Originally when we launched a show, we were looking for something that had gay content front and center. I think in the future, a show like *Six Feet Under* would work very well for us.... [It's] about a group of people, and one of them is gay, and that's fine." Logo also picked up *1 Girl, 5 Gays* in 2010, a talk show produced for MTV Canada where a straight female host discussed sex and relationships with five gay men, airing four seasons.

For original content, *RuPaul's Drag Race* (*RPDR*), which began airing at the beginning of 2009, was far and away Logo's most prominent and successful series. Fashion-focused competitive reality shows were not new (*America's Next Top Model* had premiered on UPN in 2003, a year before Bravo's *Project Runway*), but *RPDR* was distinct in that contestants were consistently performing drag, and thus challenging some conventional assumptions about gender identity and expression. Although *RPDR* has been critiqued for the ways that gender was nevertheless policed, often through misogynistic language and discourses, as well as problematic approaches to race that positioned nonwhite identities as exoticized or othered,[55] it also had multiple queer people front and center, particularly host RuPaul Charles,[56] as well as many of the show's judges and contestants. Thus, to a certain extent, *RPDR* straddled the transition between Logo's earlier programming, which sought to present a spectrum of LGBTQ experience, and the shift to gaystreaming, given its reality show genre and focus on fashion and style; indeed, the show was listed in the description for the "Unconventional/Innovative" category in Logo's gaystreaming document. *RPDR* immediately became Logo's highest rated show, remaining so for the seven years it aired on the network, before it was moved in 2017 to VH1, another cable network under the MTV Networks umbrella. There have also been spin-offs: three seasons of *RuPaul's Drag University* in which women contestants were given makeovers to uncover their "inner divas," aired 2010–2012; *RuPaul's Drag Race All Stars*, bringing back past contestants of *RPDR*, began airing on Logo in 2012 before moving to VH1 in 2018;[57] and *RuPaul's Secret Celebrity Drag Race* in which celebrities compete to raise money for charities, premiered on VH1 in 2020.

Besides *RPDR*, Logo's gaystream-era programming was typified by its *The A List* shows. Clearly inspired by Bravo's *Real Housewives* franchise, the first series, premiering in 2010, was set in New York, featuring six gay or bisexual men; most well known among them was probably Reichen Lehkmuhl, who had won ABC's *The Amazing Race* competition in 2003 with his partner at the time. The episodes covered the men's professional aspirations as well as interpersonal relationships and conflicts, on occasion highlighting their questionable behavior. Thus, just as the *Real Housewives* shows often depicted straight women behaving in flabbergastingly poor ways, *The A List: New York* and then a subsequent series, *The A List: Dallas* (2011), were intended to draw viewers who wanted to see gay men behaving just as badly, fitting right into the "OMFG/JAW DROPPING" gaystream category. Logo executive John Polly commented that there has always been "an affinity in the gay community for camp, and larger-than-life women and characters and drama," explaining a commonality threading through the *Real Housewives* and *The A List* shows.

Besides *The A List*, Logo's gaystream original programming was characterized by several other reality series that dealt with style. *Pretty Hurts* (2011) followed a gay cosmetic surgery nurse serving a wealthy female clientele in Los Angeles. In *The Arrangement* (2010), a mix of contestants, the majority of whom were gay men or straight women, competed in flower arranging. *Setup Squad* (2011) featured professional dating advisers, some of whom were lesbian or gay, assisting clients in dating; the pilot paired a straight female adviser with a gay man looking for his first date, and a gay adviser with a woman looking for Mr. Right. By the 2012 season, Logo's entire slate of new shows, which included additional reality series about subjects such as a child beauty pageant star (*Eden's World*) and pop culture scandals (*Scandalicious*) did not include even a single series with gay or lesbian leads.[58]

In terms of Logo's websites, all of its acquisitions occurred in 2006–2007, before the network's turn to gaystreaming. At that time, Logo was in search of sites with LGBTQ content that were, as Logo executive Kristin Frank put it, "the best in breed for each of the demographics that we're trying to satisfy"—that is, LGBTQ-identified viewers interested in social networking, news, and entertainment of specific interest to their communities. However, even before gaystreaming, the sites varied in how strictly they stuck to explicitly LGBTQ content. In particular, AfterEllen, which quickly became Logo's most highly trafficked website, had never been fully devoted to content explicitly about lesbian or bisexual women. Although the reasons for this were not the same as the rationales for gaystreaming, AfterEllen influenced Logo's development of this strategy.

When AfterEllen first started a regular "Best Lesbianish Day Ever" column in 2007, Sarah Warn recalled that they invariably included a lot of material on straight women because there simply was not enough content on lesbian and bisexual women to fill the daily column. Five years later, that was no longer the case, but by then, AfterEllen aimed to post eight to ten new items (text or video) each weekday. This meant that AfterEllen routinely covered (1) the work of actors who had previously portrayed lesbian or bisexual women, including projects where they were not playing queer characters—for example, Alyson Hannigan, who played the lesbian character Willow on *Buffy the Vampire Slayer*, any of the stars of *The L Word*, and film actors such as Lena Headey and Julianne Moore;[59] (2) shows or films with relationships that could be read as subtextually lesbian, and/or that featured strong female characters, such as *Rizzoli & Isles* (TNT, 2010–2016), which centered on a close friendship between two women working in law enforcement, *Veronica Mars* (CW, 2004–2007) in which the lead character was a teenage girl detective, and films such as *Alice in Wonderland* (Tim Burton, 2010); and (3) the subsequent endeavors of women who had previously taken on the roles in (2), such as *Veronica Mars* star Kristen Bell.

With this range of content, AfterEllen drew many straight women, since few other websites reliably covered female entertainers or female-targeted entertainment outside of the celebrity gossip genre or the most currently "hot" (and usually young) personalities; an AfterEllen contributor had commented to Sarah Warn that all her straight female friends read the site "because they can't get stuff about the next Meryl Streep movie anywhere else, on a consistent basis." This drew the attention of other Logo executives; Claudia Gorelick commented that AfterEllen's content and readership was one initial spur for Logo to pursue gay-streaming more broadly, in that the site did not just cover "gay and lesbian things, but they'll report on *America's Next Top Model with* lesbian lens, and then some of the people that will reply are straight women . . . [so] there is the breakdown of 'we are only allowed to talk about lesbian topics, lesbian people.' There's just more of a blending that's happening."

Brother site AfterElton never lacked content about gay men in the media and popular culture, so it did not have to begin with the kind of gaystream-ready mix that AfterEllen did. However, there were some similar forms of coverage that were not about explicitly gay/bisexual men or characters but could still appeal to a queer male readership, including recaps of shows depicting close friendships between two men that many fans read as romantic, such as *Supernatural* (CW, 2005–2020) and *Merlin* (BBC One/NBC/Syfy, 2008–2012).[60] As gaystreaming progressed, there was increased coverage of non–specifically LGBTQ media on AfterEllen and AfterElton. In mid-2011, the two sites posted several reviews of movies that had neither LGBTQ characters nor actors or directors likely to be of particular interest to queer viewers, such as the comedies *Bridesmaids* (Paul Feig, 2011) and *Horrible Bosses* (Seth Gordon, 2011), and as Maria San Filippo observed, a couple of years later, *American Hustle* (David Russell, 2013), which had no lesbian content, was also covered in the Movies section alongside lesbian-themed films.[61]

Gaystreaming also pushed the websites toward shorter and lighter content versus longer, more analytical posts. Media commentators have been pointing to the diminishing attention span of audiences since the late nineteenth century with the advent of movies, then radio and comics in the 1920s–1930s, followed by television, particularly after the introduction of MTV and its derivatives,[62] but the imperative to produce content for online consumption throughout the day was new. Sarah Warn noted that AfterEllen and AfterElton had become "fluffier" as the sites had increased the frequency of posts after Logo's purchase, because "it's just frankly easier to do that stuff, and it makes more sense: people are often reading this at work or at school, and they only have time for bite-sized things, and not really super in-depth articles," thus making what another Logo executive, Kristin Frank, called "snackable content." This was epitomized by the humor-injected "Gay Girl's Goggles: TV Lesbi-fied!" recaps of shows with no canonical queer content or the "Shag, Marry, or Dump" (AfterEllen)/"Marry, Hump, or Dump" (AfterElton) questionnaires that had readers pick which fates they would choose for three actors or characters. Even though AfterEllen also introduced columns such as "Feminist Friday" that covered more news-related content and posted some longer pieces on issues such as transphobia or the decrease in butch-identified women,[63] these did not substantially counter the overall tonal shift.

365gay also did not start off gaystream and always had more than sufficient material to cover.[64] Even so, 365gay's editor in chief Jay Vanasco commented that much of the site's content consisted of relatively short opinion pieces and that such news blogs should not be equated with the more thoroughly researched reporting of traditional journalism. She contrasted the site with print gay newspapers, "which have long-standing relationships, often at a very micro local level, with political figures and local activists and community members," and are thus "able to do amazing on-the-ground long-term reporting that nobody else is doing." In the second half of 2010, 365gay introduced some fluffier content under "Living," with pieces about fashionable footwear and the best luggage appearing alongside weightier articles such as being out at one's child's school. The Living section was removed in November 2010, with content previously covered there moved to other sections such as "Ask the Expert," which also included topics such as travel destinations and personal relationships. The continuing implementation of gaystreaming in 2011 led to the closure of the entire site in September, with Vanasco announcing tersely on the site that "Logo has shifted its online strategy and so the site is closing and I am moving on to other things."

Also in September 2011, the Logo-originated site TripOutGayTravel.com was folded into Logo's NewNowNext site as a subsection that was no longer explicitly labeled as "gay" travel. Although many of its posts and advertising remained directed at primarily gay male readers, articles with more general scope were added, such as "9 Ways to Fall in Love in Prague like 'The Bachelorette,'"[65] referencing ABC's dating show setting up a woman with a man, and ads promoting other, non-LGBTQ-specific MTV Network programming, like VH1 reality show *Big Ang* (2012), centered on a straight woman. As for NewNowNext, it had always had a mix of content which editor and contributor John Polly associated with gaystreaming; as its catchy alliterative name suggested, it aimed to cover what was cool or about to become cool, thus partly fitting into the "Discovery/Next Big Thing" gaystreaming category, and Polly noted that he and other contributors sought to write about what interested them as gay men, envisioning that their tastes would to some extent be shared by their readers.

In keeping with comments by Leonard and other Logo executives that younger people were more reticent to claim labels, in July 2010 the taglines of

AfterEllen and AfterElton dropped explicit references to sexual identities and were changed to "The pop culture site that plays for your team" for both sites, replacing "News, reviews & commentary on lesbian and bisexual women" and "News, reviews & commentary on gay and bisexual men," respectively. Similarly, NewNowNext replaced its "Gay Pop Culture, Entertainment News, Music, Movies, Celebrities, Photos, and Videos—Served Fresh Daily" tagline briefly with "Serving You Celebs, Music, Gossip, & Logo TV News Direct from the Source" and "Gay Blog | Celebrity Gossip, Music & Entertainment News, Celebrity Pictures & Videos," before changing it again in September 2011 to "Beyond Trends." Only Downelink remained essentially unchanged content-wise since, as a social networking site, it had never been a site where writers produced the bulk of the content; its closure in 2014 marked the end of Logo's ownership of the LGBTQ sites it had purchased the previous decade.

Marginalizations Remade: Homonormativity and Post-Gay Discourses

While there were some divergences among the new cohort of LGBTQ cultural producers at Bravo and Logo regarding sexual expression, those with most authority tended to share dispositions around what was considered tasteful, which significantly shaped the networks' overall content strategies. Part of their discourses about programming essentialized the association of gayness, taste, and style, claiming a history dating back to, as Logo executive Chris Willey speculated, "the Renaissance era and the Greeks, that somehow the gay community was able to recognize and/or set trends and contribute to the larger pop culture." In this vein, TWoP recapper Jacob Clifton traced a line including the biblical Israelites Jonathan and David, British playwright Oscar Wilde, American fashion designer Halston and the Studio 54 nightclub, locating them within a lineage in which "gay men are understood as the sons of Apollo, totally beholden to beauty and intricacy, whether it's literary or musical or physical or comedic." A more historical explanation is that gender-nonconforming males have often been shut out from traditionally masculine occupations, leaving them to seek livings in areas such as the garment or food industries,[66] but the mystification of gay taste making, which conceals its roots in material conditions of exclusion and violence, preserves a more appealing connection between queer men and good taste that a slew of style and design programming leans into.

In drawing from and reinforcing tropes around gayness and taste, one outcome of dualcasting and gaystream programming was new marginalizations outside of what Gayle Rubin labeled the "charmed circle" of sexual and gender expression,[67] which now included a limited set of nonheterosexual forms. Thus, the well-groomed, urban gay man, entertainingly flamboyant queen, and attractive lipstick or fitness lesbian sidelined other forms of queer identity and bodies that had had a better shot at being seen especially on Logo pre-gaystreaming, even if they never enjoyed equal exposure. Furthermore, the focus on individual achievement on Bravo's and Logo's competitive reality shows, suggesting that anyone—including gays and lesbians—could succeed, also obscured the social production of talent[68] and the structural inequalities of class, race, ethnicity, and more.

Although Bravo and Logo had always had more content featuring and targeted to gay men than lesbians, the turn to lifestyle programming, and the concomitant goal of attracting straight women, solidified the diminished attention to queer women as viewers. This was exacerbated by the fact that historically, lesbians have seldom been designated as desirable consumers; Sender pithily described the way advertisers view lesbians as "neither fish or fowl"—that is, neither quite like straight women nor gay men. Even with the cultural prominence of Ellen DeGeneres and *The L Word* by the mid-2000s, the association of lesbian identity with anti-materialist ecofeminism persisted.

Having found the majority of its viewership to fit into the "Wills and Graces" and "PTA trendsetters" groups discussed earlier, Bravo further identified two audience groups that also did not specifically include lesbian/bisexual women: (1) "Metrocompetitors," described by Bravo executive Tony Cardinale as "male, young, urban social climbers who like pop culture" and (2) the "Newborn Grownups," who were "20-somethings who are fully out of college mode, buying their first couch, establishing what's going to be their house wine."[69] Not surprisingly, Bravo's lesbian reality television stars largely faded away from their main lineup. After starring on *Work Out* 2006–2008, Jackie Warner had another fitness reality series, *Thintervention with Jackie Warner*, on Bravo in 2010, but it lasted only a single season. Hairstylist Tabatha Coffey also returned to Bravo with another reality show, *Relative Success with Tabatha* in 2018, but since that was a one-season series, it did not replicate her earlier prominence with *Tabatha's Salon Takeover/ Tabatha Takes Over* (2008–2013).

AfterEllen managing editor Malinda Lo had noted in a 2008 interview that by virtue of the "three lesbians who run Logo"—general manager Lisa Sherman and senior executives Kristin Frank and Sarah Warn—that "even though there is a lot of content for gay men, there will be content for lesbians." However, gaystreaming, which began to be implemented after Frank and Warn had left Logo, changed those circumstances considerably. Chris Willey pointed to reruns of *Queer as Folk*, which featured primarily gay male characters, although it did have a lesbian couple, drawing a strong lesbian audience as one reason why Logo did not need to continue programming specifically for lesbians the way it had in earlier years with original series such as *Curl Girls* (2007), *Exes and Ohs* (2007, 2011), and *Gimme Sugar* (2008). And, commenting that gay men and straight women shared a good deal in regards to their viewing preferences while describing Logo's target demographics as LGBTQ people and heterosexual women twenty-five to forty-nine years old, Marc Leonard noted that "obviously, we're continuing to serve the lesbian audience, as well as bi and trans.... But the younger generation isn't as interested in the buckets of 'lesbian,' 'gay,' 'bisexual,' 'transgender'; you're hearing increasingly, 'I don't know what I am and don't ask me.'" In fact, it was not obvious how Logo's gaystream programming did serve lesbian viewers overall or indeed other LGBTQ viewers who were not interested in the lifestyle series that came to dominate. Furthermore, an aversion to claiming an identity label did not mean that viewers did not differ in their sexual practices or the kinds of media content they sought.

Beyond sexual and gender expression, there was also a decrease in representing other forms of diversity. As mentioned above, Bravo has targeted a primarily white viewership, with content that occasionally appeals to an African American audience less by design than happenstance. Logo's executives, on the other hand, had expressed pride in the network being a responsible corporate citizen with respect to diversity; Chris Willey commented that Logo had intentionally programmed for the African American gay community, which was "underserved," in multiple ways through *The Click List*, short films about Black gay men in *Best in Short Film*, as well as *Noah's Arc*. Willey also mentioned the importance of other culturally specific LGBTQ representation, such as a Korean American lesbian coming out to her mother.[70]

While one queer African American musician I spoke to at the 2009 NewFest, New York's annual LGBTQ film festival, praised Logo for *Noah's Arc* and some of the movies it aired, the network drew criticism from other Black cultural producers for being problematically white in its management and overall content. One Black lesbian filmmaker was scathing, commenting that "I can't f-cking tell a young Black sixteen-year-old lesbian to check out Logo because you're not going to see yourself," particularly since "Logo has gone nuts with the reality TV, like *Drag Race* and . . . the gay *Real World* stuff that they put out." Another Black independent filmmaker also noted that Logo "seems to be a lot of white people, a lot of white men" who had responded problematically to his race in his interactions at the festival.

Logo was initially more inclusive at its websites even as gaystreaming began to be implemented, particularly with its ownership of Downelink and the explicit mandate laid down by Sarah Warn for AfterEllen and AfterElton to promote racial diversity at the sites and advocate for it in other mainstream media. Still, Warn recounted how much research was often required in order to write a piece not about white women or the same handful of women of color entertainers who garner mainstream attention, recalling an occasion where it took her "five hours to find a post about a woman of color!" since she was reliant on mainstream websites such as *E! Online, Entertainment Weekly*, and *TV Guide*, which generally covered "either all white people or the same five Black people, and Salma Hayek."[71] In any case, gaystreaming ended up exerting pressures on its websites as well, and particularly after Sarah Warn stepped down as both AfterEllen's editor in chief and Logo's director of online editorial in 2009, there was not the same kind of editorial commitment to provide diverse coverage.

Beyond the shifts of programming at Logo's outlets, how Logo executives discussed gaystreaming also included generalizations about the extent of social and political progress that did not address how the intersections of sexuality, gender, class, and race produced differential outcomes for LGBTQ people. One persistent theme was that gays and lesbians no longer clustered together in isolated "ghettos." For example, Marc Leonard commented that "the gay audience . . . [is] moving back into the suburbs, they're raising families, their best friends are straight, they're close with their families, they have lots of straight coworkers who know that they're gay and they're okay with that." Logo head Lisa Sherman characterized the outcome of this as Logo's audience seeking media content that mirrored their integration into the general populace, so that the network was "inviting gays and lesbians and their friends and families, who just like good entertainment, to come and watch."[72] However, the idea of the "gay ghetto" was itself a construct that imagined LGBTQ people as clustered only in urban settings, when many have always lived and continue to live outside cities.[73]

A related thread concerned claims that traditional categories of sexuality were becoming less relevant due to greater mainstream integration and acceptance with, as Marc Leonard commented, "the younger set" not interested in programming such as *Queer as Folk* that continually suggested that "being gay is hard." Marketing executive Claudia Gorelick suggested that we were now in a "post-gay" era, meaning that "anyone who's investing in gay and lesbian" needed to reconsider their long-term strategies as segregations along the lines of sexual identity were breaking down. However, a sense that labels are not necessary frequently marks relative privilege, as scholars have noted about white enthusiasm for "color blindness";[74] thus, programming directions that downplayed explicit labels of sexual identity also constituted a shift away from addressing persistent inequalities.

In some ways, the commentary of Logo's executives here reflected broader trends in discourses about sociopolitical (in)equality. For example, Amin Ghaziani discussed how college organizations devoted to LGBTQ students and issues had been increasingly forgoing names that contained terms such as *gay*, *lesbian*, or *queer* as they negotiated emphasizing sameness versus difference or assimilation versus diversity. However, although such a post-gay moment could "entail a multiculturalist blurring of modernist boundaries and a move toward expanded tolerance and freedom," the use of "post-" terms risked augmenting discourses that were "blissfully ignorant of a group's historical and present-day struggles" and characterized by "a neoliberal, class- and racially inflected, and surface blurring that redefines the contours of hetero- and homonormativity."[75] Similarly, claims about being in a post-feminist era have frequently been premised on the inroads made in professional employment and political participation by disproportionately white, middle- and upper-class women, without addressing class differences, institutional racism, and other structural barriers.[76] And post-racial discourses, which became prevalent in the United States after Barack Obama's Democratic nomination and successful election as president, valorized "anyone can make it" narratives that held up the achievements of individuals as evidence that racism was merely historical, no longer a barrier for contemporary America.[77]

From a more global perspective, Bravo's and Logo's programming and discourses about it exemplified homonormativity, particularly given the turn toward reality genres centered on consumption and interpersonal relationships rather than issues of structural inequality or injustice. Such contingent integrations of gays and lesbians in the United States (and other Western states), however, have been predicated on the subjugation of subjects elsewhere. As theorized by Jasbir Puar, "homonationalism" has threaded through various projects of nation-state formation in the Global North that deployed homonormative discourses. This includes claiming the moral mantle of gay rights while subjecting those in the Global South to homophobic, racist, and often violent othering, such as exposed by the abuse of inmates by U.S. soldiers at the Abu Ghraib prison in Afghanistan.[78] Bravo's and Logo's content strategies would seem worlds removed from these practices, yet nevertheless were predicated on discourses of a sexually progressive West, while remaining silent about Global North–South disparities of economic and political power. As it turned out, the specific U.S. contexts that facilitated dualcasting and gaystreaming also ended up pushing Logo, and to a lesser extent Bravo, away from the production of LGBTQ content, resulting in a decrease in even homonormative programming.

Beyond Dualcasting and Gaystreaming

At one level, dualcasting and gaystreaming can be seen as signifiers of gains that had already occurred for LGBTQ media and its viewers. That there was sufficient LGBTQ-centric content to set aside in favor of programs with one or two LGBTQ characters, that LGBTQ individuals routinely appeared on a slew of reality programming comprised a notable contrast to a decade or two earlier, when mining the subtext and reading against the grain were the major methods for gleaning queer representation from mainstream texts.[79] In addition, executives were probably right that their network's new content better reflected the lives and interests of many viewers: fluffier, entertaining stories and lifestyle series rather than chronicles about coming out or earnest pitches for acceptance.

However, one of the threads in this chapter has been a critique of network and mainstream media discourses associated with dualcasting and gaystreaming, particularly the claims about what was already going on in terms of LGBTQ integration and mainstreaming, when these programming strategies also reinforced hierarchies of gay identity, visibility, and inclusion. External commentators attributed much of Bravo's programming to president Lauren Zalaznick's infusion of her own visions of tasteful consumption[80] and the mythologization of the affluencer through a Bravo advertising campaign,[81] while network staff explained Bravo's success as due to its ability to target desirable demographic groups. The gayness of (some) Bravo viewers, when discussed explicitly, was bundled in with the characteristics of being educated and hip, an unacknowledged mirror of programming and development executives such as Andy Cohen. Logo's aspirations to emulate Bravo's success were shaped in part by a number of its key staff sharing similar backgrounds and dispositions, although Logo initially had more lesbians in executive positions.

Despite how network staff often framed it, then, Bravo's and Logo's programming during the periods of rebranding examined in this chapter was not the outcome of an inevitable progression from more niche to more mainstream. Rather, specific conditions of production, particularly a new cohort of cultural gatekeepers for LGBTQ media, alongside selective inclusions of LGBTQ people tied to the arenas of consumption and style, were central to the content shifts of Bravo and Logo. Also, even though having digital outlets meant that Bravo and Logo could at least potentially provide more diverse programming to different audience segments through their websites, the network-level directions eventually sealed the fate of the websites as well, changing their content alongside the channels or shuttering them altogether.

Currently, only Bravo's content remains largely similar to the directions it took during the period of rebranding detailed here; it remains a bastion of reality series, some of which feature LGBTQ participants, including *Top Chef*, and— after a long absence when the series aired on rival cable network Lifetime, *Project Runway*,[82] as well as Andy Cohen's long-running talk show *Watch What Happens Live with Andy Cohen*, but there are no longer any LGBTQ-centric shows. A stable of *Real Housewives* series continues to anchor the network's regular programming, with multiplatform tie-ins involving stars extending narrative elements of the shows (such as interpersonal feuds) via social media posts as well as encouraging viewer participation.[83]

For Logo, another overhaul took place when Lisa Sherman, who had headed the network as its general manager since 2008, resigned in 2013 and was succeeded by Chris McCarthy. In a 2015 interview,[84] McCarthy acknowledged that *RPDR* continued to be its highest rated series but recommitted Logo to LGBTQ-centered programming, including acquiring the British comedy-drama series *Cucumber* and *Banana*. McCarthy also addressed Logo's failure to attain the popularity of Bravo, noting that "they're not going after gays; they just happen to get them. We're targeting gays . . . and we're outpunching our weight class well beyond any network that's in our size." *Cucumber* and *Banana* seemed to promise a return to the kind of distinctive scripted programming that Logo had begun with, akin to *Noah's Arc* or *Exes and Ohs*. Created by Russell T. Davies, who had also produced the UK *Queer as Folk* (Channel 4, 1999–2000) series and then the revival of sci-fi classic *Doctor Who* in 2005 and spin-off *Torchwood* (BBC One/Two/Three, 2006–2011), which starred a pansexual lead, *Cucumber* and

Banana were part of a trio of shows, along with *Tofu*, whose titles referenced a scale for the hardness of male erections; *Cucumber* focused on middle-aged gay men, while *Banana* was about several young LGBTQ characters in contemporary Britain. However, *Cucumber* and *Banana* premiered in April 2015 to miniscule ratings, even with *RPDR* as a lead-in.[85]

Logo also returned to the production of reality series, with dating show *Finding Prince Charming* in 2016, which, like ABC's *The Bachelor*, involved a number of male suitors seeking to be the final choice of the star; unlike Bravo's *Boy Meets Boy*, there was no twist that some of the men were not gay. The premiere was simulcast on both Logo and VH1, which drew in a cumulative viewership similar to an episode of *RPDR*,[86] but when the show aired only on Logo, ratings were mediocre, and the show was not renewed. *Fire Island* (2017) (unrelated to the 1999 Stephen Fry series of the same name mentioned earlier),[87] featuring six gay men sharing a house at the popular gay vacation locale near Long Island, New York, further pushed the formula of *The A List* (which had of course in turn borrowed this from the *Real Housewives* on Bravo, MTV's *Jersey Shore*, and others) in showcasing its stars engaged in questionable behavior and relationship drama. Again, despite being scheduled after *RPDR*, the ratings never attained even a 0.1 in the important 18–49 age demographic,[88] and only one seven-episode season was made.

Logo featured some short LGBTQ videos for the Pride month of June at its LogoTV website in 2016, but that year McCarthy was promoted to president of VH1 and MTV as well, and after *Fire Island*, original production under his purview was pursued at only those two networks.[89] By fall 2017, Logo, once again, not only lacked any LGBTQ-centric series but did not air any original series at all, scripted or reality, and its airtime became devoted to marathon reruns of older network sitcoms, such as *Married with Children* and *Three's Company*.

As efforts to move away from a queer niche approach to programming, dual-casting and gaystreaming illustrated the successes as well as challenges faced by advertiser-supported cable, with mixed outcomes with respect to what content has endured or what has not. Two developments help illustrate the broader industry shifts that the trajectories of Bravo's and Logo's LGBTQ-centric content presaged. First, at Logo, Marc Leonard, who had been with the network since the planning stages before its 2005 launch, left in 2016 for a senior position on linear and multiplatform programming at Fuse TV,[90] a newer network that had rebranded in 2015 to target young viewers of color. Its mix of original reality series and music-based programming reflected Fuse's origins as a music video channel and its merger just prior to its rebranding with NuvoTV, which had programmed English-language content for a "bicultural" Latino audience; it also had an adult animated series *Sugar and Fuse* (2019) akin to *Rick and Steve*, and one of its reality series, *Big Freedia: Queen of Bounce* (2013–2017), was centered on a Black gay man and drag queen. The new Fuse did increase its ratings to some extent with the implementation of a niche programming approach similar to Logo's, but it was dropped from the channel lineups of both Comcast and Verizon at the beginning of 2019 due to what those carriers deemed insufficient viewership compared to other "multicultural" networks such as BET.[91] After emerging from a bankruptcy filing, Fuse continued with a more limited set of original series focused on musicians and celebrities of color mostly airing at 11:00 P.M. or later,[92] with the bulk of its airtime filled, like Logo's, with reruns of old sitcoms, although its earlier original content is also viewable online through its website, as a mobile app, or streamed on the Pluto TV live television website. Still, the targeting of a niche audience—even one relatively expansive like young viewers of color—appears to be a challenging way to thrive long term for a cable network.

Second, Bravo's signature show of the 2000s, *Queer Eye*, was rebooted on Netflix in 2018 to strong critical and viewer reception. Beyond the fact that all of the cast of experts were different, many of the criticisms of the original show did not apply or apply nearly as strongly. Michael Lovelock argued that "instead of relying on distinct *differences* between the consumer-savvy, style-oriented gay hosts and the uncouth heterosexual makeover subjects," the reboot emphasized "the apparent *similarities* between the hosts and their subjects."[93] Thus, the episodes did not denigrate a contestant's taste in problematically classed or racialized ways, but were grounded on the premise that the subject simply needed assistance to become their best authentic selves. Furthermore, while the original *Queer Eye* had steered clear of discussions about structural inequality, episodes in the reboot have acknowledged issues such as Christian homophobia, internalized homophobia, and police violence against African Americans.[94] Part of this reflects a degree of improvement in mainstream media in regard to critically informed approaches to gender, sexuality, race, and ethnicity, particularly after prominent movements such as Black Lives Matter and the renewed #MeToo activism surged in the mid-2010s. However, it is noteworthy that this show is now streaming on Netflix, which had earlier contributed significantly to LGBTQ programming through scripted series. The fact that the reality show that created such a pop culture splash for a particular kind of gay representation in the 2000s was remade for the premier streaming service the following decade speaks to a broader dissemination of LGBTQ-themed programming through streamers. Indeed, media commentator (and former TWoP recapper) Joe Reid identified several recent Netflix reality shows that are metaphorically "coming to eat Bravo's lunch," including "high-end real estate porn" reality shows in the ilk of Bravo's *Million Dollar Listing* and candid reality shows similar to the *Real Housewives* series.[95]

It was not just Bravo and Logo but all of legacy television that began facing competition from streaming services like Netflix that had adopted what Amanda Lotz called a "conglomerated niche" strategy; this included specifically targeting LGBTQ viewers with greater diversity of representation than available elsewhere in commercial media.[96] Indeed, with "LGBTQ" listed as a content category by Netflix, Hulu, and Amazon Prime, Himberg commented that LGBTQ programming had attained the status of a genre, like older classifications such as drama and comedy.[97] Thus, a key question is how the place of LGBTQ content has shifted since Bravo and Logo implemented dualcasting and gaystream programming, as well as the implications such changes have for accounts of contemporary television, audience segments, and the relationships between traditionally marginalized groups and commercial media. These issues are taken up in the next chapter as part of a broader discussion on LGBTQ media and its remaking of the mainstream.

4

Beyond Queer Niche

•••••••••••••••••••••••

Remaking the Mainstream

Rethinking the Mainstream/Independent Distinction

In Logo's early years, it forged associations with NewFest,[1] the New York LGBTQ Film Festival, since the network was looking to acquire content to stream, and in 2009, Logo became the largest "presenting" sponsor. Marc Leonard, a senior Logo executive, was on the programming committee, and he suggested I check out the festival. I decided to attend NewFest as a venue where I could observe encounters between independent producers and commercial media more concretely, given that so much of the website-network interaction happened over email or in circumstances I was not privy to.

My first event was an evening mixer at the School of Visual Arts Theater, where I made it past the door staff by dropping Leonard's name even though I was not a registered filmmaker "on the list." Inside, the foyer's low-level lighting showed most of the people to be men in their thirties and forties, smartly dressed, talking in pairs and small groups. Along one wall was a bar with water and red and white wine in plastic cups; along the other, a table with unappetizing hors d'oeuvres. It was not really my scene; I wanted to approach a young African American woman wearing a filmmaker's badge, but she was in conversation with an older white man, and I caught the drift of their conversation being about the possibilities of distribution for the woman's film. The first people I talked to were festival volunteers—the photographer who was an exchange student from Spain, and a post-college trio, two men and a woman, who were hanging together in a

small group. An older woman, Raquel Solomon, turned out to have been volun-
teering for NewFest for ten years, so I asked her how the festival had changed. It
had acquired a new director at some point[2] and gotten more "corporate" in the
last couple of years, she said, but attendance and participation had always been
dominated by men. As I picked up my backpack to leave after an hour or so, the
African American woman I saw initially was alone, and when we made eye contact, she asked me if I was a filmmaker. We introduced ourselves—it was my first
conversation with Tiona McClodden—and as an opening, I borrowed Raquel's
characterization and noted that the festival seemed pretty corporate. McClodden agreed immediately and said emphatically that almost everyone here was a
gay white man; she was the only African American lesbian. She had made *black./
womyn.*, a documentary about lesbians of color, and said that her style and
subject matter were not particularly commercial, yet it was work like this that
gave Logo its edge. She felt compelled to screen her film at venues like this so
that it had some legitimacy—that is, curated by a major festival—which is
where an independent filmmaker needed to start from to even begin negotiating distribution.

Earlier chapters addressed various facets of LGBTQ media developing within
the auspices of Bravo and Logo as major commercial networks. Chapter 1 traced
how convergence culture brought LGBTQ cultural agents into mainstream
media production. Chapter 2 examined how Bravo's and Logo's websites offered
new digital spaces for queer expression and community. Chapter 3 discussed the
evolution of Bravo's and Logo's channel programming strategies with respect to
LGBTQ content. Building on these threads, this chapter presents multiple
sources of data and analysis—my interviews with Bravo and Logo workers, recent
television industry trends regarding where LGBTQ content now appears,
and previous accounts of media production—to explain how the key developments at Bravo and Logo demonstrate not simply the move of LGBTQ producers,
users, and content into the mainstream, but also how this remade the very delin-
eations between "mainstream" and "independent." A new model of media production, I argue, is needed to account for the contemporary media landscape.

Certainly, Bravo and Logo were "corporate," as my interviewees at NewFest
noted, and there were some predictable dynamics in their interactions with
independent queer producers. At the same time, although dichotomies to do
with content, the motivations of cultural workers, and the scale of production are commonly assumed to position commercial media unfavorably with
respect to artistically authentic and politically resistive expression, Lisa Henderson has argued that such a "commercial repressive hypothesis" overlooks the
bidirectional—though uneven—flows between (more) subcultural and (more)
mainstream spaces, as well as the complex positionings and trajectories of cultural agents in the field that more careful examination of production contexts
reveals.[3] And as the introduction chapter noted, Sarah Thornton's work on subcultures demonstrated how mainstream culture and subcultures were mutually

co-constructed, even as the mainstream was frequently invoked as a denigrated comparison point by those active in the music subcultures she examined.[4]

In this vein, the next section of this chapter considers how Bravo's and Logo's network and site staff negotiated the commercial contexts of their work, discussing how they framed the mainstream/independent distinction and how they addressed the lower prestige of the mainstream, compared to the cachet of subcultural production and content. These producer discourses provide telling insights into the tensions at the intersections of commercialism and LGBTQ content creation, where queer is no longer niche but still retains the cultural and political charge of independent and subcultural domains.

In the longer run, Bravo's and Logo's integrations of LGBTQ cultural agents and media presaged a diversification of queer content creation in the industry more broadly, and the second part of the chapter moves to explain why LGBTQ-centric programming approaches by cable networks like Bravo and Logo did not end up to be sustainable despite novel conjunctures of commercial and independent media. Two overlapping developments in the television landscape have been central: (1) the immense growth of reality TV, including shows, across multiple cable networks, featuring LGBTQ stars and (2) the emergence of the "peak TV" era of scripted television, with greater diversity than ever before. Thus, not only could LGBTQ content no longer serve as a distinctive hallmark for any one network, but scripted series with strong queer narratives provided viewing options that Bravo's and Logo's embrace of the reality genre did not.

How can these developments around commercial integrations of LGBTQ media be represented in a way that reflects more general dynamics across the commercial-independent and mainstream-subcultural spectrums? As the introduction chapter noted, Pierre Bourdieu's model of the field of cultural production[5] offers a starting point, given its explicit attention to unequal distributions of capital and the differential positioning of cultural agents, but it fails to reflect the conditions of contemporary media, including those involving LGBTQ content and producers. Taking account of the production characteristics and content of Bravo's and Logo's channels and websites, I present a revised model of the cultural field that is inclusive of two key shifts: an expansion beyond queer niche in mainstream media, showing that the changes at Bravo and Logo prefigured future developments in the production of LGBTQ media more generally, and the diversification of television distribution modes, which is now a more complex landscape that includes not just broadcast and cable networks but also streaming platforms of varying scale themselves.

Negotiating Commercial Contexts: The Discourses of Bravo's and Logo's Cultural Producers

Broadly glossed, mainstream and independent media have inverse relationships in terms of economic capital and subcultural capital; mainstream media enjoys relatively high economic capital but relatively low subcultural capital. With queer producers and content only beginning to be integrated into major commercial media, staff at Bravo and Logo acknowledged inequalities of economic capital that favored the networks, but they generally sought to downplay this asymmetry, framing it in the most positive light. Logo executives also talked down the artistic prestige often accorded to independent production, reframing the relationship that Logo had with independent media as one where the network provided a crucial venue for performers who otherwise would not enjoy wide exposure. And, while recognizing the profit imperative of commercial media, they highlighted the nonfinancial motivations for their work, particularly in serving the LGBTQ community. Some of these discourses were self-serving and did not acknowledge the ways that the networks benefited from the creative and economic value of independent queer labor. Yet, as Julia Himberg has argued from her own interview research with LGBTQ industry insiders, rather than assuming that such cultural agents are inevitably beholden only to commercial interests, "many openly lesbian and gay workers in positions of power have been able to navigate and operate within the corporate media industry space in explicitly political ways, accruing agency and authority," at times effecting politically significant changes.[6] Hollis Griffin similarly noted that professionals working on gay and lesbian cinema, television, and online media often "understand their professional labor as serving important political and cultural functions."[7]

Scale was a common theme in the discourses of site and network staff that I discuss separately, given the frequency with which Bravo's and Logo's workers described their companies as "small," particularly in reference to their earlier days. At one level, this reflects a familiar framing of smallness as a disadvantage or challenge that was overcome. In his ethnographic research on workers in the media industry, John Caldwell heard many narratives of "making it" despite the odds or difficult conditions.[8] Coming from Bravo's and Logo's site and network staff, such narratives sometimes served to assert skills or career decisions that both made the successes possible and marked them as distinctive. Beyond this, though, commentary about the relative scale of the networks or websites also reflected the complexities of the cultural field, especially with respect to the incorporation of websites aimed at what would formerly have been termed "niche" audiences. The fragmentation of the "mass" audience had already begun with the emergence of cable television but was accelerated with the rise of the internet; thus, as Joseph Turow has discussed, advertisers introduced segmented targeting of online consumers after the internet became commercially significant in the 1990s and continued to develop these strategies in the 2000s.[9] What this section considers, however, is how to rethink the character of major commercial media itself when it cannot simply be defined as monolithically "large scale," and the role of digital technologies in these changes.

Mainstream/Independent Engagements

The tensions of being a commercial media network for which LGBTQ content was important were most evident, unsurprisingly, for Logo. Even as Logo was reliant on independently produced queer media for the network's programming and subcultural capital, several network staff sought to deromanticize its cachet. Thus, Chris Willey challenged assumptions about the creative richness of independent versus mass commercial content, describing most indie films as "horrific" and "unwatchable," with festivals like Sundance providing a filtering process that audiences are generally unaware of, out of which a few stand-out products can emerge. Although his assessment was reasonable, Willey talking down independent production also signaled his position as a programming and development executive at Logo, someone invested in both Logo's position as an institutional agent and how his network's programming was received in relation to content produced elsewhere.

Logo executives also cast the network's programming of music videos and independent film, on *The Click List* music video and short film shows, as a service to their creators: "just something we have to do," as Marc Leonard put it, despite other programming presumably being able to draw more viewers. Chris Willey commented that for independent artists who would otherwise not get airplay on a major network, "we're connecting the money of advertising . . . to an independent filmmaker and storyteller world that had never had that connection before, and you start to see films now being produced, knowing 'I have a chance now of licensing this to Logo, and I have a chance of actually making some of this money back.'"[10]

Senior Logo executives also noted that the network provided the LGBTQ community with a voice and a broader range of stories and characters that it had not previously enjoyed on mainstream media. In public comments, Logo head Lisa Sherman expressed satisfaction that the network's content "reflect[s] the diversity of our audience," and in this vein, Chris Willey pointed to the channel's early original programming, which included *Noah's Arc*, a drama about queer African American men, *Curl Girls*, a show about lesbian surfers, and *The Ride*, a documentary about a charity AIDS bike ride, which "might not have been the most commercial, hitting-all-those-buttons choices, but they were really significant to our audience, and they were things we felt like they would really enjoy and watch."

Website staff provided examples of improving LGBTQ representation as well, through both giving positive coverage to shows and films that helped those "who are doing a good job . . . do more of those sorts of things," as AfterElton editor in chief Michael Jensen put it, and critiquing problematic media texts, sometimes by directly communicating with content creators. For example, Jensen had spoken with producers at industry events such as the Television Critics Association meetings, and noted that he expected a science-fiction show that had not yet aired at the time would reflect such conversations.[11] Such behind-the-scenes practices to improve LGBTQ representation exemplify what Himberg has termed "under-the-radar activism,"[12] instances of which occur out of public sight and are not referenced in any publications, such as GLAAD's annual reports on LGBTQ media, yet are ways that cultural workers within commercial media are able to effect meaningful change.

Site runners also mentioned the importance of their sites for facilitating LGBTQ community, with both Sarah Warn and Danny Nguyen emphasizing that AfterEllen/AfterElton and Downelink retained their missions to serve LGBTQ users even after being purchased by Logo. In addition, tying them to a tradition of television airing material in "the public interest," Bravo's and Logo's websites participated in gay and lesbian community projects and produced public service announcements; OutZoneTV's collaboration with the Human Rights Campaign in 2007 for National Coming Out Day as discussed in chapter 2 was one example.

As for the channels, Claudia Gorelick commented that although Logo had been "upping the entertainment factor" in its regular programming, it was producing LGBTQ-focused messages for the channel and websites as part of MTV Networks' "social initiatives," which addressed issues including bullying, homophobia, being out, and HIV/AIDS prevention. These initiatives were examples of corporate social responsibility (CSR) practices that, as Himberg noted, have become widespread as a way to mitigate concerns that media conglomeration would severely reduce the diversity of voices on the most highly viewed media outlets. While critics have been skeptical about CSR contributing toward substantial social change, Himberg pointed to a gay media executive speaking off the record who had successfully advocated for multiple causes through a CSR division he established, including homeless LGBTQ youth, anti-bullying, and same-sex adoption campaigns.

Still, such approaches did not completely compensate for continuing asymmetries associated with the shift of LGBTQ production into network domains. Logo in particular derived both economic and subcultural capital from its exchanges with queer cultural producers on the edges of commercial media: its compensation for filmmakers was poor, and the network did not pay out residual fees or even for liability insurance, according to independent producers I spoke to. Filmmaker Tiona McClodden, whose work had played at NewFest, was told that Logo "doesn't pay you jack shit," though this was part of a broader picture of meager offers from commercial enterprises that distribute independent film; McClodden had also fielded DVD distribution deals where the company wanted an exclusive license, including all digital rights, while offering cheap packaging and demanding a substantial cut of 40–50 percent.

There was a similar dynamic at websites like AfterEllen. Sarah Warn noted that it was not easy to secure advertising support for online programming, which meant that AfterEllen could offer video contributors exposure but not financial compensation. Even though it was true that websites like AfterEllen faced challenges to be profitable, at the same time, AfterEllen obtained for free content that drew visitors to the site, as well as enjoying the credibility of having original lesbian video, which also helped shape its brand for Logo. Furthermore, LGBTQ digital content was not uncompensated everywhere; SheWired, for example, was paying vloggers even when AfterEllen was not, as Dalila Ali Rajah mentioned when explaining why she moved her talk show *Cherry Bomb* there after it had initially been hosted on AfterEllen. In fact, a fundamental inequality is that bandwidth is still much cheaper compared to the resources required for producing video content. This is particularly true for scripted shows like *Anyone but Me*, which AfterEllen hosted for a time; Rajah estimated that it would cost around $400,000 an episode were it produced under normal studio conditions, but even one of the talking head vlogs on AfterEllen still required the costs of at least the equipment for filming and food for those involved.

Logo's news site 365gay had a different but parallel relationship with independent gay and lesbian newspapers. Asked about a comparison between Logo and small-scale print gay media, Kristin Frank cast Logo as assuming the role of LGBTQ representation on a larger scale, with independent LGBTQ newspapers being "the foundation for what was created," but "all Logo was doing was taking it to the next step and giving voice to a community, in a much larger way, that didn't have that reach before." 365gay editor in chief Jay Vanasco, however, was not so sanguine, seeing online news sites as riding "the backs of gay papers" in the sense that these papers carried out the actual journalism for producing stories rather than just publishing news content from other sources. However, Logo did little to sustain these publications financially at a time when many were folding or struggling to survive.[13]

In short, it was not simply that Logo and its websites were investing resources into independent media; the network also benefited substantially from its capacity to obtain this content cheaply or for free. In addition, having the work of unknown or emerging artists graced Logo with a measure of subcultural prestige that its corporate status would otherwise make it hard to claim.

On the other hand, the interactions of independent queer producers with Logo could also yield benefits to those producers. Some examples were discussed in the section on LGBTQ digital video in chapter 2, with AfterEllen and AfterElton hosting and promoting a number of video blogs and web series, but it was also possible for queer artists more on the margins. In May 2011, AfterEllen posted an article about an ongoing document project about Black lesbian elders spearheaded by Tiona McClodden, the filmmaker I met at NewFest. To generate funding and publicity, McClodden had used various online spaces such as Facebook, Tumblr, Twitter, and Indiegogo. However, coverage on AfterEllen when it was the most highly trafficked site about lesbian entertainment probably provided the most significant exposure, so even though McClodden did not successfully negotiate the distribution of her first documentary, *black./womyn.*, to Logo, Logo nevertheless had a tangible impact on the career of a queer producer whose work was among the least "commercial" of those I spoke to.[14]

Questions of Scale

Given that Bravo's and Logo's statuses as cable networks belonging to large media conglomerates, it was striking how commonly network executives described them as being "small." Of course, even within commercial media, scale is relative; one media corporation may be small fry compared to another, and these narratives reflected these conditions even though such descriptions also obscured the ways that the networks drew on free or cheap labor. Still, what was also at play was how Bravo's and Logo's websites functioned as units that were indeed smaller and modestly resourced, something partially enabled by the conditions of digital media production.

One theme from Bravo and Logo executives was characterizing their organizations as small in comparison to their parent companies or other units therein. Logo vice president of digital media Dan Sacher compared his network to other channels under the Viacom umbrella, saying that "the stuff we do, we do it on a shoestring budget. . . . We don't have money on the scale of MTV or VH1, or even CMT." In a similar vein, Claudia Gorelick called Logo "the little engine that could," outperforming its size in "doing things with smaller budgets in successful ways." Kristin Frank acknowledged the relative bounty of Logo vis-à-vis non-network-supported ventures, but described Logo as built up from scratch as a start-up with "very few resources" via tight organization and efficient multitasking by a small number of employees. Echoing much of this, Jay Vanasco pointed out how adaptable and innovative staff at Logo were and noted that it was "crazy" that 365gay was more poorly funded than "this very small community gay paper" that she had worked on over a decade ago as her first writing job.

Bravo staff also provided narratives of smallness. Discussing Bravo's early days as it rebranded itself into one of NBC Universal's most prominent successes, Bernard Grenier summed up its space in NBC's 30 Rock building as staffed by "a very small team of people: fourteen people total, working on [floor] fourteen . . . in a space half the size of this part of the [current] floor." Aimee Viles, vice president of emerging media, said that her team was "not nearly big enough," consisting of only two dedicated staff, an assistant shared with her immediate superior Lisa Hsia (senior vice president of digital media), although she also had two to five interns at any given time.[15]

On this note, although the number of regular staff is an obvious measure of size, like other commercial networks, both Bravo and Logo had numerous interns, usually each providing twenty hours per week working on website or channel content, including creative input,[16] in return for college credit but little or no financial remuneration. The networks could attract interns based on brand appeal to youthful applicants; thus, as Jay Vanasco commented, MTV was "notorious" for paying poorly since it had long drawn young people who wanted to work there, and Logo benefited from this as well, often with the additional attraction of producing content for a traditionally underrepresented group. At Bravo, Mari Ghuneim, vice president of digital media, also noted the importance of interns to the network and to her unit in particular, with new and emerging media appealing to applicants who wanted to do "cutting edge" work. Thus, at the network level, Logo, and even more so Bravo, were not as small as their staff characterized them, even if their budgets and profit margins were more modest than many other media companies.

The fact that websites like OutZoneTV and Television Without Pity (TWoP) were owned by Bravo and AfterEllen, AfterElton, and 365gay were Logo properties was also pertinent to the scale characteristics of the networks as a whole. Just as for the networks, a repeated theme among website founders was making do or succeeding with limited resources, certainly during the pre-purchase establishment of their sites but even when the sites were part of Logo or Bravo. With respect to staff, one to three people were typically doing the bulk of the work: Sarah Warn, Malinda Lo, and Karman Kregloe were the three mainstays in the early days of AfterEllen, Danny Nguyen worked with two other cofounders at Downelink, Zac Hug became the only dedicated staff member for Out-ZoneTV, and Jay Vanasco noted that she had been the sole full-time staff member for 365gay after coming onboard as editor in chief, with only limited funds for paying freelance writers. Such circumstances were possible due to the affordances of digital media, which enabled a few people to produce and disseminate content widely without the same level of infrastructure required by legacy media.

Still, the relative spectrum of scale also held for the websites; they were by no means the least well-resourced ones as a whole. The initial creation of TWoP, AfterEllen, and Downelink depended on the founders having the training and occupations that furnished them with the skills and time to develop and manage websites on their own. Furthermore, before being purchased by networks, several sites were already in the process of becoming more commercialized. When TWoP struggled financially a few years prior to Bravo's purchase, the owners raised the possibility of user fees, which were averted when the site secured sufficient advertising revenue, primarily through an association with Yahoo!. Also, as Michael Jensen recalled, when Sarah Warn approached him to become editor of AfterElton, she told him that she wanted to develop the sites and then "eventually have them be acquired by someone bigger." In other words, these sites were founded and run by cultural agents who were already relatively well positioned in the field prior to their encounters with networks.

This disparate set of conditions for scale is indicative of a key point about contemporary media which I identified earlier: how the relationship between the amount of capital associated with producing media texts is no longer as strongly tied to the extent of their distribution or their audience sizes, compared to the network or even early post-network eras. Bravo and Logo were undeniably corporate-owned companies and there were clear elements of those resources, both in terms of physical workspaces (30 Rock is still 30 Rock, after all) and the number of workers, paid and unpaid. Nevertheless, the outlets under each network did vary in size, with the production of LGBTQ content through the websites having some characteristics of the independent media that several of these sites had been prior to being purchased.

It is worth stepping back for a moment to take stock of what was going on at Bravo and Logo with respect to LGBTQ media. A number of LGBTQ-identified producers were now producing LGBTQ content, targeted at least in part to LGBTQ consumers. As the last chapter discussed, these developments were occurring as much of the LGBTQ community was increasingly part of mainstream culture more generally. Yet even as the integrations of LGBTQ websites to Bravo and Logo reshaped the character of mainstream media in terms of its producers and content, these programming directions were not ultimately sustained at those networks. Instead, as the next section describes, what Bravo and Logo had initially been at the vanguard of is part of a longer story of where commercial LGBTQ media has ended up thriving and what this means for conceptualizing the field of cultural production.

Beyond Queer Niche: The Contemporary Landscape

Bravo's and Logo's strategies around LGBTQ-centric programming confronted two overlapping developments in the television landscape: (1) the increase of LGBTQ content in network and cable television more generally, including in the reality genres that Bravo and then Logo had built their programming on; (2) as chapter 2 discussed, the emergence of streaming services such as Netflix that carried a catalog of LGBTQ series. Thus, not only could LGBTQ content no longer serve as a hallmark of distinction for any one cable network, but there were a number of scripted series with strong queer narratives in the "quality TV" ilk that reality programs generally fell outside of.

The Limits of the "Real Gay People" Appeal: Reality Television Saturation Collides with Peak TV

RuPaul's Drag Race, which had anchored Logo's ratings for so long, shifted to VH1 in 2017. At one level, this move was a consequence of Logo chief Chris McCarthy also heading up VH1 and MTV and, as the last chapter discussed, overseeing the abandonment of Logo's original programming pursuits. However, it was also indicative of the broader expansion of reality shows across broadcast and cable television. Although there have several such shows that have sustained strong audience numbers, most reality series, as Amanda Lotz noted—even the ones that made a splash in terms of ratings or critical attention—were short-lived, so they were not particularly useful for helping a network to increase the fees paid to it by cable service providers and did not re-air well the way that various

scripted genres did. There were occasional shows that became breakout hits—
Queer Eye for Bravo and *RuPaul's Drag Race* for Logo, certainly—but even successful reality series did not necessarily end up establishing a clear, long-term
brand for their networks, which sometimes went on to produce other shows similar to the first hit that failed to bring in the same kinds of audience numbers.[17]
Lotz identified Bravo, as well as MTV, as exceptions in being able to build successful network brands from reality programming—Bravo with a mix of
makeover shows, competitive reality, and its *Real Housewives* series, and MTV
with candid reality series such as *The Osbournes* (2002–2005), *Laguna Beach*
(2004–2006), and *Jersey Shore* (2009–2012), as well as dating show *A Shot at Love
with Tila Tequila* (2007–2009). However, the trajectory of cable overall demonstrates that reality programming has not been a guarantor of sustainable success for any one network.

What about the LGBTQ-centric elements of Bravo's and Logo's programming? First, the fashion and design, music and dance, food, and travel themes
of Bravo's reality slate, which Logo sought to replicate in broad strokes during
gaystreaming, also became common elsewhere. As Katherine Sender noted,
because these programs are "cheap to produce, use non-actors, and tend to be
preoccupied with domestic and feminized concerns," the "upscale associations"
of tasteful gays "helps deflect the trashy shadow of reality television,"[18] and a
number of such reality shows with LGBTQ stars emerged in the 2010s outside
of Bravo and Logo. More generally, LGBTQ participants across different reality television genres became prevalent, thus also diluting the distinctiveness of
the reality series that Bravo and Logo had been the first to offer.

VH1's *TRANSform Me* (2010) was a riff on *Queer Eye*, featuring three trans
women, including Laverne Cox, making over a female contestant. E!'s *EJNYC*
(2016) was centered on EJ Johnson, a gay Black man seeking a career in fashion
design in New York City. On Oxygen, *The Prancing Elites Project* (2015–2016)
featured a troupe of queer African American dancers, and *Strut* (2016) profiled
a modeling agency in New York City that specialized in representing transgender
models.[19] Trans women were also the stars of *I Am Cait* (E!, 2015–2016), which
followed the life of Caitlyn Jenner, and *I Am Jazz* (TLC, 2015–present),
which began airing when star Jazz Jennings was still a teenager. Fuse, a network
that rebranded itself in 2015 to target young people of color, had *Transcendent*
(2015–2016), about a group of transgender dancers in San Francisco, and *Big
Freedia: Queen of Bounce* (2013–2017), about the musical pursuits of the show's
star, a Black gay man and drag queen reminiscent of RuPaul (and with whom
Big Freedia performed on occasion). New York's drag community was also the
theme of two shows for other newer cable networks aimed toward millennials:
Shade: Queens of NYC (2017), which aired for one season on Fusion, an English-
language cable network launched in 2013 by Spanish-language television giant
Univision, and *My House* (2018), which ran for a single season as well, on Viceland, a network majority-owned by AMC Networks that launched in 2016.

Viceland also aired two seasons of the travel show *Gaycation* (2016–2017), starring Elliot Page.[20] Other reality series starring lesbians included *The Real L Word* (2010–2012) on Showtime, seeking to capitalize on its scripted drama *The L Word*; *Make or Break: The Linda Perry Project* (VH1, 2014), following Perry's work in the music industry; and Food Network's *I Hart Food* (2017), starring Hannah Hart, who had started off with a YouTube vlog. Gay male couples were featured on Planet Green's *The Fabulous Beekman Boys* (2011–2012), following a couple's professional and life endeavors on a farm; OWN's *10 Kids, 2 Dads* (2012); and more recently, Netflix's *Styling Hollywood* (2019), about a celebrity stylist–interior designer couple.

In addition to such shows have been a plethora of series with at least one or two LGBTQ participants, including some high-profile winners in competitive genres, from Richard Hatch taking the first season of CBS's *Survivor* in 2000 to Melissa King's victory on *Top Chef* in 2020. Indeed, as Michael Lovelock noted, so many LGBTQ contestants have appeared on reality television that there are numerous "Top 10"–type lists about them.[21] Thus, there may be a certain degree of reality show ennui, even though, as scholars have discussed, viewers watch the shows for multiple kinds of general reasons that might seem able to outlast the tenure of particular shows. For example, in her audience study of four makeover series, including *Queer Eye*, Sender's interviewees recounted getting fashion and style tips for themselves or family members, using the shows as "free psychotherapy," for the entertainment value of the show itself, and the social interactions and other activities associated with online fandom. Thus, the question is what the implications of reality television saturation are for viewers looking for LGBTQ representation.

First, although gay and lesbian characters had begun appearing much more frequently on U.S. scripted series in the 1990s, most of that content targeted straight viewers and was deficient in various ways as queer representation.[22] The significant increases and improvements in the 2000s and 2010s were partly due to the burgeoning reality genre; even though reality programming is often problematic in terms of discourses around gender and sexuality, it has also been a site of more complex representations for these, as Sender and others have pointed out.[23] Thus, one of the novel draws for the first few reality series that showcased LGBTQ stars, like *Queer Eye* and *RuPaul's Drag Race*, was seeing LGBTQ people in ways they had not previously been depicted, such as designated experts in the position of giving advice or judging skills-based competitions, and not simply contestants. However, as reality show genres were remade with only slightly different variations in settings, the appeal of seeing real-life LGBTQ people may have worn off.

Second, for LGBTQ audiences, research about viewer identification and perceived authenticity of show participants has particular resonances. Contestants on makeover or competitive shows as well as participants in candid reality series are often shown in vulnerable, even humiliating situations, subject to judgment within the show environment as well as by audiences, so one issue is how viewers relate to these participants. Although some viewers may enjoy the shaming and downfall that contestants often experience, feeling well distanced from those suffering on-screen, a substantial amount of research "suggests that identification between viewers and candidates [i.e., reality show participants] might be the norm, despite sometimes very different class positions and in contrast to the assumption that schadenfreude epitomizes reality show viewing."[24] For groups that have been historically underrepresented in the media, such as LGBTQ people, who experience such identification, the extent to which participants are viewed as authentic may be particularly important.

Of course, audiences generally understand that reality shows are partially scripted and strategically edited,[25] so the "realness" of participants is mediated by the processes of production. Nevertheless, many viewers still judge these participants on how true to their selves they appear to be; as Sender pointed out, even if they assume that reality show star personas and storylines are partly constructed, viewers are often invested in the "emotional authenticity" of the participants, judged by various elements of their emotional expressiveness.[26] This point underlies not just makeover reality television but also competitive fashion and design shows, where contestants are supposed to also find their true selves with which to project distinct style identities. In this vein, Lovelock argued that "the drive towards authenticity, rather than particular, normative formations of sexuality and gender" has become the overarching trope for reality television, overriding the earlier dominance of heteronormative and gender-conforming representations.[27]

Authenticity, however, is double-edged especially when it comes to candid reality series. Such shows often base their appeal on the stars behaving badly, and there is clearly still a market for this content, what Dana Heller notes has been labeled "trainwreck TV" in her discussion of Showtime's *The Real L Word*.[28] However, LGBTQ viewers may be particularly critical of these kinds of depictions—even if participants are being their "true" selves—given the historical and contemporary deficits of queer representation. For example, both *The A List* and *Fire Island* (2017)[29] garnered scathing reviews in mainstream and LGBTQ outlets, with *Gawker* sniping that *The A List* showcased the worst sort of "fame-hungry, attractive, horrible people you could have imagined,"[30] while *The Advocate* blasted the *Fire Island* trailer for its "screaming fights, slamming doors, gossiping, the use of the f word (although bleeped out) and an opening line simply of 'cocktails, sunshine, boys'";[31] whether these were gay men being their actual selves or deliberately play-acting less than admirable traits, it was not something a lot of gay viewers wanted to watch. In addition, Logo's gaystream reality programming was relatively derivative, and perceived authenticity might also be diminished when a show was seen as overly similar to earlier series. If being real partly means not copying others for the cool factor, for example, then shows that are more or less imitations of preexisting successes might be received skeptically; how authentic could participants be when the very premise of their show was a replica?

Bravo's and Logo's websites did also offer a range of what the industry terms "alternative" programming, which groups together with reality series other non-fully scripted genres such as talk shows. As chapter 2 discussed, AfterEllen and AfterElton streamed a number of series that were mostly in this category: talking head shows featuring either just the host(s) or including interviewees. With this content provided mostly for free, the financial arrangements were different than channel programming, and these web series as a whole were successful in helping AfterEllen and AfterElton grow. The decline of the sites under Logo was therefore not due to the fact that the video content did not appeal to site visitors so much as the network's overall change in direction precipitated by gaystreaming.

A small number of scripted shows centering multiple LGBTQ characters, such as *Queer as Folk* and *The L Word*, had already aired on premium cable networks by the early 2000s when Bravo and Logo began their own forays into LGBTQ-centric series. In addition, Here TV evolved from a pay-per-view LGBTQ channel to a premium cable network in 2004, with a couple of scripted series of note such as sci-fi drama *Dante's Cove* (2005–2007), but the vast majority of television viewers at the time had only advertiser-supported cable packages. Other broadcast and non-premium cable networks were offering an increasing number of dramas and comedies with LGBTQ characters and storylines. Tellingly, GLAAD's annual "Where We Are on TV" reports, which it began compiling in 1995, listed by name all U.S.-aired scripted series with regular lead or supporting LGBTQ characters until its 2014 report; according to its statistics, the number of scripted series with regular LGBTQ characters (lead or supporting) on broadcast networks increased from five in 2007–2008 to twenty-seven in 2014, while for all cable networks, both premium and advertiser-supported, this number changed from twenty-one to forty-three in the same period.[32] Many LGBTQ viewers saw these options as superior to what Logo offered, lamenting online that the network had strayed regrettably far from serving the communities it had previously. In a Queerty article critical of Logo's 2012 slate, reader comments included "I have been wishing for a long time that [Logo] would feature quality gay programming, like a PBS for gay viewers," while another wrote similarly that ideally, Logo would be "like a gay HBO with compelling dramas about gay lives in context.... [Logo's staff] don't aim that high or don't want to."[33]

In her account about the relationships and changes involving broadcast, advertiser-supported cable, premium cable, and streaming services, Lotz pointed to the failures of many cable networks to sufficiently differentiate themselves from other channels and, most recently, to effectively compete with streamers, several of which have taken a multi-niche strategy in terms of content type.[34] As chapter 2 discussed, streamers with original programming emerged in the early 2010s, as Logo was implementing gaystreaming and, led by Netflix, began offering well-budgeted shows with LGBTQ narratives outshining any scripted series that Logo had programmed in terms of production values and critical attention. Furthermore, monthly subscription fees for the big three—Netflix, Amazon, and Hulu—were less than even the cheapest cable packages, making them appealing even to viewers who wanted to gain access to only one or two shows.[35] Thus, the integrations of LGBTQ content into commercial media that Logo comprised, which had been noteworthy when they occurred in the mid-2000s, contributed to conditions where such content in itself did not ultimately sustain an advertiser-supported cable network. This was true even given the broader brushstrokes of gaystreaming, as this period overlapped with viewers beginning to shift away from traditional cable packages, which bundled broadcast and advertiser-supported cable television in minimally configurable ways, toward streamers and subscription services more broadly.[36]

A New Model of Media Production

Having discussed the complex ways that LGBTQ media and its production shaped the trajectories of Bravo and Logo, two major commercial networks, this section proposes a new model of media production that can account for the expanded presence of LGBTQ content in staking distinction (what Bourdieu termed symbolic capital) and securing profitability (in terms of economic capital), taking account of the fact that television is available through multiple forms of delivery, particularly digital platforms that vary immensely in character and scale. First, it should be noted that content distinctiveness and Bourdieusian distinction are not identical, nor are industry notions of niche audiences the same as traditionally disempowered groups. Thus, distinctive content is not always high prestige; although the quest for viewers in the post-network era has often tapped the "quality" television domain, as Lotz and other television scholars have discussed, it has also involved content with less symbolic capital.[37] Also, even if industry insiders might similarly describe LGBTQ viewers and, say, lovers of jewelry, as "underserved," Bravo and Logo were not programming just to any niche but to a historically marginalized community that was being significantly integrated into mainstream culture.

Lotz has proposed a "subscriber model of cultural production," arguing that the most consequential change for television in the last decade has been the rise of subscriber-supported services.[38] This has altered many aspects of the industry compared to when it was dominated by advertiser-supported broadcast and cable television, in terms of not just how content is offered to consumers, which is perhaps most obviously different, but also the economic configuration of these services and how income is generated, how market segments are targeted, and the logistical and financial arrangements for content creation. These are developments especially important to understanding the business of television and how the explosive growth of streamers occurred, but in centering her account on major commercial media, Lotz does not focus on how digital technologies have brought content that had previously been marginalized into mainstream media, or on the relationships between mainstream and independent production and the unequal distribution of capital across the field of cultural production more broadly.

As I noted in earlier chapters, Bourdieu's well-known representation of the field of cultural production offers a way of representing hierarchies and differences of power as structuring the field, and both economic and symbolic capital are crucial to capturing the status of queerness (and outsider-insider status in general) within media and culture. However, the four-quadrant division poorly reflects the conditions of contemporary media. Bourdieu's model better fit LGBTQ content when it was primarily produced outside of major commercial domains; experimental or avant-garde films that attracted little or no critical reception of any sort—the independent works dismissed by Chris Willey as "unwatchable"—that Bourdieu placed in the "Bohemia" segment, while more accessible works would draw the attention of an "intellectual" audience and enjoy higher symbolic capital. Yet, as the first section of this chapter laid out, the divide between mainstream and independent was never absolute, and the convergences of legacy television with digital media have further complicated demarcations of Bourdieu's "large-scale" and restricted ("small-scale") production.[39] David Hesmondhalgh suggested that "restricted production has become introduced into the field of mass production,"[40] maintaining the original terms of Bourdieu's model, but these terms themselves require reconceptualization when the incorporation into mainstream media of previously "niche" content with diverse economic, cultural, and symbolic capital has become the norm.

While there is still a spectrum of linear scale for individual criteria such as budget or audience size, those factors alone do not correlate with Bourdieu's descriptions of small- and large-scale production as characterized by low economic capital/high symbolic capital and high economic capital/low symbolic capital, respectively. Media texts with high production costs used to require large audiences, who could be sold to advertisers, in order to be profitable; conversely, media texts that attracted large audiences were generally those that were relatively expensive to make: network shows, Hollywood films. However, now a show with a significant budget may not cost a lot to access; Netflix's *Orange Is the New Black* had a budget of about $50 million per season[41] but could be watched for a monthly subscription of less than $10. Also, a media text that attracts a large audience may not necessarily have a huge budget, given what digital media and the internet enable. As for prestige and distinction, previously, queerness was largely marginalized, both in media and culture more broadly. As LGBTQ elements became selectively included in mainstream culture, their cachet initially derived in part from queerness's edginess—the fact that it was still on the margins. Over the last couple of decades, LGBTQ content—from reality shows to acclaimed films and television series, modest web series to Netflix-funded shows—has come to span the cultural field, distributed through broadcast networks, premium cable, advertiser-supported cable, digital media, and streamers, garnering mixed commercial success and status.

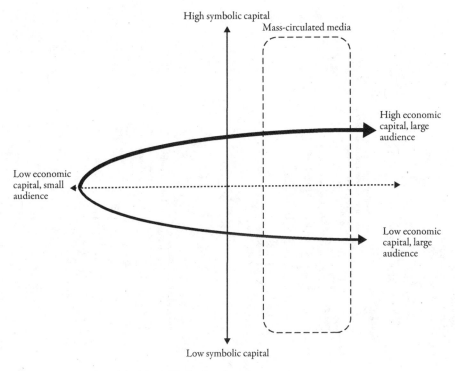

High symbolic capital

Mass-circulated media

High economic capital, large audience

Low economic capital, small audience

Low economic capital, large audience

Low symbolic capital

FIGURE 5 Revised model of the field of cultural production.

Revising Bourdieu in a way that avoids overpolarizing large-scale and restricted-scale production allows the complexities of scale as well as producer trajectories and textual characteristics to be captured. Drawing from the outlines of Bourdieu's model, figure 5 presents such a representation of the field of cultural production. This model contains a parabolic axis—which can be thought of as Bourdieu's original horizontal axis distinguishing large-scale from restricted production curved around—such that there is also a subfield of low economic capital with large audiences. In addition, in lieu of Bourdieu's various field subdomains and audience segments,[42] on the right side of the revised diagram, a space of mass-circulated media is indicated: defined by larger audiences but not necessarily high economic capital or low symbolic capital but a range of possible variation for both. This allows the representation of conditions where attaining large audiences is not necessarily tied to big-budget production, precisely what digital media has enabled. Delivery platform types—for example, broadcast, advertiser-supported cable, premium cable, websites and streamers for television, as well as film—are noted but not demarcated, because while they differ with respect to certain content and financial characteristics, what is crucial here is how LGBTQ media from different platforms can end up as mass-circulated media.

Figure 6 provides a more elaborated version of the field and shows how different types of LGBTQ content associated with Bravo and Logo are positioned

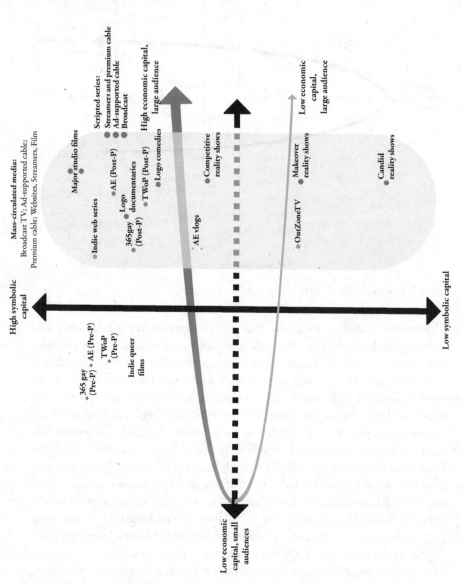

High symbolic capital

Low symbolic capital

Mass-circulated media:
Broadcast TV; Ad-supported cable;
Premium cable; Websites, Streamers, Film

Scripted series:
● Streamers and premium cable
● Ad-supported cable
● Broadcast

High economic capital,
large audience

Low economic capital,
large audience

Low economic capital,
small audiences

● Major studio films

● Indie web series

● AE (Post-P)

● Logo
● 365gay documentaries
(Post-P)

● TWoP (Post-P)

● Logo comedies

● Competitive
reality shows

● AE vlogs

● OutZoneTV

● Makeover
reality shows

● Candid
reality shows

● 365 gay
(Pre-P)   ● AE (Pre-P)

● TWoP
(Pre-P)

Indie queer
films

FIGURE 6   The revised field of cultural production: LGBTQ content of Bravo and Logo—websites and content types.

relative to each other as well as LGBTQ media types elsewhere.[43] The domain of mass-circulated media, on the right side of the diagram, is shaded gray. For the parabolic axis, the larger red end marks higher economic capital while the smaller blue end marks lower economic capital; thus, the dots that are red are media texts associated with relatively high economic capital, the blue dots are media texts associated with relatively low economic capital, and the purple dots are media texts associated with a medium amount of economic capital.

In terms of the main websites, AfterEllen, AfterElton, and TWoP pre-purchase (abbreviated "Pre-P" in the diagram) had lower economic capital, somewhat higher symbolic capital, and fewer users than post-purchase (Post-P); thus, their pre-purchase positions are in the top-left quadrant, while post-purchase they have moved to the top-right quadrant. The video blogs that AfterEllen solicited and hosted after Logo's purchase are in the domain of mass-circulated media, though associated with low economic capital and thus represented as blue dots. Scripted independent web series are generally associated with more economic capital than vlogs, and several have high symbolic capital (see the labeled purple dot in the top-right quadrant). As a news site, 365gay had fewer users than the entertainment-focused websites, although post-purchase, that increased, along with a higher amount of economic capital. With its primary coverage being on the attractive personalities of Bravo's reality shows, Out-ZoneTV had relatively low symbolic capital, and also never enjoyed as much economic support from Bravo as TWoP (or as much as any of Logo's sites); it is located in the bottom-right quadrant.

In terms of channel content, Logo's original comedies and documentaries (both in the top-right quadrant) had moderate amounts of economic capital relative to much other content within mass-circulated media, with the documentaries enjoying more symbolic capital than the comedies. Mainstream reality series, all instances of mass-circulated media, can vary significantly in terms of symbolic capital: competitive reality shows generally outrank makeover shows, which in turn are better regarded than candid reality shows. Mainstream scripted series can also span a range of symbolic capital, but for simplicity, in this diagram I only label them in the top-right quadrant as shows available on broadcast, advertiser-supported cable, and premium cable and streaming services. Finally, film can also span the field for economic capital, symbolic capital, and audience sizes; in this diagram, I have noted two positions in the field, one for independent queer films with moderate economic capital and high symbolic capital, in the top-left quadrant, and one for prestigious mainstream films, in the top-right quadrant.

The diagram is further elaborated with specific media texts in figure 7, including more recent LGBTQ content that helps illustrate the scope of what has become available. First, for Bravo's and Logo's programming, the web series hosted on AfterEllen and AfterElton varied in their amounts of capital and

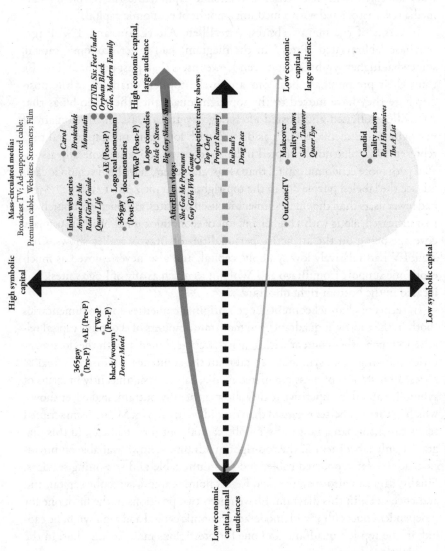

FIGURE 7   The revised field of cultural production: LGBTQ content of Bravo and Logo—with more specific examples.

audience. *Anyone but Me* became the best known and was relatively expensive to make, being a scripted series filmed in various indoor and outdoor locations, while a number of talk show series, such as *Gay in the UK* on AfterElton and *Gay Girls Who Game, She Got Me Pregnant*, and *Walking Funny with Jennie McNulty* were cheaper to produce while also being popular. For channel programming around the time that the websites were all up, Logo's *Real Momentum* documentary series had relatively higher symbolic capital than the channel's comedies, such as *The Big Gay Sketch Show* and the animated series *Rick and Steve: Happiest Gay Couple in the World*, although all of the channel series had more economic capital than the websites. For reality series, Logo's successful competitive reality show *RuPaul's Drag Race* shared similar field position to shows such as *Top Chef* and *Project Runway* on Bravo, while its candid reality series *The A List* was similar to Bravo's *Real Housewives* series, and *Queer Eye* as a makeover show was in the middle in terms of symbolic capital.

Figure 7 includes additional examples to show how Bravo's and Logo's content was positioned in relation to other LGBTQ content circulating in the same time period. Critically acclaimed films such as *Brokeback Mountain* (Ang Lee, 2005) and *Carol* (Todd Haynes, 2015) have relatively high symbolic and economic capital; conversely, independent queer film produced by those with less professional cachet, such as the *Desert Motel* short that Lisa Henderson discussed or Tiona McClodden's *black./womyn.* documentary on Black lesbians, is situated in a space of much lower economic capital and smaller audiences, though still enjoying some symbolic capital. A number of critically well-received television series with prominent LGBTQ content available on major networks or streamers, such as *Glee* and *Modern Family* on broadcast television, *Orphan Black* on advertiser-supported cable, *Six Feet Under* on HBO, and *Orange Is the New Black* on Netflix, are variously situated on the right side of the space of mass-circulated media. Independently produced web series are associated with lower economic capital but can also attract moderate viewership, even without being promoted by a network-owned website like AfterEllen did for *Anyone but Me*; for example, Aymar Jean Christian discusses the trajectory of several series about queer African Americans, including *The Real Girl's Guide to Everything Else* (Carmen Elena Mitchell and Reena Dutt, 2011) and *quare life* (M Shelly Conner, 2017), which streamed on platforms for independent television.[44]

As should be evident, LGBTQ media has become situated across the field of cultural production, associated with varying economic capital, symbolic capital, and audience sizes, with a plethora of options available across different distribution platforms. Notably, digital media spans the field, from independently produced content and websites, some of which occupy a similar part of the field as independent films, to major streamers and their series within mass-circulated media. Bravo and Logo played key roles in bringing some of this content into the major commercial realm, through a combination of channel and digital programming, even as most of their LGBTQ-centric programming has now been eclipsed by the range of LGBTQ content available elsewhere.

Bravo's and Logo's LGBTQ Media: Bridging Past and Present

In the last few years, a select number of LGBTQ producers have solidified their successes within mainstream media through multiyear deals with the largest streamers. In 2018, Ryan Murphy agreed to produce multiple shows for Netflix in a deal reportedly worth up to $300 million.[45] Given Murphy's status as a cisgender, gay white man, this was perhaps less noteworthy than Lena Waithe's contract with Amazon in 2019, which, though reportedly for a lower but still substantial eight-figure amount, provided a non-gender-conforming, African American lesbian with the kind of financial support and creative space that have long been out of reach for queer media producers. Waithe moved to Amazon already enjoying critical prominence from her 2018 Emmy writing for *Master of None* (Netflix, 2015–2017) and then for her show *The Chi*, the first season of which aired in 2018 to strong critical reception on Showtime.[46] Indeed, Christian argued that within an intensely competitive media landscape, Waithe and other young queer producers successfully "secured [commercially significant] deals after years of producing short-form digital work"[47] in smaller scale, independent web series, with diverse programming having become more attractive to "both legacy and streaming TV channels" with "a renewed appetite for cultural difference," to such an extent that "the distance between margins and center, on the surface, appears to be narrowing."[48]

In the 2010s, major commercial subscription-based networks and platforms offered such producers substantial creative freedom, allowing the development of series that centered characters diverse by race/ethnicity, sexuality, and class. In a feature article on HBO's LGBTQ-centric programming, the creators of *We're Here*, a reality series featuring three drag queens who had competed on *RuPaul's Drag Race*, *Betty*, a drama about several young women skateboarders, and *Legendary*, a competitive reality series on voguing with a gay host and a panel of mainly LGBTQ judges, all praised the network, with *Betty* creator Crystal Moselle commenting, "They barely gave me any notes, and when they did, they said 'you can take them or not.' They're really there for the artists. They wanna do powerful work that's groundbreaking, different, and new."[49] Netflix was also part of this trend; for example, in 2016 it acquired the rights to *Eastsiders*, a comedy following a gay couple and their friends, which had begun as a web series on YouTube in 2012, then was acquired by Logo to stream on its LogoTV site in 2013, and made available on a number of other paid platforms, including Wolfe Video and Vimeo; Netflix subsequently funded the production of seasons 3 and 4.[50]

Queer, it would seem, is no longer niche—or at least, not at the moment in the U.S. media landscape (and if television is not hospitable to certain kinds of queer media, the art world might provide an alternative; in recent years, Black filmmaker Tiona McClodden has screened her work at the Museum of Modern Art, Philadelphia's Institute of Contemporary Art, and at the 2019 Whitney Biennial art exhibit).[51] Still, in framing the developments at Bravo and Logo as comprising shifts going beyond queer niche, the argument is not that independent queer content targeted to and consumed by a small viewership no longer exists. Rather, in the commercial domain, LGBTQ media became productively and not just problematically enmeshed with networks like Logo and Bravo at a moment when digital media was also becoming much more commercialized, setting the scene for the rather more mixed cultural field today. Mainstream and independent realms of production, while unequally positioned, are not as different as common dichotomies about them in popular and scholarly discourses would suggest. Thus, while some elements of LGBTQ content production at Bravo and Logo were in line with an account of commercial takeover and appropriation, the bidirectional exchanges facilitated by the channels and even more so the websites, how cultural workers negotiated the commercial imperatives alongside the political significance of media representation for a historically marginalized group, and the different layers of production size and scale underscore the complexity of the landscape.

Furthermore, the developments at Bravo and Logo did not occur in isolation. Although there were distinctive, even unique elements about their LGBTQ content at the time of its production—having the first reality show with multiple gay experts on *Queer Eye*, for example, or AfterEllen and AfterElton streaming multiple queer-themed web series for free—media with significant LGBTQ content became more and more common in the years just after the prominence of *Queer Eye* and Logo's turn to gaystreaming, both in genres similar to and different from Bravo and Logo. Thus, the LGBTQ-centric programming that had helped these two networks stand out initially was no longer sufficient. Bravo successfully pivoted away from LGBTQ-front-and-center shows, with its *Real Housewives* franchise replacing *Queer Eye* in most strongly defining the network from the second half of the 2000s onward, while being home to other reality shows that continued to feature LGBTQ participants without being seen as "gay" shows. There have been other, "lifestyle" cable networks with a broadly similar slate—Oxygen, OWN—so Bravo's continued ratings successes are also about its programming maintaining distinct appeal to viewers despite comparable series elsewhere. But it is still notable that its current achievements were built on earlier deployments of more front-and-center LGBTQ content supported at the network level when such content was much less mainstream; as former Bravo executive Rachel Smith recalled, *Boy Meets Boy* emerged as an idea "out of [NBC president] Jeff Gaspin's head" in the wake of ABC's success with *The Bachelor*, and Gaspin also committed a huge amount of money to marketing *Queer Eye* before its debut—"the one bullet in the arsenal approach"—and signed off on the use of "queer" in the show title when this term was laden with more stigma.

As for Logo, its early programming epitomized the queer niche approach and was unique to advertiser-supported television in the United States. Its acquired sites, particularly AfterEllen, AfterElton, and 365gay, also contributed to this content, and there was a period of coexistence of the websites with their continued LGBTQ-centric focus and the gaystream programming on the channel in the late 2000s through to the early 2010s. This kind of potpourri did not prove financially viable, yet its presence for several years nevertheless demonstrated how mixed commercial LGBTQ media production had become, even just for a single network, in terms of who the cultural producers were, the kinds of content they produced, and the platforms that it was distributed on, with some enduring legacies and political significance even for short-lived efforts. The fact that the Logo-originated website Visible Vote '08 coordinated with its acquired 365gay website to report on LGBTQ issues for the 2008 U.S. elections remains noteworthy as an example of queer political coverage on mainstream media,[52] and Logo's short film and music *Click List* programming as well as its sponsorship of NewFest and thus the network's engagements with independent filmmakers demonstrates how expansive "queer niche" could be in terms of content characteristics and the cultural agents involved. *Noah's Arc*, the first television series centered on a group of queer African American men, canceled by Logo in 2006 after just two seasons (although a wrap-up movie was released in 2008), retained sufficient popularity that the original cast performed an online special, *Noah's Arc: The 'Rona Chronicles*, in July 2020 in part as a fundraising event.[53]

I have proposed one approach to represent the contemporary landscape for LGBTQ media, and media production more generally, drawing from the insights of Bourdieu in recognizing the uneven distributions of capital but revised to reflect the fact that different modes of production and delivery contribute to a much more complex, crowded arena of mass-circulated media. Digital media is important both in terms of facilitating low-budget content to be made and circulated—occasionally hitting it big financially but even if not, at least potentially still widely seen, alongside the media texts of legacy television (and film)—and with respect to the new dominance of streaming services. Put another way, digital technologies can bring niche content to mainstream audiences, as well as bringing big-budget content to multiple audience segments.

Finally, framing the developments at Bravo and Logo as a bridge between legacy and streaming does not mean either that the current period is better than the past—that is, assuming a model of linear progress for LGBTQ media—or that the past was better than the present—that is, arguing that LGBTQ culture was previously less diluted or contaminated by the commercial mainstream. In fact, the revised model of cultural production discussed in the previous section can represent past and present media texts together, as figures 6 and 7 showed, as well as snapshots of specific times. Instead, my analysis has identified multiple ways that changes to LGBTQ media production at Bravo and Logo— including incorporating new cultural producers, acquiring and developing digital media, and developing programming strategies to appeal to LGBTQ and non-LGBTQ viewers in a variety of ways—arose from previous conditions of production for commercial television and independent media, as well as constituting the ground from which more recent developments for LGBTQ content have occurred.

Conclusion

• •

Legacies and Futures for
Mainstreaming Gays

I began the final chapter of my dissertation, the research for which this book draws on, comparing different versions of the *Invasion of the Bodysnatchers* movies.[1] The narrative in each was broadly similar, about much of humanity being overcome by alien spores infecting individuals and taking control of their bodies. The endings, though, varied, from the bleakness of total takeover in the 1978 film starring Donald Sutherland to the more standard Hollywood solution in the 2007 Nicole Kidman–led version, where the protagonist is able to produce a vaccine that is distributed globally and successfully eliminates the pathogen within a year. Writing this conclusion chapter now, I am wryly struck by the irony of completing my book during an actual global pandemic. In my dissertation, the different outcomes of the various *Invasion* films served as metaphors about analytical perspectives on the impact of mainstream culture and commercialism on queer subcultures. As I wrote then, "The move of LGBT cultural production into mainstream spaces entails neither a commercial takeover insidiously depriving us of agency nor the death of authentic gay culture . . ., even as mainstreaming has had significant impact on queer subcultures. . . . There is no single antidote for the ills ascribed to commercial culture (as satisfying as it was to watch Nicole Kidman's heroics), and while mainstreaming illustrates some familiarly problematic developments, the trajectories of these shifts are neither as uniform nor inevitable as the outcomes in the darker versions of [these films]."[2]

Building on the previous chapter, which addressed the complexities of mainstream/queer encounters, the first part of this conclusion highlights key impacts of the COVID-19 pandemic on LGBTQ content and interaction, how the recent financial struggles of major streaming services have affected LGBTQ content, and some trends in the global production and distribution of LGBTQ media. In an earlier period, convergences of digital and legacy media helped bring LGBTQ producers and content into the mainstream. What are the current dynamics for how new LGBTQ content and its creators enter industry spaces, with the pandemic underscoring the importance of digital media for producers across the independent-to-commercial spectrum, and the increasing transnational considerations for content distribution? Second, given that changes to the mainstreaming of LGBTQ media, producers, and users always occur within and are shaped by broader sociopolitical conditions, I review how, despite certain benchmarks of "progress" around LGBTQ issues, persistent inequalities and vulnerabilities remain. Attacks on transgender rights in U.S. politics are also reflected in the media spaces that were the subject of my analysis[3] and are part of an increasingly prominent pushback against gender and sexual nonconformity more broadly that is bound up with conservative resistance to critiques of racial inequalities as well.

The pandemic included significant disruptions for media production and distribution, initially involving a months-long stoppage affecting virtually all major commercial television and film productions in progress,[4] as well as delays and cancellations of theatrical releases, given the closures or audience size restrictions for cinemas globally. This had a disproportionate impact on LGBTQ media[5] since the abrupt loss of current productions with LGBTQ representation could not be readily replaced by airing older such content. The delays meant, for example, that the second season of *Gentleman Jack* (BBC/HBO, 2019–2022) did not premiere until three years after the first. Some shows even had renewals reversed and were canceled due to the cascading economic effects of COVID-19 on the industry, including Netflix's *I Am Not Okay with This* and CBS's *Stumptown*, which both starred queer female lead characters.[6] Still, *RuPaul's Drag Race*—once Logo's signature show though moved to VH1—was able to film its season 12 finale remotely (with each contestant recording themselves at home) in early 2020.[7]

Along with the effects on media production, widespread closures of public spaces where people normally gather in significant numbers, whether for work or leisure, and concomitant "stay at home" orders led in many countries to increased consumption of entertainment media through streaming services. Streaming had already increased over the last few years, but the pandemic contributed to significant bumps in new subscriptions for Netflix and several of its competitors, with subscribers also reporting increases in their use time in the first few months of the pandemic.[8] However, by 2021, this growth had slowed,[9] and in early 2022, Netflix reported a net loss of subscribers for the first time in ten years,[10] although numbers had rebounded by the end of the year.[11] The longer term impact of these developments for LGBTQ-centric platforms, including larger ones like Here TV and Revry,[12] as well as the smaller-scale subscriber-supported sites discussed in chapter 2, is uncertain. On the one hand, the pandemic helped normalize paying regular subscriptions for multiple streaming services.[13] On the other hand, with some consumer fatigue toward the increasing density of the streaming landscape—now additionally populated by Disney Plus, (HBO) Max, and several other network-specific services—the most appealing option for many will be choosing some combination of the streamers with the most content.

The pandemic shutdowns of corporate studio production did also open up spaces for "more organic, local, diverse, and, perhaps, sustainable" practices,[14] as Aymar Jean Christian detailed, with many queer producers long adept at making do with minimal resources. Additionally, with network talk shows being filmed from the homes of their hosts and viewers quickly becoming used to the grainy resolution of video-conferenced interviews, the lower production values of independent media became less of a strike against it, at least temporarily. Christian pointed to the use of the Twitch platform by queer performers streaming from home and the low-resolution video of Instagram Live by musicians, as well as in-person performances such as outdoor drag queen shows.

However, with much of the world's economy resuming close to pre-pandemic levels by 2022, industry production of media has come back into the foreground, and some current trends in the U.S. do not bode well for LGBTQ content. One is a marked decline in the number of original series that television networks and streaming services are greenlighting, in part due to the increased costs of production associated with COVID-19 safety protocols.[15] This more cautious approach is likely to be disadvantageous overall to programming featuring queer leads. Furthermore, with a larger number of streamers vying for a finite number of subscribers, the freer spending on overall content production and acquisition that characterized the pre-pandemic years has been significantly curtailed. The result is a turn toward more predictably appealing kinds of content, often anchored by well-known franchises such as *The Lord of the Rings* (Amazon) and *Star Wars* (Disney Plus). These strategies have likely contributed to a slew of recent cancellations of shows with queer lead characters, especially queer women, after only a season or two, including *The Baby-Sitter's Club* (2020–2021), *First Kill* (2022), and *Warrior Nun* (2020–2022) on Netflix, *Paper Girls* (2022) and *The Wilds* (2020–2022) on Amazon Prime, and *Willow* (2022) on Disney Plus.[16] Financial considerations associated with the 2022 Warner Bros. Discovery and Paramount Global merger, including diminished international sales prospects of original programming on the CW (co-owned by Warner Bros. and CBS Studios, a subsidiary of Paramount), also led to an unprecedented number of this network's shows being axed, including the superhero series *Batwoman* and *Legends of Tomorrow*, both of which had stood out for featuring queer women as leads, and *Tom Swift*, which had a gay Black man as the main character.[17]

The increasing dependence of U.S. media production on international demand has additional dimensions pertinent to LGBTQ content. With the rate of new streaming subscriptions in the United States alone being insufficient for the major streamers, adding users globally is now more pressing. The rising proportion of international subscribers has been accompanied by an increase in content produced outside of the United States, including in languages other than English, airing on major streamers.[18] For example, in the last few years, Netflix has acquired a number of Asian "boys love" (BL) series to stream in North America, Europe, and various other countries, including *2gether: The Series* (GMMTV, 2020) from Thailand and the mainland Chinese series *The Untamed* (Tencent Video, 2019), *Heaven Official's Blessing* (Bilibili, 2020), and *Word of Honor* (Youku, 2021). Many such shows illustrate a new convergence circuit for mainstreaming LGBTQ content, as they have been adapted from novels by BL fan writers first published for free online.[19] The global popularity of the BL genre has thus brought adaptations of work by authors who previously wrote for a more geographically and linguistically circumscribed online readership to audiences transnationally.

Another trend in the global distribution of LGBTQ media is the remaking of a hit series in multiple countries. Not all of these have been successful; as Katherine Sender pointed out, *Queer Eye* versions in most countries outside the United States were flops.[20] In contrast, *RuPaul's Drag Race* spin-offs in Canada (*Canada's Drag Race*, 2019–present), Thailand (*Drag Race Thailand*, 2018–present), and the United Kingdom (*RuPaul's Drag Race UK*, 2019–present) have been running for multiple seasons, and several other *Drag Race* series have recently debuted or been announced in Europe, Asia, and New Zealand.[21] For scripted content, the Norwegian web series *Skam* (Shame; NRK, 2017), with a prominent LGBTQ narrative among several storylines about a group of teenagers, has been remade in several European countries as well as in the United States, where it streamed on Facebook Watch.[22]

Revry, the LGBTQ platform that was established in 2016, has defined itself as a global network, as Julia Himberg pointed out,[23] and on its FAQ page notes that a collaboration with Queer Comrades, a community advocacy LGBTQ organization and media platform based in China, allowed it to make available "more than 50 hours of quality queer Chinese content (with subtitles)."[24] Since most of Queer Comrades' programming comes from queer-identified producers making media for "individual and community empowerment" or experimenting with stylistic elements to queer the aesthetics of their films, this constitutes a noteworthy transnationalization of LGBTQ media distribution beyond Euro-American texts circulating to the rest of the world[25] and is a process that Queer Comrades has also engaged in with other Global South queer producers.[26] Still, as Michael Wayne and Matt Sienkiewicz noted in a study of three niche Jewish/Israeli subscription video on-demand (SVOD) services, relatively little is known about how smaller commercial streaming services acquire their content and the kinds of licensing deals that are worked out.[27] Such information is also needed vis-à-vis LGBTQ media and its producers; although it seems likely that at the major streamers such as Netflix, transnational distribution deals are generally made through standard industry procedures, are there avenues that more directly involve and benefit grassroots producers?

In addition to providing media content, digital platforms have also been crucial sites of virtual connection for LGBTQ communities during the pandemic. Besides its effects on in-person dating and socializing, social-distancing public health measures led to the cancellation of Pride celebrations that normally take place during the summer months in the United States and elsewhere in 2020 and 2021. While a variety of creative alternatives arose, including interactive online Pride events, Zoom dance parties, and video dating,[28] the pandemic significantly decreased revenue for LGBTQ-centric sites and organizations—even well-known ones such as the Human Rights Campaign—due to both the cancellations of in-person fundraising events and the drop in advertising, given the lack of Pride gatherings, closures of dining and entertainment venues, and the enormous drop in travel.[29] Smaller sites also struggled; for example, in its August 2020 fundraising appeal, the independent queer website Autostraddle noted that it had experienced a 94% decrease in advertising revenue since the beginning of the pandemic;[30] it is now reliant on regular subscribers and fundraising drives.[31]

The unprecedented scale of social distancing in the first half of 2020 was emphatically interrupted by widespread protests against racial injustice triggered by the May 2020 murder of George Floyd, an African American man violently restrained by police in Minneapolis. Notably, at a time before vaccines were available, protesters "gathered across the United States and the world, risking lives and well-being to declare that white supremacy and police brutality is a much greater public health crisis than COVID can ever be."[32] Beyond demands to address the violence and racism in systems of policing and incarceration, another significant issue concerned racially problematic representations. These included both physical and mediated forms, such as statues and monuments, museum displays, team mascots, flags and coats of arms, product images, as well as the content and casting of television and film. Also placed under renewed scrutiny was the disproportionate whiteness of mainstream media behind the camera, which had been highlighted by the #OscarsSoWhite hashtag after no performers of color were nominated for the major acting categories of the 2014 Academy Awards.

With respect to Bravo and Logo, as I noted in earlier chapters, several of the independent producers I talked to as well as online commentators criticized the networks for their lack of diversity among key staff. When I conducted my research, all the senior LGBTQ executives at Bravo and Logo were white, and at Logo also mostly men, with the exception of Lisa Sherman as the network's general manager (Kristin Frank and Sarah Warn, two white lesbians, had just left Logo when I interviewed them). Logo's executive group after Sherman's departure was also exclusively white,[33] and Bravo's top positions have remained filled by white women through two recent senior staff restructurings at NBCUniversal's Lifestyle group of channels, which also includes E!, Oxygen, and Universal Kids.[34] Revry, founded by four queer people of color,[35] provides a notable contrast, and as chapter 2 noted, its commitment to programming for the LGBTQ community and reflecting its diversity is explicitly different from the dualcasting and gaystreaming strategies that Bravo and Logo had pursued. Its size, though, positions it as somewhere in between grassroots independent platform and major commercial network.

For commercial media, Aymar Jean Christian and Khadijah Costley White have argued that in order to meaningfully address long-standing inequalities, both production and distribution should be thought of through reparational terms. This would involve "organic representation," with members of historically disempowered communities "hav[ing] ownership over the entire production process, from who is writing the story, producing it, acting or speaking in it, and editing it," ideally "practiced as either local or community-based" rather than by global media corporations, and "organic distribution" enabled by state and commercial support for changes that lead to members of those communities distributing the content they produce. With major telecommunications companies being legally required to carry channels owned by people of color, "organically" produced diverse content would then be available on major commercial media alongside independent and community-based outlets.[36] If this seems like a pipe dream, the stimulus packages in numerous countries to combat pandemic-related economic slowdowns have demonstrated that governments have substantial spending capacity above the norm, and the barriers to doing so are therefore more political than economic. Indeed, pandemic measures in the United States such as universal stimulus checks and moratoriums on evictions seemed to indicate a moment for significantly redressing long-standing socioeconomic inequities. The fact that the status quo has been reimposed for now only signals the underlying power of current structures, not their immutability. Christian's new Media and Data Equity (MADE) Lab, established in 2022, is intended to investigate "inequity in media & technology systems" and "experimen[t] with cultivating equitable systems."[37]

Recent political developments in the United States underscore how tenuous the status of marginalized social groups are (even when certain legal rights have been attained) and the ways that this ties into media content. In the conclusion to her 2018 book on LGBTQ media and mainstream culture, Julia Himberg noted a return to the prominence of identity and identity politics—belying the assumptions of post-gay discourses—and pointed to transgender rights as a key site of contestation in the United States, given political struggles over bathroom bills and other legal protections.[38] Since then, there have been multiple federal and state-level government actions against transgender people, particularly under the Trump administration, although the election of Democrat Joe Biden to the presidency has also failed to stem numerous U.S. state legislatures passing bills constraining the rights of transgender individuals as well as targeting parents and healthcare providers for gender-affirming care and treatment.[39]

Moreover, it is not only heteronormative institutions that have attacked transgender rights; the transgender community has also been vulnerable to tensions and fissures within the LGBTQ umbrella. The changes to AfterEllen are illustrative, which under the editorship and ownership of Memoree Joelle has established a transphobic position at the website as well as on Twitter; trans women in particular have been accused of abusing their privilege as "men" in seeking to infiltrate and take over (cisgender) lesbian spaces, even though statistics show that, if anything, transgender people experience greater rates of discrimination and violence than cisgendered LGB people.[40] As I discussed in chapter 3, Logo executives Kristin Frank and Marc Leonard used the metaphors of creating a larger tent for viewers and the dissolution of "buckets" containing distinct identity categories to discuss the march of progress that Logo's establishment as a network and programming directions exemplified. Yet the fact that hostility toward transgender people is being directed to them by some lesbians illustrates how LGBTQ integrations into the mainstream have always been partial and contingent, and disparities between different subgroups of the LGBTQ community persist.

An *Out* magazine article identified possible reasons for transphobia among cis lesbians as stemming from anxieties around the decline of many lesbian spaces, such as bars and bookstores, and the shuttering of the Michigan Womyn's Music Festival in 2015,[41] coupled with "the struggle of scarcity," where lesbians continue to lack the resources and media representations that gay men (and straight people) enjoy.[42] Furthermore, as transgender representation has increased in the last few years on U.S. media, both in scripted and reality television series and in news coverage,[43] this very visibility may be subjecting transgender people to more hostility—including from some gays and lesbians[44]—even as it signals a measure of acceptance.[45] At the same time, there has been condemnation of the transphobia posted by AfterEllen (and prominent figures such as author J. K. Rowling), including from Autostraddle and several other publications aimed at queer women,[46] expressions of solidarity that recognize the stratified privileges and vulnerabilities within the LGBTQ community.

Pushbacks to feminist and queer critiques of traditional gender and sexuality are not limited to transphobic actions but have included opposition that seeks to reinforce gender and sexual conformity more broadly. Disturbingly, the June 2022 *Dobbs v. Jackson* U.S. Supreme Court decision, which overturned the earlier 1973 *Roe v. Wade* ruling that had established abortion as a constitutional right, may signal future reconsiderations of rights premised on readings of the Fourteenth Amendment's statements about the right to privacy, including consensual queer sex and marriage equality, as one justice argued.[47] For now, conservative efforts to shore up conventional gender and sexuality include restricting student access to books addressing identities outside gender-normative and heteronormative binaries—in 2021 and 2022, the most banned book in the United States was Maia Kobabe's 2019 memoir *Gender Queer*, about a young person exploring their nonbinary gender identity, and others on the top ten banned books also center on queer protagonists.[48] These actions are deeply entwined with rejections of books and educational content addressing structural inequalities of race and racism, frequently decried as "critical race theory"[49] and interwoven with threads of white nationalist discourse, such as claims that critical race theory is "un-American."[50]

Nor are these kinds of regressive measures and discourses confined to the United States. Notably, in response to the huge popularity of many male idols with a "soft masculinity" demeanor, the Chinese government has sought to rein in "effeminate men," homoerotic "boys love" (BL) media, and their fans in the last few years. In 2021, official state dictates led to the suspension of production on Chinese BL series, as well as increased constraints and surveillance on fandom sites.[51] Government and other commentary in China has also exemplified how such policing of gender expression in popular culture is intimately linked to the propagation of a more muscular, heteronormative nationalism, another example of how identities of gender, sexuality, and nation are co-constructed.[52]

In light of these snapshots of contemporary media, culture, and politics, I end by pivoting back to what in many ways is the central question of this book: What does it mean for LGBTQ media to go mainstream, both as it happened at Bravo and Logo, and for the current and future conditions of a mainstream arena more complexly layered than ever in terms of producers, platforms, and distribution? Beyond the unprecedented shadow of a global pandemic, there are likely to be new ebbs and flows for the prominence of LGBTQ content and their creators. I have detailed how specific contexts of digital technologies and commercial production transformed LGBTQ media in the United States in various ways, showing how the recent past has crucially structured the present landscape without ridding it of enduring issues around intersectional inequalities. Alongside the rise of new digital platforms and the more global distribution of LGBTQ content in the past decade, these hierarchies continue to be challenged as well as reinforced through processes of media production, distribution, and use. In framing some of these disparities in larger terms, this concluding chapter highlights the fact that the contours and contestations of power in media domains reflect and comprise broader social, economic, and political conditions, therefore underscoring what the stakes are for meaningful inclusion in mainstream culture.

Appendix

• •

List of Research Interviews and Events

Interviews and Interviewees

I interviewed the research participants during a period from July 2008 to July 2011, in person (usually singly but occasionally in pairs or groups), by phone, on Skype video call, or via email. Their positions or relationships to the relevant organizations are given as they were at the time of the interviews.

Alexandra Albright: intern, Programming, Logo (in-person interview, April 15, 2010)

Jeff Alexander (pseudonym M. Giant): recapper, Television Without Pity (phone interview, May 12, 2010)

Heather Allison: intern, Development and Production, Bravo (in-person group interview, March 19, 2010)

Dennis Ayers: associate editor, AfterElton (phone interview, April 29, 2010)

Trish Bendix: blogs editor, AfterEllen (phone interview, March 10, 2010)

Ashley Birt: site user, AfterEllen and blogger, Pink Purple Blue (phone interview, May 26, 2010)

Rebecca Brown: intern, Development and Production, Bravo (in-person group interview, March 19, 2010)

Grace Chu: blogger, AfterEllen (emails, February 11–March 3, 2010)

Jacob Clifton: recapper, Television Without Pity (emails, June 29–July 7, 2010)

Tabatha Coffey: show star, *Tabatha's Salon Takeover*, Bravo (in-person interview and panel questions, April 1, 2010)

David Cole: founder, Television Without Pity (emails, April 15, 2010)

John Corvino: columnist, 365gay (phone interview, February 12, 2010)

Sekiya Dorsett: production coordinator, Marketing, and Out@NBCU, NBC (phone interview, May 12, 2010)

Shari Einstein: intern, Development and Production, Bravo (in-person group interview, March 19, 2010)

Kristin Frank: formerly Senior VP of Multiplatform Distribution and Marketing, Logo (phone interview, July 31, 2009)

David Gale: Executive VP, MTV New Media, MTV Networks (phone interview, October 26, 2010)

GD (pseudonym): independent musician (phone interview, July 18, 2010)

Mari Ghuneim: VP of Digital Media, Bravo (phone interview, March 30, 2010)

José Gomez: employee, Operations (in-person interview, June 8, 2009)

Claudia Gorelick: VP of Business Development, Logo (in-person interview, June 8, 2009)

Bernard Grenier: Manager of Development, Bravo (in-person interviews, July 7, 2009 and March 19, 2010)

Brent Hartinger: writer, AfterElton (phone interview, March 10, 2010)

Ryan Haynes: creator and presenter, "Gay in the UK" web series (Skype group interview, April 23, 2010)

Dennis Hensley: writer and vlogger, OutZoneTV and AfterElton (phone interview, September 3, 2010)

Heather Hogan: writer, AfterEllen (emails, March 11–April 8, 2010)

Zac Hug: formerly senior writer, OutZoneTV (phone interview, September 3, 2010)

Michael Jensen: editor in chief, AfterElton (phone interview, June 16, 2009)

Lauren Kuester: Creative Operations, New Media/Graphics Project Manager, Logo (in-person interview, June 9, 2009)

Anthony Langford: contributor, AfterElton (phone interview, March 11, 2010)

Marc Leonard: Senior VP of Multiplatform Programming, Logo (in person interviews, individual and group, May 21, 2009, June 9, 2009, and July 9, 2009; emails, February 2, 2010)

Malinda Lo: writer and former managing editor, AfterEllen (in-person interview, March 31, 2008)

Tim Macavoy: creator and presenter, "Gay in the UK" web series (Skype group interview, April 23, 2010)

Daniel MacEachern: recapper, Television Without Pity (phone interview, May 11, 2010)

Dan Manu: director, Television Without Pity (phone interview, November 3, 2009)

Tiona McClodden: independent filmmaker (phone interview, July 10, 2010)

Jennie McNulty: creator and presenter, "Walking Funny" web series (phone interview, Apr 21, 2010)

David Barclay Moore: independent filmmaker (phone interview, July 2, 2010)

Dara Nai: senior writer, AfterEllen (phone interview, February 25, 2010)

Danny Nguyen: founder and producer, Downelink (phone interview, March 1, 2010)

John Polly: editor, LogoONLINE (in-person interview, June 9, 2009 and July 22, 2009)

Dominick Pupa: co-executive producer, *The A List*, Logo (in-person interview, June 26, 2010)

Dalila Ali Rajah: founder and presenter, *Cherry Bomb* web series (phone interview, April 8, 2010)

Douglas Ross: founder and partner, Evolution Media (phone interview, May 5, 2010)

Dan Sacher: VP of Digital, Logo (in-person interview, June 9, 2009)

Nicki Schultz: production set assistant, TNT (phone interview, October 31, 2010)

Lauren Shotwell: recapper, Television Without Pity (phone interview, June 3, 2010)

Rachel Smith: former Director of Development, Bravo (in-person interview, April 15, 2010)

Dorothy Snarker: blogger, AfterEllen (emails, March 11–September 13, 2010)

the linster: blogger, AfterEllen (emails, March 9–16, 2010)

Jay Vanasco: editor in chief, 365gay (in-person interview, June 9, 2009)

Aimee Viles: VP of Emerging Media, Bravo (in-person interview and panel questions, March 3, 2010)

Sarah Warn: founder and former editor in chief, AfterEllen (phone interview, October 27, 2009)

Chris Willey: Head of East Coast Development and Programming, Logo (in-person interviews, individual and group, June 9, 2009, July 9, 2009, and July 22, 2009)

James Withers: contributing editor, 365gay (emails, May 12–July 30, 2011)

Lauren Wood: site user, AfterEllen and blogger, My Take On All Things Lesbian (emails, June 1–2, 2010)

Research Events

I attended the following events as part of my research:

NewFest, the New York LGBTQ film festival, in June 2009 and June 2010. Logo was its major sponsor in 2009 (Marc Jacobs, the fashion company, took over this role in 2010).

The New York Television Festival, September 2009. Its cosponsors included MTV Networks and Bravo.

The TV of Tomorrow Show, March 2010, San Francisco, which convened industry professionals to discuss "interactive TV."

The "Out Trailblazers in Media" panel, April 2010, New York City, whose panelists included Lisa Sherman, Logo's general manager and executive VP, and Tabatha Coffey, star of one of Bravo's reality shows.

A party being filmed for Logo's reality show *The A List*, June 2010, New York City.

Acknowledgments

The completion of every book involves a journey of sorts, but one with roots as a dissertation begins earlier than many. As *Mainstreaming Gays* draws on research that I conducted for my PhD in Communication at the University of Massachusetts–Amherst, I will start by acknowledging Lisa Henderson, the chair of my committee, for her invaluable, incomparable advising, and my other committee members Martha Fuentes-Bautista, Dan Horowitz, and Emily West for their many crucial inputs. Besides offering stellar intellectual guidance (and enduring friendship), Lisa also put me in touch with colleagues in the field, and I am especially grateful to Kathleen Farrell, Joshua Gamson, David Gleason, and Katherine Sender for discussing their research with me and their willingness to introduce me to possible interviewees. Other faculty and staff at UMass during this time who provided important support included, in WGSS, Alex Deschamps, Angie Willey, Banu Subramaniam, Karen Lederer, Linda Hillenbrand, and Nancy Patteson, and in the Department of Communication, Debbie Madigan, Kathy Ready, Mari Castañeda, Paula Chakravartty, and Shawn Shimpach.

Many executives, staff, and contributors associated with Bravo and Logo kindly agreed to speak with me (see the appendix!), so here I just name a few key people. Stacey Barbour helped set up my first interviews at Logo, and Nicole Sullivan arranged several meetings with other Logo executives. Bernard Grenier (formerly at Bravo); Marc Leonard, John Polly, and Chris Willey (formerly at Logo); and Sarah Warn, founder of the AfterEllen and AfterElton websites, were particularly gracious in their assistance and also put me in touch with other colleagues. In addition, a number of independent producers shared their time and perspectives generously, including Dalila Ali Rajah and Tiona McClodden.

Not to state the obvious, but another factor that made this book possible was deciding to write it. Revising a dissertation manuscript is a different task than producing a monograph from scratch, and although I ended up completing the second kind of book first, I am glad that multiple people encouraged me to under-take this book project as well, including Jonathan Gray, Lisa Henderson, Julie Levin Russo, Adrienne Shaw, and especially Katherine Sender, who read my entire dissertation just because I asked and got me thinking about the right kinds of bigger picture questions that a book should address. Several colleagues shared advice about scholarly publishing, particularly Lynn Comella, who was always willing to chat with me, and her recommendations were invaluable. David Craig, Erin Meyers, David Oh, and Łukasz Szulc also kindly provided their insights. And I have fond memories of writing sessions with Emily West at the Smith College library when she was also working on her book, each sitting in one of those delightful spherical cubicles!

I spent part of my sabbatical writing this book and am grateful that both my academic units at Ohio University—the School of Media Arts and Studies and the Women's, Gender, and Sexuality Studies Program—granted me the full academic year of faculty fellowship leave.

I have been fortunate to work with several people at Rutgers University Press. Lisa Banning was the first to receive my inquiries and then a book proposal, and her enthusiasm and advocacy on my behalf were important early on. Kimberly Guinta connected me to Nicole Solano after Lisa left the press, and Nicole has been a consistent and reliably encouraging editor, with her assistant Bianca Battaglia also providing prompt and useful guidance. I also much appreciate the competent efficiency of the production team, led by Sherry Gerstein and Vincent Nordhaus. And the detailed, insightful feedback from two anonymous reviewers on earlier drafts of the manuscript was immensely useful.

Writing a book is time intensive, but no one can work on it at every moment. I have especially enjoyed conversation and activities along the way with the Baird-Sears family (Stephanie, Ben, and Lyra), whose company for meals, movies, hikes, and other fun has been such a wonderful constant for the last few years; Becca and Mike for being the best neighbors ever when we were all on the East side; Cathy Vollinger, who never said no to my dinner invites even though vegetarian food was not her thing; Marion Lee and Stephanie Wu for our once-monthly gatherings around *qingzheng longliyü* (thanks for always letting me take the leftovers); Meghan Andrews for discussions about football, fandom, and more; Myrna Perez Sheldon, especially the heartfelt reflections on parenting and recommendations for fiction; the Peck-Suzuki household (Lynette, Taka, Miyo, and Theo) for many nights of delicious dinners (ah, fatty meat!) and games; Shakuntala (Fugu) Ray, Sreela Sarkar, Steph Kent, and Sunny Lie over all those Zoom meetings that sustained us through the pandemic, as well as Fugu and Steph in various in-person modes as the COVID-19 response moved through its different phases; and my parents, Siang Ng and Yew Kwang Ng, and sister, Aline Shaw, who I owe a lot of catch-up in-person visiting with in the summers ahead.

Sreela, you deserve a special shout-out for being the one who knows more about this book journey than anyone else. Your grounded encouragement and support have bolstered me when I most needed it, and I wish I could still make my way through the ice and snow on a dark winter evening to pick up some of your amazing banana bread.

Finally, Quinn, you were there when my doctoral research planted the seeds for this book, and you are here now to help me celebrate its publication. I am lucky that you drew on your incredible artistic vision to help me think through cover designs. I am even luckier to share so much of the journey of life with you that began when you were born.

Notes

Introduction

1 See Alessandra Stanley, "Sex and the Gym: 'Work Out' and the Gaying of Bravo," *New York Times*, July 19, 2006, http://www.nytimes.com/2006/07/19/arts /television/19watc.html; Reuters, "Bravo Tops Survey of Gay-Friendly Companies," *Reuters*, May 13, 2008, http://www.reuters.com/article/2008/05/13/industry-gay-dc -idUSN1343338320080513.

2 See Ron Becker, *Gay TV and Straight America* (Piscataway, NJ: Rutgers University Press, 2006).

3 Katherine Sender, *Business, Not Politics: The Making of the Gay Market* (New York: Columbia University Press, 2004).

4 See Jim Carnegie, *Television Business Report*, May 11, 2006, https://www.rbr.com /tvepaper/issue93-06-thu.html.

5 See New York Times, "Webdenda: People and Accounts of Note," *New York Times*, June 19, 2006, https://www.nytimes.com/2006/06/19/business/media/19adco -webdenda.html.

6 In lay terms, "producer" often connotes a professional position for a film or television series. Within media studies scholarship and especially production studies, however, "producer" is a more general term referring to someone involved in processes of media production, sometimes as a content creator, but also in other positions associated with production work, including both "below the line" media workers and company executives. The term *cultural agent* includes "producer" in this broader sense as well referring to media users.

7 Pierre Bourdieu, *The Field of Cultural Production: Essays on Art and Literature*, trans. Randal Johnson (New York: Columbia University Press, 1993).

8 His *On Television* book (New York: New Press, 1998; original French edition *Raisons d'agir*, Liber, 1996), which primarily comprises transcriptions of two lectures, focuses on how the characteristics of television production in France have transformed journalism.

9 Henry Jenkins, "Convergence? I Diverge," *Technology Review*, June 1, 2001, https://www.technologyreview.com/2001/06/01/235791/convergence-i-diverge/.

10 For example, see Ben Bagdikian, *The New Media Monopoly* (Boston: Beacon, 2004); Jeffrey Blevins, "Source Diversity after the Telecommunications Act of 1996: Media Oligarchs Begin to Colonize Cyberspace," *Television & New Media* 3, no. 1 (2002): 95–112; David Croteau, William D. Hoynes, and Stefania Milan, "The Economics of the Media Industry," in *Media/Society: Industries, Images, Audiences* (Thousand Oaks, CA: Sage, 2011), 31–71; Andrew Leyshon et al., "On the Reproduction of the Musical Economy after the Internet," *Media, Culture & Society* 27, no. 2 (2005): 177–209.

11 In later years, these were eclipsed by the acquisitions by other digital media giants, such as Facebook's 2014 acquisition of WhatsApp for $19 billion.

12 This is the case not just in popular culture but also areas such as food and household products; around the time of Bravo's and Logo's website acquisitions, for example, the "natural" personal care brands Burt's Bees and Tom's of Maine were purchased by Clorox and Colgate, respectively (see Katherine Manchester, "12 'Natural' Brands, Owned by Giant Corporations—Here's the Breakdown," *Groundswell*, January 30, 2015, https://groundswell.org/12-natural-brands-owned-by-giant-corporations-heres-the-breakdown/; Cornucopia, "Who Owns Organic," *Cornucopia*, n.d., https://www.cornucopia.org/who-owns-organic/).

13 Lisa Henderson, "Queer Relay," *GLQ: A Journal of Lesbian and Gay Studies* 14, no. 4 (2008): 569–597. The term is a riff off Michel Foucault's original concept of the "repressive hypothesis" concerning popular assumptions about the pre-twentieth century as more sexually repressed than contemporary times, which Foucault argued erroneously simplified much more complex conditions (see Michel Foucault, *The History of Sexuality, Volume 1*, trans. Robert Hurley [New York: Pantheon, 1978]).

14 Dick Hebdige, *Subculture: The Meaning of Style* (London: Methuen, 1979). See also Thomas Frank, *The Conquest of Cool: Business Culture, Counterculture, and the Rise of Hip Consumerism* (Chicago: University of Chicago Press, 1997). Frank argued that an aversion to sameness was deliberately and profitably tapped by corporate capital through the fostering of "hip consumerism" practiced by those attracted to what was perceived as novel, yet who did not "buy to fit in or impress the Joneses, but to demonstrate that they were wise to the game, to express their revulsion with the artifice and conformity of consumerism" (31).

15 Sarah Thornton, *Club Cultures: Music, Media and Subcultural Capital* (Hanover, NH: University Press of New England, 1996).

16 Henry Jenkins, *Convergence Culture: Where Old and New Media Collide* (New York: New York University Press, 2006).

17 Jenkins, *Convergence Culture*, 63.

18 See, for example, Christian Fuchs, "Competition and Cooperation in the Internet Economy," in *Internet and Society: Social Theory in the Information Age* (New York: Routledge, 2008), 148–212.

19 Nico Carpentier, "Theoretical Frameworks for Participatory Media," in *Media Technologies and Democracy in an Enlarged Europe*, ed. Nico Carpentier et al. (Tartu, Estonia: Tartu University Press, 2007), 105–122, 110–111.

20 See, for example, Camille Bacon-Smith, *Enterprising Women: Television Fandom and the Creation of Popular Myth* (Philadelphia: University of Pennsylvania Press, 1992); Henry Jenkins, *Textual Poachers: Television Fans and Participatory Culture* (London: Routledge, 1992).

21 Suzanne Scott, *Fake Geek Girls: Fandom, Gender, and the Convergence Culture Industry* (New York: New York University Press, 2019), 119.

22 See Edward Castronova, *Synthetic Worlds: The Business and Culture of Online Games* (Chicago: University of Chicago Press, 2005); T. L. Taylor,

Play between Worlds: Exploring Online Game Culture (Cambridge, MA: MIT Press, 2006).

23 See Mark Coté and Jennifer Pybus, "Learning to Immaterial Labour 2.0: MySpace and Social Networks," *Ephemera* 7, no. 1 (2007): 88–106; Tiziana Terranova, "Free Labor: Producing Culture for the Digital Economy," *Social Text* 18, no. 2 (2000): 33–58.

24 Alex Lothian, "Living in a Den of Thieves: Fan Video and Digital Challenges to Ownership," *Cinema Journal* 48, no. 4 (2009): 130–136.

25 Kristina Busse, "Fan Labor and Feminism: Capitalizing on the Fannish Labor of Love," *Cinema Journal* 54, no. 3 (2015): 110–115.

26 Abigail De Kosnik, "Should Fan Fiction Be Free?" *Cinema Journal* 48, no. 4 (2009): 24.

27 Suzanne Scott, "Repackaging Fan Culture: The Regifting Economy of Ancillary Content Models," *Transformative Works and Cultures* 3 (2009), https://doi.org/10.3983/twc.2009.0150.

28 Scott, *Fake Geek Girls.* The "affirmational"/"transformative" terminology was first proposed by Livejournal user obsession_inc in a Dreamwidth blog post; see obsession_inc, "Affirmational Fandom vs. Transformational Fandom," *Dreamwidth*, June 1, 2009, http://obsession-inc.dreamwidth.org/82589.html.

29 Megan Condis, "No Homosexuals in *Star Wars*? BioWare, 'Gamer' Identity, and the Politics of Privilege in a Convergence Culture," *Convergence: The International Journal of Research into New Media Technologies* 21, no. 2 (2015): 198–212.

30 Henry Jenkins, Gabriel Peters-Lazaro, and Sangita Shresthova, "Popular Culture and the Civic Imagination: Foundations," in *Popular Culture and the Civic Imagination: Case Studies of Creative Social Change,* ed. Henry Jenkins, Gabriel Peters-Lazaro, and Sangita Shresthova (New York: New York University Press, 2020), 15.

31 For an example of media corporations seeking to suppress fan writing, see Henry Jenkins's discussion of the Harry Potter franchise in "Why Heather Can Write," in *Convergence Culture: Where Old and New Media Collide* (New York: New York University Press, 2006), 169–205. One show that invited a fan author to write for the show is *Xena: Warrior Princess,* which asked well-known Xena fan fiction writer Melissa Good to write two season 6 scripts (see Bret Ryan Rudnick, "An Interview with Robert Tapert," *Whoosh* 52 [2001], http://whoosh.org/issue52/itapert1b.html).

32 See John Campbell, "Outing PlanetOut: Surveillance, Gay Marketing and Internet Affinity Portals," *New Media & Society* 7, no. 5 (2005): 663–683; Serkan Gorkemli, "'Coming Out of the Internet': Lesbian and Gay Activism and the Internet as a 'Digital Closet' in Turkey," *Journal of Middle East Women's Studies* 8, no. 3 (2012): 63–88; David Phillips, "Negotiating the Digital Closet: Online Pseudonymity and the Politics of Sexual Identity," *Information, Communication, and Society* 5, no. 3 (2002): 406–442; Nikki Usher and Eleanor Morrison, "The Demise of the Gay Enclave, Communication Infrastructure Theory, and the Transformation of Gay Public Space," in *LGBT Identity and Online New Media,* ed. Christopher Pullen and Margaret Cooper (New York: Routledge, 2010), 271–287.

33 *The Advocate* and *Out* are now owned by the Equal Entertainment company, which in 2017 (as Pride Media) bought out the parent company of both magazines, Here Media. *Curve* was purchased by the Avalon Media company in 2010.

34 See Ben Aslinger, "PlanetOut and the Dichotomies of Queer Media Conglomeration," in *LGBT Identity and Online New Media,* ed. Christopher Pullen and Margaret Cooper (New York: Routledge, 2010), 113–124; Joshua Gamson, "Gay Media Inc.: Media Structures, the New Gay Conglomerates, and Collective Sexual

Identities," in *Cyberactivism: Online Activism in Theory and Practice*, ed. Martha McCaughey and Michael Ayers (New York: Routledge, 2003), 255–278.

35 D. Travers Scott, "Queer Media Studies in the Age of the E-invisibility," *International Journal of Communication* 5 (2011): 96, http://ijoc.org/ojs/index.php/ijoc /article/view/1055/510.

36 Ben Aslinger, "Creating a Network for Queer Audiences at Logo TV," *Popular Communication* 7, no. 2 (2009): 111.

37 See Bravo, "The Bravo Affluencer Effect," Bravo (2008), formerly up at http://www .affluencers.com.

38 For example, FanFiction.net started off as a repository for user-submitted stories, and readers could leave comments. It later acquired the features of liking and/or following favorite authors and stories as well as maintaining user profiles and contacting other site users via private messages.

39 See Aymar Jean Christian, "Open TV Distribution," in *Open TV: Innovation beyond Hollywood and the Rise of Web Television* (New York: New York University Press, 2018), 156–211.

40 Aslinger, "Creating a Network for Queer Audiences," 107–121.

41 Trish Bendix, "Does LGBT Media Have a Future?" *BuzzFeed*, January 25, 2019, https://www.buzzfeednews.com/article/trishbendix/future-of-lgbt-media-out -advocate-autostraddle-into-grindr.

42 Jonathan Gray and Amanda Lotz, *Television Studies* (Malden, MA: Polity, 2012); Amanda Lotz, *The Television Will Be Revolutionized*, 2nd ed. (New York: New York University Press, 2014); Amanda Lotz, *We Now Disrupt This Broadcast: How Cable Transformed Television and the Internet Revolutionized It All* (Boston: MIT Press, 2018).

43 ABC, CBS, and NBC have existed as broadcast television networks since 1948, 1941, and 1939, respectively. Fox came on air in 1986; the WB, partly owned by Warner Brothers, and UPN, partly owned by Viacom, which was CBS's parent company at the time, both launched in 1995 and then both ceased airing in 2006, whereupon the CW was launched as a network co-owned by ViacomCBS and WarnerMedia.

44 Joseph Turow, *Breaking Up America: Advertisers and the New Media World* (Chicago: University of Chicago Press, 1997).

45 See Ron Becker, *Gay TV and Straight America* (Piscataway, NJ: Rutgers University Press, 2006).

46 Bonnie Dow, "*Ellen*, Television, and the Politics of Gay and Lesbian Visibility," *Critical Studies in Media Communication* 18, no. 2 (2001): 136.

47 Lynne Joyrich, "Epistemology of the Console," *Critical Inquiry* 27, no. 3 (2001): 450.

48 See Larry Gross, *Up from Invisibility: Lesbians, Gay Men, and the Media in America* (New York: Columbia University Press, 2001); Vito Russo, *The Celluloid Closet: Homosexuality in the Movies* (New York: Harper, 1987); Suzanna Danuta Walters, *All the Rage: The Story of Gay Visibility in America* (Chicago: University of Chicago Press, 2001).

49 Lotz, *We Now Disrupt This Broadcast*.

50 See, for example, Robin Nabi et al., "Reality-Based Television Programming and the Psychology of Its Appeal," *Media Psychology* 5 (2003): 303–330.

51 See Shannon Kelly, *Hot Topics: Reality TV* (Detroit: Lucent Books, 2013), especially 14–18.

52 Jenkins, *Convergence Culture*, 60.

53 Lynne Joyrich, "Queer Television Studies: Currents, Flows, and (Main)streams," *Cinema Journal* 53, no. 2 (2014): 133.

54 See Melanie Kohnen, *Queer Representation, Visibility, and Race in American Film and Television: Screening the Closet* (New York: Routledge, 2016).

55 Hollis Griffin, *Feeling Normal: Sexuality and Media Criticism in the Digital Age* (Bloomington: Indiana University Press, 2016), 12, 13.

56 Bourdieu, *The Field of Cultural Production*.

57 The term *cultural capital* has been used widely outside of Bourdieu's work with different inflections in its meaning, often losing the critical analytical slant in Bourdieu's account in which cultural capital arises from and reflects economic and social inequalities.

58 Nicolas Garnham, "Bourdieu, the Cultural Arbitrary, and Television," in *Bourdieu: Critical Perspectives*, ed. Craig Calhoun, Edward LiPuma, and Moishe Postone (Cambridge: Polity, 1993), 178–192.

59 David Hesmondhalgh, "Bourdieu, the Media, and Cultural Production," *Media, Culture & Society* 28, no. 2 (2006): 223.

60 More specifically, Bourdieu describes a habitus as both a means through which an individual perceives and engages with the social world and the product of the press of social structures on individuals—that is, both a "structuring structure" and a "structured structure." Bourdieu, *The Field of Cultural Production*, 100.

61 See Leo Rosten, *Hollywood, the Movie Colony, the Movie Makers* (New York: Harcourt Brace, 1941); Hortense Powdermaker, *Hollywood, the Dream Factory: An Anthropologist Looks at the Movie-Makers* (London: Secker & Warburg, 1951).

62 See Julie D'Acci, *Defining Women: Television and the Case of* Cagney & Lacey (Chapel Hill: University of North Carolina Press, 1994); Paul Espinosa, "The Audience in the Text: Ethnographic Observations of a Hollywood Story Conference," *Media, Culture & Society* 4 (1982): 77–86; Lisa Henderson, "'Storyline' and the Multicultural Middlebrow: Reading Women's Culture on National Public Radio," *Critical Studies in Mass Communication* 16, no. 3 (1999): 329–349; Catherine Lutz and Jane Collins, *Reading* National Geographic (Chicago: University of Chicago Press, 1993); Janice Radway, *A Feeling for Books: The Book-of-the-Month Club, Literary Taste, and Middle-Class Desire* (Chapel Hill: University of North Carolina Press, 1997).

63 See Howard Becker, *Art Worlds* (Berkeley: University of California Press, 1982); Barry Dornfeld, *Producing Public Television, Producing Public Culture* (Princeton, NJ: Princeton University Press, 1998); Nina Eliasoph, "Routines and the Making of Oppositional News," *Critical Studies in Mass Communication* 5, no. 4 (1988): 313–334; Herbert Gans, *Deciding What's News: A Study of* CBS Evening News, NBC Nightly News, Newsweek *and* Time (New York: Vintage, 1979); Henry Kingsbury, *Music, Talent, and Performance: A Conservatory Cultural System* (Philadelphia: Temple University Press, 1988); Roger Silverstone, *Framing Science: The Making of a BBC Documentary* (London: British Film Institute, 1985); Gaye Tuchman, *Making News: A Study in the Construction of Reality* (New York: Free Press, 1978).

64 Vicky Mayer, Miranda Banks, and John Caldwell, *Production Studies: Cultural Studies of Media Industries* (New York: Routledge, 2009), 2. See also John Caldwell, *Production Culture: Industrial Reflexivity and Critical Practice in Film and Television* (Durham, NC: Duke University Press, 2008); Vicki Mayer, *Below the Line: Producers and Production Studies in the New Television Economy* (Durham, NC: Duke University Press, 2011).

65 Alfred L. Martin Jr., "Introduction: What Is Queer Production Studies/Why Is Queer Production Studies?" *Journal of Film and Video* 70, no. 3–4 (2018): 3–7.

66 Sender, *Business, Not Politics*.
67 Vincent Doyle, *Making Out in the Mainstream: GLAAD and the Politics of Respectability* (Montreal: McGill-Queen's University Press, 2015).
68 Julia Himberg, *The New Gay for Pay: The Sexual Politics of American Television Production* (Austin: University of Texas Press, 2018).
69 Anne O'Brien and Páraic Kerrigan, "Gay the Right Way: Roles and Routines of Irish Media Production among Gay and Lesbian Workers," *European Journal of Communication* 35, no. 4 (2020): 361, italics in the original.
70 Thirty-one of my interviewees identified as women and twenty-six as men; thirty-eight explicitly identified themselves as gay, lesbian, or bisexual; and as far as I know, seven were African American, six Asian American, one Latino, and the others (non-Hispanic) white. Appendix 1 gives a list of the people I communicated with, their positions and organizational affiliations (if any), and the type and dates of communication.
71 These included the 2009 New York Television Festival, the 2009 and 2010 NewFest LGBTQ film festivals, and the 2010 Television of Tomorrow Show. See the appendix for more details.
72 Jenkins, *Textual Poachers*; Jenkins, *Convergence Culture*.
73 See, for example, Nancy Baym, *Tune In, Log On: Soaps, Fandom and Online Community* (London: Sage, 2000); Elizabeth Bird, *The Audience in Everyday Life: Living in a Media World* (New York: Routledge, 2003).
74 Laura Nader, "Up the Anthropologist: Perspectives Gained from Studying Up," in *Reinventing Anthropology*, ed. D. Hymes (New York: Random House, 1969), 284–311.
75 Sherry Ortner, "Studying Sideways: Ethnographic Access in Hollywood," in *Production Studies: Cultural Studies of Media Industries*, ed. Vicky Mayer, Miranda Banks, and John Caldwell (New York: Routledge, 2009), 186.
76 One interviewee, former Bravo executive Rachel Smith, was also Australian, and three AfterEllen staff or contributors—Grace Chu, Malinda Lo, and Dara Nai—were Asian American.
77 Sender, *Business, Not Politics*, 400.
78 One strand of this perspective is seen in the work of the Frankfurt School, especially that of Theodor Adorno and Max Horkheimer; see, for example, Theodor Adorno and Max Horkheimer, *Dialectic of Enlightenment* (New York: Herder and Herder, 1972; original German edition *Dialektik der Aufklärung*, Amsterdam: Querido Verlag, 1944). In her study of subcultures, Sarah Thornton also critiqued various British cultural studies scholars, including Stephen Evans, Dick Hebdige, and Geoff Mungham, for their "reductive" assumptions about mainstream culture; see Sarah Thornton, *Club Cultures: Music, Media and Subcultural Capital* (Hanover, NH: University Press of New England, 1996), 92–96. Some scholars writing more specifically about queer culture have also subscribed to the position that mainstream culture is, in contrast, a homogeneous commercialized mass; see, for example, Alexandra Chasin, *Selling Out: The Gay and Lesbian Movement Goes to Market* (New York: Palgrave Macmillan, 2000).

Chapter 1   New Convergences in LGBTQ Media Production

1 One of the regular characters on *Buffy*, Willow, had been in a lesbian relationship since the 1999–2000 (fourth) season.
2 As Vincent Doyle noted in his study of the gay and lesbian media advocacy organization GLAAD, the internet had begun facilitating the entry of "agents with

the right kinds of cultural capital to challenge the dominance of powerful players even in the absence of large amounts of economic capital" in the 1990s; Vincent Doyle, *Making Out in the Mainstream: GLAAD and the Politics of Respectability* (Montreal: McGill-Queen's University Press, 2016), 243.

3 For example, Raph Koster, developer of the official *Star Wars Galaxies* video game, interacted regularly with fans online during the development phase; see Henry Jenkins, *Convergence Culture: Where Old and New Media Collide* (New York: New York University Press, 2006), 162. Neil Perryman found some similar kinds of producer-fan interactions for the *Doctor Who* franchise; Neil Perryman, "*Doctor Who* and the Convergence of Media: A Case Study in 'Transmedia Storytelling,'" *Convergence: The International Journal of Research into New Media Technologies* 14, no. 1 (2008): 21–39.

4 Pierre Bourdieu, *The Field of Cultural Production: Essays on Art and Literature,* trans. Randal Johnson (New York: Columbia University Press, 1993).

5 Suzanne Scott, *Fake Geek Girls: Fandom, Gender, and the Convergence Culture Industry* (New York: New York University Press, 2019), 145.

6 Scott, *Fake Geek Girls,* 171–172.

7 Katherine Sender, *Business, Not Politics: The Making of the Gay Market* (New York: Columbia University Press, 2004), 65.

8 Sender, *Business, Not Politics,* 68.

9 Sender, *Business, Not Politics,* 207.

10 Bravo was purchased from Cablevision's Rainbow Media division (subsequently AMC Networks) in 2002, and Trio, originally jointly owned by the Canadian Broadcasting Corporation and Power Broadcasting, also Canadian, had been purchased by the cable arm of NBC (then known as USA Networks) in 2000. Trio was transferred to the French-based Vivendi Universal when that corporation acquired Universal Studios the same year, and then back to the NBC fold when NBC and Vivendi merged in 2004 to form NBC Universal (renamed NBCUniversal in 2011).

11 At a dedicated site, www.gettrio.com.

12 Television Without Pity was up at www.televisionwithoutpity.com. The first site was Dawson's Wrap (www.dawsonswrap.com), the second Mighty Big TV (www.mightybigtv.net). Besides *Dawson's Creek*, Mighty Big TV offered recaps of *7th Heaven* (WB/CW, 1996–2007), *Angel* (WB/UPN, 1999–2004), *Buffy the Vampire Slayer* (WB/UPN, 1997–2003), *Charmed* (WB, 1998–2006), *Felicity* (WB, 1998–2002), *Judging Amy* (CBS, 1999–2005), *Law & Order: SVU* (NBC, 1999–present), *NYPD Blue* (ABC, 1993–2005), *Popular* (WB, 1999–2001), *Roswell* (WB, 1999–2002), *Sports Night* (ABC, 1998–2000), *The Practice* (ABC, 1997–2004), and *The West Wing* (NBC, 1999–2006). Ariano and Cole, a couple, were living in Toronto, and Bunting in New York City; Ariano and Bunting had met through a fan message board for the teen drama *Beverly Hills 90210* (Fox, 1990–2000).

13 Using their online handles—"Wing Chun" for Ariano, "Sars" for Bunting, and "Glark" for Cole.

14 See Christy Carlson, "Is This because I'm Intertextual? *Law and Order, Special Victims Unit,* and Queer Internet Fan Production," in *Queer Online: Media Technology & Sexuality,* ed. Kate O'Riordan and David Phillips (New York: Peter Lang, 2007), 177–195; Jessica Stilwell, "Fans Without Pity: Television, Online Communities, and Popular Criticism," (master's thesis, Georgetown University, 2003).

15 TWoP had always had rules that posters could not restate their arguments over and over again; in addition, it had a no "boards on boards" rule, which forbade commenting about discussions taking place in other online spaces. I observed the

application of both these rules significantly cutting down the amount of discussion on HoYay threads, with posts such as "Readers at AfterEllen are not as critical of lesbian character X as you guys are here at TWoP" or debates about homoerotic subtext on various series censored by the moderator.

16 These included Tim Gunn and Daniel Vosovic (judge and contestant on *Project Runway*, respectively), Ted Allen (one of the stars of *Queer Eye*, and at the time a judge on *Top Chef*), Dale Livitski and Sandee Birdsong (contestants on *Top Chef*), Jesse Brune (a trainer on *Workout*), and Ryan Brown (a realtor on *Flipping Out*), who talked about being out television stars.

17 Hug knew Kris Slava, the Bravo executive who oversaw OutZoneTV, through a mutual friend, while Hensley had worked with Andy Cohen on an unaired Bravo pilot.

18 In fact, Hug was the only full-time staff member, becoming the site's de facto editor in chief without ever gaining additional editorial staff. In comparison, although none of Logo's or Bravo's other websites enjoyed huge staff numbers, TWoP had about half a dozen dedicated staff as well as dozens of freelance contributors; AfterEllen and AfterElton each had a managing editor and assistant editor in addition to the editor in chief as well as freelance writers.

19 See Queerty, "William Sledd Was Going to Be Bravo's YouTube Star," *Queerty*, February 2, 2010, https://www.queerty.com/william-sledd-was-going-to-be-bravos -youtube-star-then-everything-fell-apart-20100202.

20 For example, with Comcast, the tier at which Logo was available was Digital Preferred, which was one tier above the basic digital package.

21 According to Logo head Lisa Sherman at the "Out Trailblazers in Media" panel, New York City, April 1, 2010.

22 This point was noted by Logo's vice president of digital media, Dan Sacher, in a 2009 interview with me.

23 This then changed to "New Music Videos, Reality TV Shows, Celebrity News, Pop Culture"; currently, there is no byline.

24 The site went through several different labelings. As part of Logo's 2009–2010 rebranding, the byline was changed to "Serving you celebs, music, gossip, Logo TV news direct from the source," with the browser tagline "Gay Blog | Celebrity Gossip, Music & Entertainment News, Celebrity Pictures & Videos." In October 2011, NewNowNext was revamped with a broader focus, absorbing another Logo site, TripOutTravel, and the Ask an Expert section from newly defunct sister site 365gay, changing its byline to "Beyond Trends" and dropping its browser tagline. Most recently, the site was titled "Logo NewNowNext" with the browser tagline "LGBT News, Entertainment & Current Events." It was folded into the LogoTV site in July 2022, with the NewNowNext URL redirecting to www.LogoTV.com /news.

25 Will Pulos, who started as a NewNowNext intern in spring 2010, was hired as a freelancer for the site afterward and contributed posts for a couple of years.

26 All six participating presidential candidates were Democrats (Republican candi- dates were also invited but did not accept the invitation): eventual president Barack Obama, Hillary Rodham Clinton, Senator John Edwards, former senator Mike Gravel, Representative Dennis Kucinich, and Governor Bill Richardson (NM). The forum panelists were Human Rights Campaign president Joe Solmonese, singer/ songwriter Melissa Etheridge, and journalist Jonathan Capeheart, with journalist Margaret Carlson serving as moderator.

27 The original tagline was "An online LGBTQ community that provides ways for people to interact with others through network of friends," which was replaced in

2010 by "A social networking community for the LGBTQ (lesbian, gay, bisexual, transgender and queer/questioning) community."

28 According to an archived page of Gay Ottawa Now!, in the 1990s there were only four online gay news sites, including the Gay Globe, published by Darry Marengere and formerly online from 1999–2000 at gayottawanow.com, and 365gay.

29 For a discussion of the affective dimensions of 365gay's content, see Hollis Griffin, *Feeling Normal: Sexuality and Media Criticism in the Digital Age* (Bloomington: Indiana University Press, 2016), 86–91.

30 A 2011 Logo-wide rebranding changed the tagline of both sites to "The pop culture site that plays for your team"; this rebranding is discussed further in chapter 3.

31 Richard Ohmann, "The Shaping of a Canon: U.S. Fiction, 1960–1975," *Critical Inquiry* 10, no. 1 (1983): 199–223; Barbara Ehrenreich and John Ehrenreich, "The Professional-Managerial Class," in *Between Labor and Capital*, ed. Pat Walker (Boston: South End Press, 1979), 5–45.

32 Katherine Sender, "Gay Readers, Consumers and a Dominant Gay Habitus: 25 Years of the *Advocate* Magazine," *Journal of Communication* 51, no. 1 (2001): 73–99; Sender, *Business, Not Politics*.

33 Both MacEachern and Shotwell are straight, but I discuss their trajectories as examples of how website contributors joined the sites through personal connections.

34 Catherine Kirkland, "For the Love of It: Women Writers and the Popular Romance" (PhD diss., University of Pennsylvania, 1984).

35 Edward Castronova, *Synthetic Worlds: The Business and Culture of Online Games* (Chicago: University of Chicago Press, 2005); T. L. Taylor, *Play between Worlds: Exploring Online Game Culture* (Cambridge, MA: MIT Press, 2006); Nick Yee, "The Labor of Fun," *Games and Culture* 1, no. 1 (2006): 68–71.

36 For example, *Xena: Warrior Princess* fanfiction writer Melissa Good wrote two season 6 episodes for the show. See SLK, "The Good Life," *Ausxip*, 2000, https://www.ausxip.com/interviews/mgood.html.

37 In terms of a per-word rate. The exact amount was confidential.

38 MTV's management has since been reorganized, and Frank's position no longer exists.

39 This is a pseudonym, a pun on the twentieth-century American writer and critic Dorothy Parker.

40 At http://dorothysurrenders.blogspot.com; Chu's site at http://www.gracethespot.com is no longer active.

41 An acronym for "Chicago's Hip Independent Lesbian Lifestyle."

42 Dorothy Snarker asked that her specific occupation not be identified.

43 Several other site workers were hired by the networks on acquisition, but these arrangements were confidential.

44 AfterEllen's managing editor Malinda Lo and contributors Grace Chu, Dara Nai, and another who prefers to remain anonymous are Asian American; Dalila Ali Rajah and Gloria Bigelow, two presenters on the *Cherry Bomb* vlog, are African American; and AfterElton contributor Anthony Langford is African American. Also, 365gay writer James Withers is African American, and two of the founders of Downelink are gay men of color (Danny Nguyen is Asian American and Ronald Mabagos is Latino).

45 *Cherry Bomb* moved to SheWired, another lesbian entertainment website owned by Regent Media (later Here Media), in March 2010 and streamed there until October 2010.

46 Manu left a position as editorial director at TV Guide Online and prior to that had been at AOL. In addition, Angel Cohn, who had also worked at *TV Guide* as well as AOL, joined TWoP as managing editor; Zach Oat, with experience as an editor for a couple of online publications, was hired as editor; and Mindy Monez, from AOL, came on as assistant editor. (Oat was later replaced by Ethan Alter, a film critic and journalist who had written for entertainment publications including *TV Guide* and *Entertainment Weekly*.)

47 Jenkins, *Convergence Culture*.

48 Short for "homoeroticism, yay!" the term originated on the TWoP message boards when TWoP was called MightyBigTV, but its origins are traceable to the *Buffy the Vampire Slayer* fandom on the Usenet server. See Arnold Zwicky, "Hoyay!" *Linguist List*, January 20, 2005, http://listserv.linguistlist.org/pipermail/ads-l/2005-January/044924.html.

49 Also, Brian Graden, the former head of MTV Networks, of which Logo was one network, is gay.

50 Sherman was Logo's general manager and executive vice president until 2014, Kristin Frank the senior vice president of multiplatform distribution and marketing, and Sarah Warn the director of online editorial.

51 From 2004 to 2010 for AfterEllen, from 2005 to 2010 for AfterElton.

52 See, for example, John Edward Campbell's discussion of online spaces for gay dating in *Getting It on Online: Cyberspace, Gay Male Sexuality, and Embodied Identity* (New York: Haworth, 2004).

53 Bendix is referencing a stereotype that gay men (but not lesbians) enjoy the genre of musicals.

54 Perez Hilton is a gay man who runs a very popular celebrity gossip site at www.perezhilton.com.

55 Daniel Rosovic, on season 2.

56 See Alexandra Chasin, *Selling Out: The Gay and Lesbian Movement Goes to Market* (New York: Palgrave Macmillan, 2000) for an example of the assumption of a formerly untainted LGBTQ culture, and Sender, *Business, Not Politics* for a critique of this position.

57 Several Logo network executives are also no longer working to produce specifically LGBTQ content. This includes former network head Lisa Sherman, who is now president and CEO at the Ad Council, and Marc Leonard and Chris Willey, who are now executives at companies targeting online content to millennial viewers (Fuse Media and DEFY Media, respectively).

58 Lisa Henderson, "Queer Relay," *GLQ: A Journal of Lesbian and Gay Studies* 14, no. 4 (2008): 569–597.

59 At the time, Soloway produced *Transparent* as Jill Soloway.

60 See, for example, discussions by Urvashi Vaid, *Virtual Equality* (New York: Anchor, 1995); Michael Warner, *The Trouble with Normal: Sex, Politics, and the Ethics of Queer Life* (New York: Free Press, 1999).

Chapter 2   The New Queer Digital Spaces

1 The article used the term rather loosely to mean websites that offer commentary and/or analysis.

2 Amanda Lotz, *We Now Disrupt This Broadcast: How Cable Transformed Television and the Internet Revolutionized It All* (Boston: MIT Press, 2018), 150–151.

3 One of the first notable examples for television involved the science fiction series *Heroes* (NBC, 2006–2010), whose producers cultivated immersive fan engagement.

See Denise Mann, "Does 'Heroes 360' Represent NBC's Blistering Vision of the Future?" *Flow TV*, July 10, 2009, http://flowtv.org/2009/07/does-heroes-360-represent-nbcs-blistering-vision-of-the-futuredenise-mann-university-of-california-los-angeles/.

4 See Suzanne Scott, *Fake Geek Girls: Fandom, Gender, and the Convergence Culture Industry* (New York: New York University Press, 2019).

5 See, for example, Kristina Busse, "Fan Labor and Feminism: Capitalizing on the Fannish Labor of Love," *Cinema Journal* 54, no. 3 (2015): 110–115.

6 See Bertha Chin, "Sherlockology and Galactica.tv: Fan Sites as Gifts or Exploited Labor?" *Transformative Works and Cultures* 15 (2014), http://doi.org/10.3983/twc .2014.0513.

7 Gay.com, originally dominated by personal ads and chat rooms for men seeking other men, absorbed rival PlanetOut.com in 2000 and was later purchased by Here Media in 2009, whose television station Here TV was a direct rival to Logo; see John Edward Campbell, "Virtual Citizens or Dream Consumers: Looking for Civic Community on Gay.com," in *Queer Online: Media Technology & Sexuality*, ed. Kate O'Riordan and David Phillips (New York: Peter Lang, 2007), 197–216. Here Media was purchased by the Equal Entertainment company in 2017, which maintains Advocate.com, Out.com, and Pride.com as sites with LGBTQ content; Gay.com now redirects to the LA LGBT Center at https://lalgbtcenter.org.

8 Discussing how Logo sought to differentiate its digital properties, Logo executive Kristin Frank commented to me in an interview that "Gay.com was very much of a dating and hookup site . . . [while] a company that also has Nickelodeon [i.e., Logo's parent company Viacom] isn't going to be in that business."

9 See Mark Coté and Jennifer Pybus, "Learning to Immaterial Labour 2.0: MySpace and Social Networks," *Ephemera* 7, no. 1 (2007): 88–106; Diana Anselmo, "Gender and Queer Fan Labor on Tumblr: The Case of BBC's *Sherlock*," *Feminist Media Histories* 4, no. 1 (2018): 84–114.

10 See, for example, Katherine Sender, "Evolution, Not Revolution," in *Business, Not Politics: The Making of the Gay Market* (New York: Columbia University Press, 2004), 24–63; Tracy Baim, ed., *Gay Press, Gay Power: The Growth of LGBT Community Newspapers in America* (Scotts Valley, CA: CreateSpace, 2012).

11 Alfred L. Martin Jr., "Introduction: What Is Queer Production Studies/Why Is Queer Production Studies?" *Journal of Film and Video* 70, no. 3–4 (2018): 4; see also Alfred L. Martin Jr., "Queer (In)frequencies: SiriusXM's OutQ and the Limits of Queer Listening Publics," *Feminist Media Studies* 18, no. 2 (2018): 1–15.

12 See Denise Mann, "It's Not TV, It's Brand Management TV: The Collective Author(s) of the *Lost* Franchise," in *Production Studies: Cultural Studies of Media Industries*, ed. Vicki Mayer, Miranda Banks, and John Caldwell (New York: Routledge, 2010), 99–114; Carlos A. Scolari, "Lostology: Transmedia Storytelling and Expansion/Compression Strategies," *Semiotica* 195 (2013): 45–68.

13 See, for example, Henry Jenkins, "Searching for the Origami Unicorn: The Matrix and Transmedia Storytelling," in *Convergence Culture: Where Old and New Media Collide* (New York: New York University Press, 2006), 93–130.

14 The annual poll was held until 2016 for AfterEllen and 2013 for AfterElton (which by then was called TheBacklot).

15 Warn recounted that Logo had told her that she did not need to be as circumspect about sexual content, "but I'm insistent on it, not them." On occasions when she declined to post "racy" material on AfterEllen that Logo staff wanted her to, she took the position, "Fine, put it on LogoONLINE.com. I don't want it on the AEs [AfterEllen and AfterElton]."

16 After Logo's purchase, Lo became managing editor, while Kregloe served as editor in chief after Warn stepped down in 2009, until 2014.

17 The column provided a rundown of shows and actors that site staff judged to be of particular interest to the site's readers, even if they did not overtly involve lesbian storylines or personalities.

18 Analytical articles covered topics such as being queer and religious, debates about homosexuality as a choice, as well as more entertainment-focused pieces such as representations of female law enforcement characters. See Heather Hogan, "Beyond Visibility: A Good Christian Girl in a Big Gay World," *AfterEllen*, September 1, 2010, formerly up at http://www.afterellen.com/beyondvisibility/09-01-2010, archived at https://web.archive.org/web/20121127151835/http://www.afterellen.com/beyondvisibility/09-01-2010; Marcie, "Pop Theory: What's (Legally) in a Choice?" *AfterEllen*, December 1, 2011, formerly up at http://www.afterellen.com/column/pop-theory-3, archived at https://web.archive.org/web/20111204001932/http://www.afterellen.com/column/pop-theory-3; Mia Jones, "De-butching Female Cops on TV's Crime Dramas," *AfterEllen*, November 23, 2010, formerly up at http://www.afterellen.com/TV/2010/10/de-butching-female-cops-on-tvs-crime-dramas/, archived at https://web.archive.org/web/20101124134246/http://www.afterellen.com/TV/2010/10/de-butching-female-cops-on-tvs-crime-dramas/. Interviews included both those conducted by AfterEllen staff as well as posts' repurposed content drawn from interviews in other publications.

19 This point was noted by both Sarah Warn and Malinda Lo in interviews with me.

20 The others were journalist Chagmion Antoine, who worked for the *CBS News on Logo* program that later became *365gay News*, writer Lauren Blitzer, and poet/activist Staceyann Chin.

21 Although AfterElton also hosted some video, in being aimed at gay and bisexual men, it had much more competition than AfterEllen and did not expand as much as AfterEllen after the Logo acquisition, including in terms of video. Series at AfterElton, none of which were scripted, included the talk shows *Doin' It with Ethan*, *Gay in the UK*, *Louis Virtel Weekly*, *Rantasmo Presents*, and *Tell Dennis Everything*, and for a couple of years, episodes of the *Logo Drama Club*, where stars of Broadway shows were interviewed, were also posted at the site, although these streamed at LogoONLINE as well.

22 Additionally, there was a single "series finale" episode in July 2011, then several new episodes in 2015 and another few episodes in 2017.

23 She was managing editor from 2014 to 2016.

24 According to Trish Bendix in an interview with me in her capacity as AfterEllen's blogs editor.

25 Ben Aslinger, "PlanetOut and the Dichotomies of Queer Media Conglomeration," in *LGBT Identity and Online New Media*, ed. Christopher Pullen and Margaret Cooper (New York: Routledge, 2010), 119.

26 Amanda Lotz notes that the ability for streaming services to deliver video over the internet was accompanied by the introduction of consumer tablets in 2010 as another viewing screen option besides televisions and computer screens, which also helped popularize the streaming of video content. See Lotz, *We Now Disrupt This Broadcast*, 114.

27 As mentioned in the introduction chapter, Netflix's earlier signature series had strong queer representation, especially *House of Cards* (2013–2018), *Orange Is the New Black* (2013–2019), and *Sense8* (2015–2018).

28 Aymar Jean Christian, *Open TV: Innovation beyond Hollywood and the Rise of Web Television* (New York: New York University Press, 2018), 141–142. See also Aymar

Jean Christian, "The Value of Representation: Toward a Critique of Networked Television Performance," *International Journal of Communication* 11 (2017): 1552–1574.

29 See, for example, Michael Lovelock, "'Is Every YouTuber Going to Make a Coming Out Video Eventually?': YouTube Celebrity Video Bloggers and Lesbian and Gay Identity," *Celebrity Studies* 8, no. 1 (2016): 87–103; Faithe Day, "Between Butch/ Femme: On the Performance of Race, Gender, and Sexuality in a YouTube Web Series," *Journal of Lesbian Studies* 22, no. 3 (2018): 267–281.

30 See Dee Lockett, "*Brown Girls* Is Now an Emmy-Nominated Show Well Ahead of Its HBO Debut," *Vulture*, July 13, 2017, https://www.vulture.com/2017/07/brown -girls-emmy-nominated-well-ahead-of-its-hbo-debut.html.

31 See Aymar Jean Christian, "OML and Tello Join Forces for More Lesbian Programming Online," *TubeFilter*, January 16, 2013, https://www.tubefilter.com/2013/01 /16/one-more-lesbian-tello-join-forces-film-tv/; Winnie McCroy, "Wish There Was a Netflix for Lesbians? Tune into Tello!" *Edge*, March 27, 2015, https://www .edgemedianetwork.com/news/national//174055.

32 OML did host a fan video competition at the 2019 ClexaCon convention, an annual event for queer women and trans/nonbinary entertainment fans, but does not generally support content creation itself.

33 See Revry, "Questions," Revry.tv, n.d., https://www.revry.tv/support, para. 5.

34 Julia Himberg, "Revry: Making the Case for LGBTQ Channels," in *From Networks to Netflix: A Guide to Changing Channels*, 2nd ed., ed. Derek Johnson (New York: Routledge, 2022), 272.

35 See Revry, "Questions," para. 4.

36 See Kona Equity, "Revry Inc," *Kona Equity*, December 14, 2022, https://www .konaequity.com/company/revry-inc-4395709467/.

37 As Julia Himberg described it, Revry operates a "tribrid" model consisting of ad-free subscription, ad-supported video on demand, and ad-supported live TV options; see Himberg, "Revry," 274. Revry has since also become available as a linear channel through certain cable TV subscription packages.

38 GagaOOLala has since expanded into additional Southeast and South Asian countries, carrying an inventory of both Western and Asian films and television series, although it also produces some original content. See Shannon Power, "Forget Netflix, There's a New Asian Streaming Service That's 100% LGBTI," *Gay Star News*, July 21, 2017, https://www.gaystarnews.com/article/forget-netflix-theres-new -streaming-service-100-lgbti/; Reiss Smith, "The 'Netflix of Queer Content' Launches across Asia Despite Gay Sex Bans," *Pink News*, January 2, 2020, https:// www.pinknews.co.uk/2020/01/02/gagaoolala-lgbt-streaming-service-asia/.

39 For example, Dekkoo is available through Amazon as well as its own website; Revry can be added as an app for Apple TV, Roku, and Amazon Fire, as well as an add-on via Comcast in the United States or through other television channels such Pluto TV (see Jaclyn Cosgrove, "Revry Wants to Be the Streaming Service for and by LGBTQ People," *Los Angeles Times*, March 15, 2019, https://www.latimes.com /business/la-fi-ct-revry-lgbtq-streaming-20190315-story.html).

40 Conversely, dating platforms have also been used for other forms of interaction or information exchange, which may be particularly important for queer migrants. For example, Andrew Shield has discussed how immigrants to Europe use Grindr for logistical as well as dating purposes, such as seeking leads on employment, housing, and other local information; see Andrew Shield, "'I Was Staying at the Camp, and I Met This Guy on Grindr, and He Asked Me to Move in with Him': Tourists,

Immigrants, and Logistical Uses of Socio-sexual Media," in *Immigrants on Grindr: Race, Sexuality and Belonging Online* (London: Palgrave Macmillan, 2019), 111–142.

41 Earlier scholarship examined platforms such as bulletin board system (BBS) bulletin boards, internet relay chat (IRC) chat rooms, and internet message boards which allowed queer users to connect through text-only communication; see, for example, Jon Campbell, *Getting It on Online: Cyberspace, Gay Male Sexuality, and Embodied Identity* (New York: Haworth, 2004), for a study on gay men using IRC. Research then largely shifted to internet-based platforms, including social media and mobile platforms that have come to dominate online interaction more generally; see, for just a few examples, Sally Munt, Elizabeth Bassett, and Kate O'Riordan, "Virtually Belonging: Risk, Connectivity, and Coming Out On-line," *International Journal of Sexuality and Gender Studies* 7, no. 2/3 (2002): 125–137; Sharif Mowlabocus, *Gaydar Culture: Gay Men, Technology and Embodiment in the Digital Age* (Farnham, UK: Ashgate, 2010); and Stefanie Duguay, "'He Has a Way Gayer Facebook than I Do': Investigating Sexual Identity Disclosure and Context Collapse on a Social Networking Site," *New Media & Society* 18, no. 6 (2016): 891–907.

42 Jacquelyn Arcy, "The Digital Money Shot: Twitter Wars, *The Real Housewives*, and Transmedia Storytelling," *Celebrity Studies* 9, no. 4 (2018): 487–502.

43 Peter Kafka, "AMC to Twitterers: Please Don't Market 'Mad Men' for Us," *Business Insider*, August 26, 2008, http://www.businessinsider.com/2008/8/amc-to-twitterers -please-don-t-market-madmen-for-us.

44 See Inger-Lise K. Bore and Jonathan Hickman, "Continuing *The West Wing* in 140 Characters or Less: Improvised Simulation on Twitter," *Journal of Fandom Studies* 1, no. 2 (2013): 219–238; Kathryn L. Lookadoo and Ted M. Dickinson, "Who Killed @TheLauraPalmer? Twitter as a Performance Space for *Twin Peaks* Fan Fiction," in *Television, Social Media, and Fan Culture*, ed. Alison F. Slade, Amber J. Narro, and Dedria Givens-Carroll (Lanham, MD: Lexington), 337–351.

45 At the time, Scott identified as a gay man but currently identifies as transgender and nonbinary, using they/them pronouns.

46 At the same time, social media cannot do everything in regard to distribution and networking. Thus, GD commented that while she had submitted her music to the lesbian-themed web series *Venice*, which enjoyed an audience of millions, entry into mainstream commercial media still largely depended on who you happened to know. In a similar vein, another independent filmmaker, David Moore, whose work screened at Newfest 2010, saw networking rather than promotion or distribution as the most important aspect of using Facebook.

47 Henry Jenkins, *Convergence Culture: Where Old and New Media Collide* (New York: New York University Press, 2006), 26.

48 See, for example, Campbell, *Getting It on Online*.

49 Maria San Filippo, "Before and after AfterEllen: Online Queer Cinephile Communities as Critical Counterpublics," in *Film Criticism in the Digital Age*, ed. Mattias Frey and Cecilia Sayad (New Brunswick, NJ: Rutgers University Press, 2015), 117–136.

50 Based on this kind of feedback, *Cherry Bomb* creator Dalila Ali Rajah commented that international audiences constituted a lucrative market of possible consumers of LGBTQ media, given that "in a lot of these places, they have nothing. . . . There isn't enough freedom for them to create, so they need a place where they can go to find it."

51 For example, AfterEllen's and AfterElton's "Hot 100" lists, determined by user votes, as well as staff-crafted lists, such as AfterElton's "The History of U.S. Daytime Gay Soap Kisses" (snicks, *AfterElton*, August 16, 2012, formerly up at http://www

.afterelton.com/tv/2012/08/gay-soap-kisses-oltl-atwt-dool, archived at https://web
.archive.org/web/20120817223703/http://www.afterelton.com/tv/2012/08/gay-soap
-kisses-oltl-atwt-dool) or AfterEllen's "The Top 25 Lesbian/Bi Characters on TV
(Right Now)" (Heather Hogan, *AfterEllen*, November 4, 2013, formerly up at
https://www.afterellen.com/tv/201217-the-top-25-lesbianbi-characters-on-tv-right
-now, archived at https://web.archive.org/web/20181217013750/https://www
.afterellen.com/tv/201217-the-top-25-lesbianbi-characters-on-tv-right-now).

52 A particular galling instance cited by Warn was when she had stayed up for hours
writing a post about an episode of the ABC series *Flashforward* and posted it at
5:00 A.M. the day after it aired, yet still received indignant tweets and comments on
the website asking why AfterEllen had missed coverage of it.

53 See, for example, Luca Iandoli, Simonetta Primario, and Giuseppe Zollo, "The
Impact of Group Polarization on the Quality of Online Debate in Social Media:
A Systematic Literature Review," *Technological Forecasting & Social Change* 170
(2021): 1–12.

54 Data from Quantcast and Logo's internal figures were about 110,000 unique visits
per month for 365gay, 430,000 unique visits per month for AfterElton, and 760,000
unique visits per month for AfterEllen.

55 In 2008, at the height of its site proliferations, Here owned the general sites
LambdaSearch.com, billed as a "Gay and lesbian search engine," and LambdaEvents
.com, "Calendar listing of local LGBT happenings and events"; sites targeted to
specific communities—AsianGayNet.com, "An online community for gay Asian
and Pacific Islanders," BlackGLO.com, "Online destination for the African
American community," LatinoGLO.com, "Where gay Latino and Hispanics gather
online," LesbiaNation.com, "One of the largest online lesbian communities,"
CountryGayWeb.com, "A top site for the rural and Country Western gay community," GrayAndGay.com, "Online community for gay seniors," QueerFuture.com,
"Where gay youth can interact with their peers," and LeatherAndBears.com,
"Online stop for the leather and bear communities"; interest-oriented sites
GayWired.com, "A premiere gay entertainment website," and GaySports.com,
"A must-see for the gay sports enthusiast"; travel sites 247gay.com, "Up-to-minute
gay and lesbian news portal," LambdaTravel.com, "Gay and lesbian travel packages,
tours and cruises," NaviGaytion.com, "Find travel hot spots for the LGBT
community," and QTMagazine.com, "Online gay and lesbian travel guide";
relationship-oriented sites MonkeyMatch.com, "A premiere matchmaking site for
the LGBT community," and Gay MarriageWorld.com, "Marriage advice for the
LGBT couple"; and business and employment sites GayBusinessWorld.com,
"A news and networking site for the gay business professional," GayJob.biz, "Up-to-
date job listings for the gay job hunter," LambdaBusiness.com, "The premiere source
for locating gay friendly business in your area," and LambdaShopping.com, "Local
gay and lesbian retailers and shopping spots."

56 SheWired.com started to redirect to the https://www.pride.com/women link at
that time and continues to do so.

57 Jennifer Beals, Katherine Moennig, and Leisha Hailey were cofounders; see Pete
Cashmore, "OurChart.com—*The L Word* Launching Lesbian Social Network,"
Mashable, December 18, 2006, https://mashable.com/2006/12/18/ourchartcom-the
-l-word-launching-lesbian-social-network/.

58 Candace Moore, "Liminal Places and Spaces: Public/Private Considerations," in
Production Studies: Cultural Studies of Media Industries, ed. Vicki Mayer, Miranda
Banks, and John Caldwell (New York: Taylor & Francis, 2009), 125–139. FanLib,

which had also launched in 2007, had been notorious among fandom circles for seeking to monetize fan fiction that writers posted for free on the site (and to which they ceded copyright), and its collaboration with Showtime exemplified this; see Scott, *Fake Geek Girls*, 117.

59 Dalila Ali Rajah, producer of the *Cherry Bomb* talk show, also noted the challenges of finding advertisers given stereotypes that lesbians "like to wash our pads out in a stream on a rock; we wash our hair in the ocean. . . . If we like nature, we can just go pick an herb and wash our hair. There's nothing for somebody to sell us."

60 See, for example, Alexander Cho, "Default Publicness: Queer Youth of Color, Social Media, and Being Outed by the Machine," *New Media & Society* 20, no. 9 (2018): 3183–3200; Dustin Goltz, "It Gets Better: Queer Futures, Critical Frustrations, and Radical Potentials," *Critical Studies in Media Communication* 30, no. 2 (2013): 135–151; Brandon Miller, "'They're the Modern-Day Gay Bar': Exploring the Uses and Gratifications of Social Networks for Men Who Have Sex with Men," *Computers in Human Behavior* 51 (2015): 476–482.

61 See, for example, Advocate, "OurChart.com Pulls the Plug," *Advocate*, November 22, 2008, https://www.advocate.com/news/2008/11/22/ourchartcom-pulls-plug.

62 Many viewers of *TLW* were disappointed with its uneven quality, particularly how the final season ended, and saw Chaiken as having exercised excessive creative influence. Chaiken's subsequent show, the reality series *The Real L Word*, which aired three seasons on Showtime from 2010 to 2012, was also subject to much criticism among lesbian (and other) viewers.

63 Warn noted that "almost nobody knows that I'm the director of editorial for all of Logo['s websites]. . . . They don't know that Michael [Jensen, editor in chief of AfterElton] technically works for me, they don't know that Jay [Vanasco, editor in chief of 365gay] works for me. . . . Basically, except for the 'AfterEllen on Logo-ONLINE,' the little 'on LogoONLINE' part you see on that, you can't really tell that we're owned by Logo. And that's very, very intentional."

64 Vanasco commented, "People don't always realize that we're owned by Logo, or they kind of do but they don't know what that means, or they don't imagine that I'm actually in the office, at Logo! So I think we try to keep the brand separate from Logo, because I am *not* influenced, day to day, by what happens at Logo or what people want me to put on the site."

65 According to Cutestat.com.

66 See Valerie Anne, "Exclusive: 'The 100' EP Jason Rothenberg on This Week's Game-Changing Episode, 'Thirteen,'" *AfterEllen*, March 2, 2016, https://www.afterellen.com/tv/476855-exclusive-100-ep-jason-rothenberg-weeks-game-changing-episode-thirteen; J. Halterman, "Exclusive: 'Person of Interest' EPs on Tonight's Shocking Episode," *AfterEllen*, May 31, 2016, https://www.afterellen.com/entertainment/490045-person-of-interest-exec-producers.

67 Emrah Kovacoglu, "False Rumor: We Are Not Shutting Down!" *AfterEllen*, September 21, 2016, https://www.afterellen.com/general-news/514543-false-rumor-not-shutting.

68 See Samantha Allen, "AfterEllen Is Shutting Down: Is This the End of Lesbian Media?" *Daily Beast*, September 22, 2016, https://www.thedailybeast.com/afterellen-is-shutting-down-is-this-the-end-of-lesbian-media; Marcie Bianco, "Lesbian Culture Is Being Erased because Investors Think Only Gay Men (and Straight People) Have Money," *Quartz*, October 6, 2016, https://qz.com/801501/afterellen-closing-lesbian-culture-is-being-erased-because-investors-think-only-gay-men-have-money/; Christina Cauterucci, "What's Left for Queer Women after AfterEllen?"

Slate, September 23, 2016, https://slate.com/human-interest/2016/09/afterellen-site
-of-record-for-queer-women-closes-leaving-void-in-lesbian-culture.html; Heather
Hogan, "AfterEllen Is Shutting Down," *Autostraddle*, September 20, 2016, https://
www.autostraddle.com/afterellen-is-shutting-down-352383/.

69 The website traffic site Cutestat.com estimates AfterEllen's daily unique visitors at
around 10,000; at its peak, AfterEllen had about 25,000 daily unique visitors.

70 See Mary Emily O'Hara, "AfterEllen Was a Refuge for All Queer Women—until It
Wasn't," *Out*, February 13, 2019, https://www.out.com/news-opinion/2019/2/13
/afterellen-was-refuge-all-queer-women-until-it-wasn't.

71 See, for example, Afierra, "When It Comes to Kara and Lena, the 'Supergirl'
Writers Say One Thing and Do Another," *Hypable*, October 25, 2019, https://www
.hypable.com/kara-lena-supergirl-season-2/, which has nearly one hundred
comments.

72 For example, Gayety (https://gayety.co), established in 2015, and the Gaily Grind
(https://thegailygrind.com/), established in 2013.

73 Q.Digital began as GayCities in 2007, acquiring Queerty (founded in 2005) in 2011
and LGBTQ Nation (founded in 2010), the Bilerico Project (a political blogging site
that evolved from founder Bil Browning's personal blog beginning in 1998), and
Dragaholics (a site covering drag queens) in 2015; the Bilerico Project was then
subsumed under LGBTQ Nation and Dragaholics under Queerty. See Bilerico
Project, "About Us," *Bilerico Project*, September 22, 2007, http://bilerico
.lgbtqnation.com/about/; Erik Sass, "Q.Digital Rolls Up LGBT Media Cos.,"
Media Post, September 29, 2015, https://www.mediapost.com/publications/article
/259347/qdigital-rolls-up-lgbt-media-cos.html.

74 Cutestat.com estimates over 120,000 unique daily visitors for Towleroad (https://
www.towleroad.com/, established 2003) and nearly 40,000 unique daily visitors for
Queerty (https://www.queerty.com/, established 2005). Users can comment on
Towleroad via the non-site-specific Disqus comment hosting service; for Queerty,
registered users have the option of adding a photo and text profile information to
their accounts, but there are no options to add "friends," "like" other people's posts,
and so forth. Another news site, Pink News UK (https://www.pinknews.co.uk/,
established 2005), has comparable traffic to Queerty and Towleroad (Cutestat.com
estimates over 61,000 unique daily visitors), but its posts do not attract any
significant number of user comments.

75 See Kelsey Cameron, "Constructing Queer Female Cyberspace: *The L Word*
Fandom and Autostraddle.com," in "Queer Female Fandom," ed. Julie Levin Russo
and Eve Ng, special issue, *Transformative Works and Cultures* 24 (2017), http://
doi.org/10.3983/twc.2017.846.

76 Cutestat.com estimates nearly 30,000 unique daily visitors.

77 Lori Morimoto and Louisa Ellen Stein, "Tumblr and Fandom" in "Tumblr and
Fandom," ed. Lori Morimoto and Louisa Ellen Stein, special issue, *Transformative
Works and Cultures* 27 (2018), http://doi.org/10.3983/twc.2018.1580. [2.3]

78 See, for example, Kevin Howley, "'I Have a Drone': Internet Memes and the Politics
of Culture," *Interactions: Studies in Communication & Culture* 7, no. 2 (2016):
155–175; Eve Ng, "Contesting the Queer Subfield of Cultural Production: Paratextual Framings of *Carol* and *Freeheld*," *Journal of Film and Video* 70, no. 3–4 (2018):
8–23; Carrie Rentschler and Samantha Thrift, "Doing Feminism in the Network:
Networked Laughter and the 'Binders Full of Women' Meme," *Feminist Theory* 16,
no. 3 (2015): 329–359; Limor Shifman, *Memes in Digital Culture* (Boston: MIT
Press, 2014).

79 Morimoto and Stein, "Tumblr and Fandom," [2.6], [2.5].

80 See major subreddits listed at https://subbed.org/r/fandom; see also Michael Buozis, "Doxing or Deliberative Democracy? Evidence and Digital Affordances in the Serial Subreddit," *Convergence* 25, no. 3 (2019): 357–373; The Retroist, "Reddit Has a Crazy *Game of Thrones* Community That Welcomes Fans' Biggest Fear," *Geek*, June 22, 2016, https://www.geek.com/games/reddit-has-a-crazy-game-of-thrones-community-that-welcomes-fans-biggest-fear-1658848/.

81 A few years after leaving Television Without Pity (TWoP) in 2008, TWoP founders Tara Ariano, Sarah Bunting, and David Cole founded a new television-based forum at Previously.tv, which drew many of the users who had been TWoP regulars. In 2019, Previously.tv merged with TV Tattle (formerly at www.tvtattle.com), a popular television coverage site that did not have its own message boards to form the Primetimer website (www.primetimer.com). Primetimer's first editor in chief is a former TWoP recapper, Joe Reid (Reid is now a writer for the site); after the merger, Ariano, Bunting, and Cole joined Primetimer's staff.

82 The DataLounge (www.datalounge.com) was established by U.S. media company Mediapolis, which still owns the site. The L Chat (TLC) was up for ten years at Zetaboards, a popular free, independent message board system, until Tapatalk, a company that had started out with a forum app for mobile devices, took over Zetaboard and several other forum hosting platforms (see Cision, "Tapatalk Reinvents Online Forum Management Platforms with Tapatalk Groups," *Cision*, October 4, 2018, https://www.prnewswire.com/news-releases/tapatalk-reinvents-online-forum-management-platforms-with-tapatalk-groups-300724626.html). TLC founders declined to stay with Tapatalk, which began its online forum operations in January 2019, and migrated to Jcink, another free message board system, at https://thelchat.jcink.net, before later relocating to a dedicated site at https://thelchat.net. However, Tapatalk kept TLC content it had to date and established a separate TLC message board (https://www.tapatalk.com/groups/l_anon/general-discussions-f3/).

83 Jing Jamie Zhao, Ling Yang, and Maud Lavin, Introduction to *Boys' Love, Cosplay, and Androgynous Idols: Queer Fan Cultures in Mainland China, Hong Kong, and Taiwan*, ed. Maud Lavin, Ling Yang, and Jing Jamie Zhao (Hong Kong: Hong Kong University Press, 2017), xi–xxxiii; see also Hye-Kyung Lee, "Participatory Media Fandom: A Case Study of Anime Fansubbing," *Media, Culture & Society* 33, no. 8 (2011): 1131–1147.

84 See, for example, Amin Ghaziani, *There Goes the Gayborhood?* (Princeton, NJ: Princeton University Press, 2014).

85 See Catherine Shu, "YouTube Updates Its Policies after LGBTQ Videos Were Blocked in Restricted Mode," *Tech Crunch*, June 20, 2017, https://techcrunch.com/2017/06/19/youtube-updates-its-policies-after-lgbtq-videos-were-blocked-in-restricted-mode/; Alex Bollinger, "YouTubers Say They Have Proof That the Platform Blocks LGBTQ Content," *LGBTQ Nation*, October 1, 2019, https://www.lgbtqnation.com/2019/10/youtubers-say-proof-platform-blocks-lgbtq-content/. Also, although in 2019 YouTube announced more explicit anti-harassment policies intended to protect vloggers from sexist, racist, and homophobic attacks, there remains skepticism how well and consistently the site will enforce these policies (see, for example, Daniel Villarreal, "YouTube Changes Its Policy on Anti-LGBTQ Hate Speech, but Will It Work?" *LGBTQ Nation*, October 1, 2019, https://www.lgbtqnation.com/2019/12/youtube-changes-policy-anti-lgbtq-hate-speech-will-work/).

86 Steven Thrasher, "What Tumblr's Porn Ban Really Means," *The Atlantic*, December 7, 2018, https://www.theatlantic.com/technology/archive/2018/12/tumblr-adult-content-porn/577471, para. 4, para. 6. Tumblr relaxed these restrictions in November 2022, allowing some nudity as long as it is not assessed to be "porn"; see, for example, Samantha Cole, "Tumblr Brings Back Nudity, but Not Porn," *Vice*, November 1, 2022, https://www.vice.com/en/article/xgymvj/tumblr-brings-back-nudity-but-not-porn.

87 See, for example, Older than Netfic, "A New History of Fandom Purges," *Tumblr*, October 15, 2019, https://olderthannetfic.tumblr.com/post/188360541394/a-new-history-of-fandom-purges.

88 See, for example, Aja Romano, "The Archive of Our Own Just Won a Hugo. That's Huge for Fanfiction," *Vox*, August 19, 2019, https://www.vox.com/2019/4/11/18292419/archive-of-our-own-wins-hugo-award-best-related-work.

Chapter 3   Gaystreaming, Dualcasting, and Changing Queer Alignments

Note: Parts of this chapter discussing Logo have been published in an earlier form in Eve Ng, "A 'Post-Gay' Era? Media Gaystreaming, Homonormativity, and the Politics of LGBT Integration," *Communication, Culture & Critique* 6, no 2 (2013): 258–283. https://doi.org/10.1111/cccr.12013.

1 Alessandra Stanley, "Sex and the Gym: 'Work Out' and the Gaying of Bravo," *New York Times*, July 19, 2006, http://www.nytimes.com/2006/07/19/arts/television/19watc.html.

2 Andrew Wallenstein, "Bravo Tops Survey of Gay-Friendly Companies," *Hollywood Reporter*, May 13, 2008, https://www.hollywoodreporter.com/news/bravo-tops-survey-gay-friendly-111589.

3 Katherine Sender, "Dualcasting: Bravo's Gay Programming and the Quest for Women Audiences," in *Cable Visions: Television beyond Broadcasting*, ed. Sarah Banet-Weiser, Cynthia Chris, and Anthony Freitas (New York: New York University Press, 2007), 316.

4 See, for example, Larry Gross, *Up from Invisibility: Lesbians, Gay Men, and the Media in America* (New York: Columbia University Press, 2001); Lisa Henderson, "Queer Relay," *GLQ* 14, no. 4 (2008): 569–597.

5 Although there has not been a uniform position among queer activists about how sexual and gender identities should be depicted in the media, a gradualist approach that does not come across as excessively confrontational has been dominant in mainstream LGBTQ organizations such as GLAAD, which has commended a number of problematically desexualized representations such as those on *Will and Grace* and *Queer Eye*; see, for example, Vincent Doyle, *Making Out in the Mainstream: GLAAD and the Politics of Respectability* (Montreal: McGill-Queen's University Press, 2015).

6 Ron Becker, *Gay TV and Straight America* (Piscataway, NJ: Rutgers University Press, 2006).

7 During an "Out Trailblazers in Media" panel at the LGBT Center, New York City, on April 1, 2010, Elliott noted, "The big bad recession of the '90s opened up an opportunity for a lot of gay media in that you had a great batch of advertisers back then targeting the GLBT market for the first time.... Those of you who go online and look at gay websites ... will see for the first time ... advertising from mainstream gigantic packaged good companies like Kraft and Heinz and Kellogg's and

Pepsi and Coke and so on, companies that in the past never advertised in the gay media."

8 See also Kathleen Battles and Wendy Hilton-Morrow, "Gay Characters in Conventional Spaces: *Will and Grace* and the Situation Comedy Genre," *Critical Studies in Media Communication* 19, no. 1 (2002): 87–105; Gross, *Up from Invisibility*; Katherine Sender, *Business, Not Politics: The Making of the Gay Market* (New York: Columbia University Press, 2004); Suzanna Danuta Walters, *All the Rage: The Story of Gay Visibility in America* (New York: Columbia University Press, 2001).

9 This was discussed by industry presenters at the New York Television Festival, the cosponsors for which included MTV Networks (Logo's parent network) and Bravo, that I attended in September 2009. There were several panels about digital media production on "Digital Day."

10 All of the Logo sites used asterisked replacements for words like *f-ck* in article posts, although they did not systematically remove such words in user comments or posts on forums. BravoTV allowed its bloggers to use *f-ck*, and Bravo's Television Without Pity site never moderated language on the basis of obscenity—words such as *f-ck*, *c-nt*, *c-cksucker*, and the like appeared in both recaps and on message boards. However, TWoP long enforced a strict policy around using conventional spelling and punctuation, probably to assert a certain kind of cultural capital for the site while managing a reputation for pushing the boundaries with respect to sexual language.

11 Comparing Logo to Here Media, the owner at the time of Gay.com, PlanetOut, as well as *The Advocate* and *Out* magazines, Logo executive Kristin Frank noted in an interview with me that "a company that also has Nickelodeon [one of MTV Networks' channels aimed at children] isn't going to be in [the dating and hookup] business, basically. And that's not where we also thought the value to the advertisers would be."

12 Sender, "Dualcasting."

13 See Alexander Doty, *Making Things Perfectly Queer: Interpreting Mass Culture* (Minneapolis: University of Minnesota Press, 1993); Brett Farmer, *Spectacular Passions: Cinema, Fantasy, Gay Male Spectatorships* (Durham, NC: Duke University Press, 2000); David Greven, *Representations of Femininity in American Genre Cinema: The Woman's Film, Film Noir, and Modern Horror* (New York: Palgrave Macmillan, 2011).

14 See Camille Bacon-Smith, *Enterprising Women: Television Fandom and the Creation of Popular Myth* (Philadelphia: University of Pennsylvania Press, 1992); Henry Jenkins, *Textual Poachers: Television Fans and Participatory Culture* (London: Routledge, 1992).

15 See, for example, Christopher Pullen, *Straight Girls and Queer Guys: The Hetero Media Gaze in Film and Television* (Edinburgh: Edinburgh University Press, 2016).

16 Victoria de Grazia, Introduction to *The Sex of Things: Gender and Consumption in Historical Perspective*, ed. Victoria de Grazia and Ellen Furlough (Berkeley: University of California Press, 1996), 1–10.

17 Sender, *Business, Not Politics*.

18 Lizabeth Cohen, *A Consumer's Republic: The Politics of Mass Consumption in Postwar America* (New York: Vintage, 2003).

19 Ben Aslinger, "Creating a Network for Queer Audiences at Logo TV," *Popular Communication* 7, no. 2 (2009): 107–121.

20 See Katherine Sender's discussion about how this played out in the gay and lesbian print media in Sender, *Business, Not Politics*. Other work that discusses LGBTQ workers at Logo are Aslinger, "Creating a Network for Queer Audiences"; Kathleen

Farrell, "Backstage Politics: Social Change and the 'Gay TV' Industry" (PhD diss., Syracuse University, 2008).

21 Lisa Duggan, "The New Homonormativity: The Sexual Politics of Neoliberalism," in *Materializing Democracy: Toward a Revitalized Cultural Politics*, ed. Russ Castronovo and Dana D. Nelson (Durham, NC: Duke University Press, 2002), 175–194.

22 Jasbir Puar, *Terrorist Assemblages: Homonationalism in Queer Times* (Durham, NC: Duke University Press, 2007).

23 Alfred L. Martin Jr., "Introduction: What Is Queer Production Studies/Why Is Queer Production Studies?" *Journal of Film and Video* 70, no. 3–4 (2018): 4.

24 Doug Ross, head of the production company that made *Gay Weddings* (2003) and then *Boy Meets Boy* (2003) for Bravo, also recounted in an interview with me that NBC Universal president Jeff Gaspin had been aware that "not only did [Bravo] have a lot of gay viewers, but they had a lot of viewers who would be open to gay-themed programming." See also Sender, "Dualcasting," 306.

25 This reality show is not related to the 2017 *Fire Island* reality show produced and aired by Logo or to the romantic comedy *Fire Island* (Andrew Ahn, 2022), which was released by Hulu.

26 See Alan Light, Post 35, "***Gay-Friendly DVD's, Version 5***" thread, *Home Theatre Forum*, May 31, 2001, https://www.hometheaterforum.com/community /threads/gay-friendly-dvds-version-5.17406/page-2.

27 Another Bravo executive, Rachel Smith, corroborated this in an interview with me, recalling that the concept for *Boy Meets Boy* "came out of Jeff Gaspin's head."

28 *Aussie Queer Eye for the Straight Guy* in Australia (Channel 10, 2005); *De Heren maken de Man* "The gentlemen make the man" (KanaalTwee, 2005) in Belgium; *Ojo con clase* "Classy eye" (Mega, 2013) in Chile; *Sillä silmällä* "For the eye" (Nelonen, 2005) in Finland; *Queer, cinq experts dans le vent* "Queer, five experts in the wind" (TF1, 2004) in France; *Schwul macht cool* "Gay makes you cool" (RTL 2, 2003) in Germany; *Fab 5* (Antenna 1, 2011) in Greece; *I Fantastici cinque* "The fantastic five" (La7, 2004) in Italy; *Homsepatruljen* "The gay patrol" (TV3, 2004 and 2012) in Norway; *Esquadrão G* "Squad G" (SIC, 2005) in Portugal; *El Equipo G* "Team G" (Antena 3, 2005) in Spain; *Fab 5 Sverige* "Fab 5 Sweden" (TV3, 2003) in Sweden; *Queer Eye for the Straight Guy UK* (ITV1, 2004) in the United Kingdom.

29 See, for example, Beth Berila and Devika Choudhuri, "Metrosexuality the Middle Class Way: Exploring Race, Class, and Gender in *Queer Eye for the Straight Guy*," *Genders* 42 (2005), https://www.colorado.edu/gendersarchive1998–2013/2005/08 /05/metrosexuality-middle-class-way-exploring-race-class-and-gender-queer-eye -straight-guy; Josh Gamson, "The Intersection of Gay Street and Straight Street: Shopping, Social Class, and the New Gay Visibility," *Social Thought & Research* 26, no. 1/2 (2005): 3–18; Zizi Papacharissi and Jan Fernback, "The Aesthetic Power of the Fab 5: Discursive Themes of Homonormativity in *Queer Eye for the Straight Guy*," *Journal of Communication Inquiry* 32, no. 4 (2008): 348–367; Robert Westerfelhaus and Celeste Lacroix, "Seeing 'Straight' through *Queer Eye*: Exposing the Strategic Rhetoric of Heteronormativity in a Mediated Ritual of Gay Rebel-lion," *Critical Studies in Media Communication* 23, no. 5 (2006): 426–444.

30 Bravo has not since aired any shows like *Boy Meets Boy*, although the reality dating show *Millionaire Matchmaker* (2008–2015) occasionally featured gay clients.

31 Gamson, "The Intersection of Gay Street and Straight Street."

32 Susan Dominus, "The Affluencer," *New York Times Magazine*, November 2, 2008, http://www.nytimes.com/2008/11/02/magazine/02zalaznick-t.html.

33 Sender, "Dualcasting."

34 Sender, *Business, Not Politics*.

35 See Emma Rosenblum, "How Andy Cohen Became Bravo's Face," *New York Magazine*, January 8, 2010, http://nymag.com/arts/tv/features/63010/.

36 Julia Himberg, "Multicasting: Lesbian Programming and the Changing Landscape of Cable TV," *Television & New Media* 15, no. 4 (2014): 289–304.

37 Until the middle of 2010, when it was changed to "by Bravo," such as "Style by Bravo" or "Celebrity by Bravo," depending on the programming. In 2017, another minor rebranding occurred which removed the "by Bravo" tagline from most of Bravo's content. See Elizabeth Wagmeister, "Bravo Unveils New On-Air Look, Logo in Brand Refresh (Exclusive)," *Variety*, February 6, 2017, https://variety.com /2017/tv/news/bravo-new-logo-and-tagline-1201977500/.

38 Quoted in Dominus, "The Affluencer."

39 See Jorie Lagerwey, "Bravo Brand Motherhood: Negotiating the Impossibilities of Postfeminism," in *Postfeminist Celebrity and Motherhood: Brand Mom* (New York: Routledge, 2017), 51–72; Michael J. Lee and Leigh Moscowitz, "The 'Rich Bitch': Class and Gender on the *Real Housewives of New York City*," *Feminist Media Studies* 13, no. 1 (2012): 64–82.

40 In a July 2009 interview with me, Bernard Grenier described this as viewers "identify[ing] with people that they see . . . and in that identification, they're in on the joke . . . laughing not only at the characters on our show but laughing at themselves."

41 *The Real Housewives of New York City* (2008–2011), *The Real Housewives of Atlanta* (2008–present), *The Real Housewives of New Jersey* (2009–present), *The Real Housewives of Beverly Hills* (2008–present), *The Real Housewives of New York City* (2008–2011), *The Real Housewives of DC* (2010), *The Real Housewives of Miami* (2011–2013), *The Real Housewives of Potomac* (2016–2019), and *The Real Housewives of Dallas* (2016–present) air or aired on Bravo. The most successful spin-off series are *Don't Be Tardy* (2012–present), starring Kim Zolciak from the *Atlanta* series, and *Vanderpump Rules* (2013–present), starring Lisa Vanderpump from the *Beverly Hills* series. The longest running international series are *The Real Housewives of Melbourne* (2014–present) in Australia and *The Real Housewives of Cheshire* (2015–present) in the United Kingdom.

42 There are a couple of lesbian characters: on the *Real Housewives of Orange County*, Fernanda Rocha is a lesbian who joined the show in 2011, although not as an official "housewife," and on the *Real Housewives of New Jersey*, Rosie Pierri, one of the housewives' sisters, is a recurring character who is lesbian. Also, on the *New Jersey* series, housewife Danielle Staub was reported to have had a relationship in 2010 with Lori Michaels, an out lesbian.

43 See Jessica Stilwell, "Fans without Pity: Television, Online Communities, and Popular Criticism" (master's thesis, Georgetown University, 2003).

44 In a survey of fifty-nine TWoP lurkers (users who visited regularly without posting) I conducted in 2010, whom I had contacted for follow-up from an earlier study in 2006, 84.2 percent (48) identified as women, of whom 83.3 percent (40) were straight, 10.4 percent (5) were bisexual, and 6.3 percent (3) were lesbian; and 15.8 percent (9) as men, of whom 33.3 percent (3) were gay; no one identified as transgender.

45 Rick, one half of the titular couple, was Filipino American. For the other gay male couple, Evan, partnered with Chuck, was Latino. One of the lesbian couple, Kirsten (partnered with Dana), was Black.

46 As conveyed to me in a personal interview by Logo executive Chris Willey.

47 Annemarie Moody, "Cartoons on the Bay: Pulcinella Awards 2008," *AWN*, April 14, 2008, https://www.awn.com/news/cartoons-bay-pulcinella-awards-2008.

48 See, for example, Christopher Lisotta, "The Golden Girls, Their Timelessness and Their Very Gay Legacy," *Queerty*, April 14, 2016, https://www.queerty.com/the-golden-girls-their-timelessness-and-their-very-gay-legacy-20160414.

49 Aslinger, "Creating a Network for Queer Audiences," 108.

50 Historian Jack Fritscher claims to have coined the term *gaystream*, contrasted with other subcultures such as the "bearstream" and "leatherstream," in an account of gay bear culture; see Jack Fritscher, "Bear Roots Oral History: A Pioneer Maps the Genome of Bear," *JackFritscher.com*, June 20, 2000, https://www.jackfritscher.com/FeatureArticles/Articles/Intro%20Bear%20Book%202.html, para. 46. However, there are earlier usages where "gaystream" instead refers to the more mainstream gay community versus stigmatized communities of gay men who supported sexual relations between men and boys; see Paul Mulshine, "Man-Boy Love," *Heterodoxy* 2, no. 10 (1994): 10–11, formerly up at http://archive.discoverthenetworks.org/Articles/1994%20September%20Vol%202%20No2.pdf, archived at https://web.archive.org/web/20210607162315/http://archive.discoverthenetworks.org/Articles/1994%20September%20Vol%202%20No2.pdf.

51 For example, a 2003 radio interview with hip-hop artists Paradigm (Shante Smalls) and Dutch Boy was headlined "Queer Hip-Hop Musicians Struggle against the Gaystream" (Pedro Angel Serrano, *Radio 4 All*, October 3, 2003, https://www.radio4all.net/index.php/program/7910). In the same vein, a queer activism website proclaimed in 2007 that "we are committed to celebrating our queerest selves while resisting the devastating violence inherent in the consumer driven assimilationist gaystream" (Naughty North, Header box text, http://thenaughtynorth.blogspot.com) and QueerFatFemme.com described the proceeds from a 2009 fundraising event as "go[ing] to help the Femme Family have a 'Love Your Body' themed entry into the NYC Pride Parade—so gaystream and bodyhating, generally" (Bevin Branlandingham, "Femme Pride Week Recap!!" *Queer Fat Femme*, June 10, 2009, http://queerfatfemme.com/2009/06/10/femme-pride-week-recap/).

52 Richard Butsch, "Ralph, Fred, Archie and Homer: Why Television Keeps Recreating the White Male Working-Class Buffoon," in *Gender, Race, and Class in Media: A Critical Reader*, ed. Gail Dines and Jean Humez (Thousand Oaks, CA: Sage, 2003), 575–585.

53 Sender, *Business, Not Politics*, 146.

54 See, for example, Lisa Henderson, "The Class Character of *Boys Don't Cry*," *Screen* 42, no. 3 (2001): 299–303.

55 For a summary, see Ava Parsemain, "Queering and Policing Gender: The Pedagogy of *RuPaul's Drag Race*," in *The Pedagogy of Queer TV* (London: Palgrave, 2019), 95–117.

56 RuPaul is married to a man and has said either he/him or she/her pronouns are acceptable for referring to them.

57 It then moved to Viacom's streaming service Paramount+ in 2021, for season 6.

58 Michael Ciriaco, "Logo's New Programming Slate Reveals Shift away from Gay-centric Shows," *Queerty*, February 21, 2012, http://www.queerty.com/exclusive-logos-new-programming-slate-reveals-shift-away-from-gay-centric-shows-20120221.

59 Headey starred in the lesbian romantic comedy *Imagine Me and You* (Ol Parker, 2005); Julianne Moore was one of the leads in *The Hours* (Stephen Daldry, 2002), where her character was a queer woman married to a man, and starred in *The Kids*

Are All Right (Lisa Cholodenko, 2010) as one half of a lesbian couple, later doing the same in *Freeheld* (Peter Sollett, 2015).

60 AfterElton writer Anthony Langford, who pointed out these examples to me, noted that the draw was that the men involved were "super hot" and had a "really deep intense relationship that might be perceived as if they were in love with each other."

61 San Filippo attributed such coverage to the fact that *American Hustle* was produced by Paramount, owned by AfterEllen's parent company, Viacom. However, *Bridesmaids* was produced by Apatow Productions and Relativity Media and distributed by Universal, and *Horrible Bosses* was a Warner Brothers production. See Maria San Filippo, "Before and after AfterEllen: Online Queer Cinephile Communities as Critical Counterpublics," in *Film Criticism in the Digital Age*, ed. Mattias Frey and Cecilia Sayad (New Brunswick, NJ: Rutgers University Press, 2015), 117–136.

62 See Michael Newman, "New Media, Young Audiences and Discourses of Attention: From *Sesame Street* to 'Snack Culture,'" *Media Culture & Society* 32, no. 4 (2010): 592.

63 See, for example, Marcie, "Pop Theory: Is the 'Cotton Ceiling' Theory All Fluff?" *AfterEllen*, June 11, 2012, formerly up at http://www.afterellen.com/content/2012/06/pop-theory-cotton-ceiling-theory-all-fluff, archived at https://web.archive.org/web/20120613173822/http://www.afterellen.com/content/2012/06/pop-theory-cotton-ceiling-theory-all-fluff; Marcie, "Pop Theory: The Butch in 2012," *AfterEllen*, June 18, 2012, formerly up at http://www.afterellen.com/content/2012/06/pop-theory-butch-2012, archived at https://web.archive.org/web/20120620202205/http://www.afterellen.com/content/2012/06/pop-theory-butch-2012.

64 During the site's tenure, editor in chief Jay Vanasco commented that she was limited by a small staff, or would otherwise have covered more international news as well as LGBTQ topics that did not fall under breaking news.

65 Matthew Bell, "9 Ways to Fall in Love in Prague like 'The Bachelorette,'" *NewNowNext*, June 25, 2012, http://www.newnownext.com/9-ways-to-fall-in-love-in-prague-like-the-bachelorette/06/2012/. *The Bachelorette* took place in Prague in its 2011–2012 season.

66 See Allan Bérubé, "'Queer Work' and Labor History," in *My Desire for History: Essays on Gay, Community, and Labor History*, ed. John D'Emilio and Estelle Freedman (Chapel Hill: University of North Carolina Press, 2011), 259–269.

67 Gayle Rubin, "Thinking Sex: Notes for a Radical Theory of the Politics of Sexuality," in *Pleasure and Danger: Exploring Female Sexuality*, ed. Carole Vance (New York: Routledge, 1984), 267–312.

68 See, for example, Lisa Henderson, "Directorial Intention and Persona in Film School," in *On the Margins of Art Worlds*, ed. Larry Gross (Boulder, CO: Westview, 1995), 149–166.

69 Stephanie Clifford, "We'll Make You a Star (if the Web Agrees)," *New York Times*, June 5, 2010, http://www.nytimes.com/2010/06/06/business/06bravo.html.

70 Willey is referring to episode 7, "My Traditional Korean Mom," of Logo's 2006 *Coming Out Stories* series.

71 She ended up writing about Jasmine Guy, who had directed Ntozake Shange's *For Colored Girls Who Have Considered Suicide When the Rainbow Is Enuf*, a series of twenty poems performed as an experimental play in Atlanta. Normally AfterEllen/AfterElton did not cover theater, especially experimental forms, but this performance starred Nicole Ari Parker and Robin Givens, who were both screen actors of some prominence.

72 Comments during Lisa Sherman's participation on the "Out Trailblazers in Media" panel, New York City, April 1, 2010.

73 Scholars such as Mary Gray and Scott Herring have critiqued the "metronormativity" of queer studies, and presented accounts of LGBTQ communities in the rural United States countering assumptions that cities delimit the possibilities of queer living, while Karen Tongson discussed how the suburbs of Southern California were animated in diverse ways by marginalized communities, including queers of color, immigrants, and the working classes. See Mary Gray, *Out in the Country: Youth, Media, and Queer Visibility in Rural America* (New York: New York University Press, 2009); Scott Herring, *Another Country: Queer Anti-urbanism* (New York: New York University Press, 2010); Karen Tongson, *Relocations: Queer Suburban Imaginaries* (New York: New York University Press, 2011).

74 Eduardo Bonilla-Silva, *Racism without Racists: Color-Blind Racism and the Persistence of Racial Inequality in America* (Lanham, MD: Rowman & Littlefield, 2006).

75 Amin Ghaziani, "Post-gay Collective Identity Construction," *Social Problems* 58, no. 1 (2011): 99–125.

76 See Rosalind Gill, "Postfeminist Media Culture: Elements of a Sensibility," *European Journal of Cultural Studies* 10, no. 2 (2007): 147–166; Mary Vavrus, *Postfeminist News: Political Women in Media Culture* (Albany: State University of New York Press, 2002).

77 See Kent Ono, "Postracism: A Theory of the 'Post-' as Political Strategy," *Communication Inquiry* 34, no. 3 (2010): 227–233.

78 Puar, *Terrorist Assemblages*.

79 See Doty, *Making Things Perfectly Queer*.

80 See Dominus, "The Affluencer."

81 Erin Copple Smith, "'Affluencers' by Bravo: Defining an Audience through Cross-promotion," *Popular Communication* 10, no. 4 (2010): 286–301.

82 After airing on Bravo for five seasons 2004–2008, *Project Runway*'s production company, The Weinstein Company, moved the show to then-rival cable network Lifetime, prompting a lawsuit by Bravo's parent company NBC Universal. However, in 2009, Lifetime ended up partly owned by NBC Universal when A&E Television Networks, which NBC co-owned, acquired Lifetime Entertainment Services. When The Weinstein Company became bankrupt in 2018 (precipitated by multiple charges of sexual misconduct and assault against Harvey Weinstein), NBC Universal reacquired the rights to the show. See Nellie Andreeva, "'Project Runway' to Return to Bravo," *Deadline*, May 14, 2018, https://deadline.com/2018/05/project -runway-return-bravo-lifetime-the-weinstein-co-1202390414/.

83 See Martina Baldwin and Suzanne Leonard, "Bravo: Branding, Fandom, and the Lifestyle Network," in *From Networks to Netflix: A Guide to Changing Channels*, 2nd ed., ed. Derek Johnson (New York: Routledge, 2022), 145–153.

84 Hod Itay, "Logo Chief Chris McCarthy on How the Network Returned to Its Gay Roots: Why Bravo Is Not Competition," *The Wrap*, April 8, 2015, https://www .thewrap.com/logo-chief-chris-mccarthy-on-how-the-network-returned-to-its-gay -roots-why-bravo-is-not-its-competition/.

85 See Mitch Metcalf, "ShowBuzzDaily's Top 25 Monday Cable Originals (& Network Update): 4.13.2015," *ShowBuzzDaily* [April 2015], http://www.showbuzzdaily.com /articles/showbuzzdailys-top-25-monday-cable-originals-4-13-2015.html. *RuPaul's Drag Race* earned a 0.19 rating in the 18–49 demographic (with 340,000 total viewers), while *Cucumber* premiered at only 0.02 in the 18–49 demographic (55,000 total viewers), with *Banana* even lower at 0.006 (24,000 total viewers).

86 See Mitch Metcalf, "Updated with Broadcast: ShowBuzzDaily's Top 150 Thursday Cable Originals & Network Finals: 9.8.2016," *ShowBuzzDaily* [September 2016],

http://www.showbuzzdaily.com/articles/showbuzzdailys-top-150-thursday-cable
-originals-network-finals-9-8-2016.html. The premiere earned 0.07 on Logo and
0.06 on VH1 in the 18–49 demographic, with 158,000 and 184,000 total viewers on
Logo and VH1, respectively.

87 Neither the 1999 nor the 2017 reality shows are related to the 2022 *Fire Island*
scripted romantic comedy, directed by Andrew Ahn and first released on Hulu in
the United States.

88 See Mitch Metcalf, "Updated: ShowBuzzDaily's Top 150 Friday Cable Originals &
Network Finals: 4.21.2017," *ShowBuzzDaily* [April 2017], http://www
.showbuzzdaily.com/articles/showbuzzdailys-top-150-friday-cable-originals
-network-finals-4-21-2017.html.

89 On VH1, this has been led primarily by the move of *RuPaul's Drag Race* from Logo
as well as several *Love and Hip-Hop* series franchises; on MTV, the revival of the
Jersey Shore series in 2017 was a ratings success. McCarthy also promptly canceled
MTV's scripted series for being too expensive, including the drama *Sweet/Vicious*
and the fantasy series *The Shannara Chronicles* (the latter had originally been
renewed for a second season on MTV, but this season ended up airing on Spike
instead before being fully canceled; see Madeline Berg, "The Unlikely Savior behind
MTV's Resurrection," *Forbes*, May 8, 2018, https://www.forbes.com/feature/chris
-mccarthy-mtv-resurrection/#156ad59510df).

90 Jon Lafayette, "Fuse Appoints Leonard Senior VP, Content Strategy," *Next TV*,
July 11, 2016, https://www.nexttv.com/news/fuse-appoints-leonard-senior-vp
-content-strategy-157922.

91 See Dino-Ray Ramos, "Comcast Drops Fuse after a Decade: Channel Exec Calls
Decision Is 'Surprising and Troubling,'" *Deadline*, December 30, 2018, https://
deadline.com/2018/12/comcast-drops-fuse-jennifer-lopez-michael-schwimmer
-1202527319/; Jon Lafayette, "Fuse, Dropped by Comcast, Blasts Operator,"
Multichannel News, December 31, 2018, https://www.multichannel.com/news/fuse
-dropped-by-comcast-blasts-operator.

92 See Ruben Perez Jr., "Fuse Announces Fall 2019 TV Lineup," *Entertainment Rocks*,
August 14, 2019, https://www.entertainmentrocks.com/fuse-announces-fall-2019
-tv-lineup/.

93 Michael Lovelock, *Reality TV and Queer Identities: Sexuality, Authenticity,
Celebrity* (New York: Palgrave Macmillan, 2019), 189.

94 See, for example, Glen Weldon, "New 'Queer Eye' Is a Reboot, Not a Retread,"
NPR, February 7, 2018, https://www.npr.org/2018/02/07/583676372/new-queer-eye
-is-a-reboot-not-a-retread; Laura Prudom, "Queer Eye Season 2: Why Netflix's
Reboot Is TV's Most Inspiring Show," *IGN*, June 15, 2018, https://www.ign.com
/articles/2018/06/15/netflixs-queer-eye-reboot-is-the-ultimate-feel-good-binge.

95 Joe Reid, "ICYMI, Netflix Is Coming to Eat Bravo's Lunch," *Primetimer*,
August 26, 2020, https://www.primetimer.com/features/netflix-is-coming-to-eat
-bravos-lunch.

96 Lotz also noted that not all streaming services follow the conglomerating niches
model: some also focus on genres, such as comedy or horror (e.g., Shudder), specific
types of content, such as wrestling (e.g., the WWE Network), or particular audience
segments, such as young children. See Amanda Lotz, *Portals* (Ann Arbor: Michigan
Publishing, University of Michigan Library, 2017), http://dx.doi.org/10.3998/mpub
.9699689.

97 Julia Himberg, "Revry: Making the Case for LGBTQ Channels," in *From Networks
to Netflix: A Guide to Changing Channels*, 2nd ed., ed. Derek Johnson (New York:

Routledge, 2022), 270. Given that the category is strongly audience defined, LGBTQ programming is perhaps more like a meta-genre (which includes conventional content categories such as action, comedy, drama, horror, etc.) that non-LGBTQ viewers may also seek.

Chapter 4 Beyond Queer Niche

1 The year 2009 was Logo's final year as a sponsor of the festival; the next year, Marc Jacobs took over as presenting sponsor. HBO has been the sole presenting sponsor since 2013; in 2011–2012, HBO and American Airlines were both listed as the largest sponsors.
2 Lesli Klainberg, a documentary film producer and the owner of Orchard Films, took over from Basil Tsiokos in 2008; Tsiokos had overseen NewFest since 1996.
3 Lisa Henderson, "Queer Relay," *GLQ: A Journal of Lesbian and Gay Studies* 14, no. 4 (2008): 569–597.
4 Sarah Thornton, *Club Cultures: Music, Media and Subcultural Capital* (Hanover, NH: University Press of New England, 1996).
5 Pierre Bourdieu, *The Field of Cultural Production: Essays on Art and Literature*, trans. Randal Johnson (New York: Columbia University Press, 1993).
6 Julia Himberg, *The New Gay for Pay: The Sexual Politics of American Television Production* (Austin: University of Texas Press, 2018), 6–7.
7 Hollis Griffin, *Feeling Normal: Sexuality and Media Criticism in the Digital Age* (Bloomington: Indiana University Press, 2016), 14.
8 John Caldwell, *Production Culture: Industrial Reflexivity and Critical Practice in Film and Television* (Durham, NC: Duke University Press, 2008).
9 Joseph Turow, *Breaking Up America: Advertisers and the New Media World* (Chicago: University of Chicago Press, 1997); Joseph Turow, *Niche Envy: Marketing Discrimination in the Digital Age* (Boston: MIT Press, 2006).
10 Ben Aslinger had noted that Logo's airing of such films, which would otherwise only have screened at LGBTQ film festivals at the time, served to "make GLBT cultural labor available" to a national audience of millions; Ben Aslinger, "Creating a Network for Queer Audiences at Logo TV," *Popular Communication* 7, no. 2 (2009): 111.
11 As I spoke to Jensen in 2009, I suspect the show he was referring to was the *Battlestar Galactica* spin-off, *Caprica* (Syfy, 2010), which featured a married gay couple (Sam Adama and his husband, Larry), something that had not been depicted in any earlier U.S.-produced science fiction television series.
12 See Julia Himberg, "Diversity: Under-the-Radar Activism and the Crafting of Sexual Identities," in *The New Gay for Pay: The Sexual Politics of American Television Production* (Austin: University of Texas Press, 2018), 78–105.
13 Indeed, 365gay's own demise in 2011 illustrated the precarious circumstances of LGBTQ news and political commentary websites, several others of which downsized or folded around the same time. See David Badash, "Gay News Sites: Will Your Favorite Still Be There Next Year?" *The New Civil Rights Movement*, September 28, 2011, http://web.archive.org/web/20161221072546/http://www.thenewcivilrightsmovement.com/gay-news-sites-will-your-favorite-still-be-there-next-year/news/2011/09/28/27576/; Bil Browning, "LGBT Media Shrinks Further: 365gay to Close," *Bilerico Project*, September 11, 2011, http://www.bilerico.com/2011/09/lgbt_media_shrinks_further_365gay_to_close.php.
14 Lisa Henderson has discussed the trajectory of a short queer film, *Desert Motel*, and its creators, as showing the complex relationship between mainstream-independent

production. Although negotiations with Logo for distribution did not result in a deal, several crew members ended up working elsewhere in commercial media after completing the film, and some had also come to the *Desert Motel* set already with experience working in commercial media. See Henderson, "Queer Relay," 572.

15 BravoTV was bigger, Viles estimating it having twelve to fifteen regular staff, while Television Without Pity had about five.

16 For example, Logo programming intern Alexandra Albright mentioned the role of interns as a source of internal feedback about possible program acquisitions by watching content and providing their opinions on whether they think it will "fit with the Logo brand." At Bravo, Heather Allison, a programming and development intern, spoke about making contributions to Bravo's creative content not just while they were working at the network, but "when I'm outside of Bravo, I know to notice things that maybe could be for Bravo; when you're looking through the internet, or through the newspaper, or through a magazine, or whatever, or on TV; maybe adapting another networks' program idea maybe into something for Bravo." In that sense, the unpaid labor extended beyond the twenty-hour workweek.

17 Examples that Lotz pointed out include *Ice Road Truckers* (2007–2016) for the History channel and *Jon and Kate Plus 8* (2007–2011) for TLC, both of which were successful ratings-wise but did not clearly brand their networks.

18 Katherine Sender, *Business, Not Politics: The Making of the Gay Market* (New York: Columbia University Press, 2004), 313.

19 Michael Lovelock listed these series as examples of "a queer protagonist, or group of protagonists, attempting to 'make it' within a particular industry, especially fashion or entertainment"; Michael Lovelock, *Reality TV and Queer Identities: Sexuality, Authenticity, Celebrity* (New York: Palgrave Macmillan, 2019), 177.

20 Appearing then as Ellen Page.

21 See Lovelock, *Reality TV and Queer Identities*, 3.

22 Larry Gross, *Up from Invisibility: Lesbians, Gay Men, and the Media in America* (New York: Columbia University Press, 2001); Suzanna Danuta Walters, *All the Rage: The Story of Gay Visibility in America* (Chicago: University of Chicago Press, 2001); Ron Becker, *Gay TV and Straight America* (Piscataway, NJ: Rutgers University Press, 2006).

23 See, for example, Katherine Sender, "Real Worlds: Migrating Genres, Travelling Participants, Shifting Theories," in *The Politics of Reality Television: Global Perspectives*, ed. Marwan Kraidy and Katherine Sender (New York: Columbia University Press, 2012), 1–11; Brenda R. Weber, ed., *Reality Gendervision: Sexuality and Gender on Transatlantic Reality Television* (Durham, NC: Duke University Press, 2014).

24 Katherine Sender, *The Makeover: Reality Television and Reflexive Audiences* (New York: Columbia University Press, 2012), 123–124.

25 Even without reported proof, although occasionally this has come to light, see, for example, Radar Online (2013) for revelations about the *Real Housewives of New Jersey* contracts ("'We Can Fictionalize the Footage!': Secret Bravo Contract Exposes How 'Reality' TV Shows Are REALLY Made," *Radar Online*, September 23, 2013, https://radaronline.com/exclusives/2013/09/real-housewives-new-jersey-secret -bravo-contract-exposes-reality-tv-shows-really-made-documents/).

26 Katherine Sender, "Feeling Real: Empirical Truth and Emotional Authenticity," in *The Makeover: Reality Television and Reflexive Audiences* (New York: Columbia University Press, 2012), 105–135.

27 Lovelock, *Reality TV and Queer Identities*, 192.

28 Dana Heller, "Wrecked: Programming Celesbian Reality," in *Reality Gendervision: Sexuality and Gender on Transatlantic Reality Television*, ed. Brenda R. Weber (Durham, NC: Duke University Press, 2014), 123–146.

29 This 2017 reality show is not related to the eponymous 1999 reality show made by Stephen Fry (the latter aired on Bravo) or to the romantic comedy *Fire Island* (Andrew Ahn, 2022), which was released by Hulu.

30 Brian Moylan, "Introducing the Cast of the 'Gay Housewives of New York,'" *Gawker*, June 2, 2010, https://gawker.com/5552861/meet-the-cast-of-the-gay-housewives -of-new-york, para. 1.

31 Jason Wimberly, "Logo's *Fire Island* Contributes to Gay America's Moral Decline," *Advocate*, March 9, 2017, https://www.advocate.com/commentary/2017/3/09/logos -fire-island-contributes-gay-americas-moral-decline. See also Lovelock, *Reality TV and Queer Identities*, 12–14.

32 See available reports at https://www.glaad.org/whereweareontv19.

33 Michael Ciriaco, "Logo's New Programming Slate Reveals Shift away from Gay-centric Shows," *Queerty*, February 21, 2012, https://www.queerty.com/exclusive-logos -new-programming-slate-reveals-shift-away-from-gay-centric-shows-20120221. lizcivious, comment 64; Peter, comment 79.

34 See Amanda Lotz, *We Now Disrupt This Broadcast: How Cable Transformed Television and the Internet Revolutionized It All* (Boston: MIT Press, 2018). Also, as Lotz notes, some streaming services have also opted to focus only on specific genres (e.g., the WWE Network on wrestling) or audience segments (e.g., Noggin on young children); Amanda Lotz, *Portals* (Ann Arbor: Michigan Publishing, University of Michigan Library, 2017), http://dx.doi.org/10.3998/mpub.9699689.

35 Amanda Lotz notes that while the subscription fee must be combined with paying for internet access, often "internet service and the monthly fee for one or a handful of these services can still be obtained at a lower price than basic cable service." See Lotz, chapter 2, "Implications of Subscriber-Funded Portals" section, *Portals*.

36 From 2009 to 2010, Netflix's subscriber base grew from 12.27 million to just over 20 million, no doubt spurred by the release of the first season of *Orange Is the New Black* in June 2010; growth rates were slower after that, but within five years, the number of U.S. subscribers had doubled (see Mansoor Iqbal, "Netflix Revenue and Usage Statistics [2020]," *Business of Apps*, June 23, 2020, https://www .businessofapps.com/data/netflix-statistics/). Amazon Prime subscribers had been under 5 million until the launch of its Kindle Fire tablet in November 2011, whereupon it experienced a quick increase in subscriber rates, hitting nearly 10 million a year later and reaching 25 million by the end of 2013 (see Todd Bishop, "Inside Amazon Prime's 'Explosive' Growth: 10 Million Members and Profitable," *Geek Wire*, March 12, 2013, https://www.geekwire.com/2013/amazon-prime-10m -members-counting/). Hulu's numbers were much lower, at only about 300,000 at the end of 2010 but reached 10 million by the end of 2015 (see Mariel Soto Reyes, "Hulu Is Rolling Out a Download Option for Ad-Free Subscribers on iOS," *Business Insider*, October 9, 2019, https://www.businessinsider.com/hulu-gives-ad -free-users-content-download-option-2019–10).

37 See Lotz, *We Now Disrupt This Broadcast*; Janet McCabe and Kim Akass, eds., *Quality TV: Contemporary American Television and Beyond* (New York: I. B. Tauris, 2007).

38 Lotz, *Portals*.

39 He was not completely consistent about the boundary between these two domains, saying on the one hand that the subfield of restricted production was "highly

autonomous" (53) while also briefly acknowledging that the actual practices of
cultural production result in texts with mixed characteristics, but by and large, his
model assumes that the two subfields are distinct. See Bourdieu, *The Field of
Cultural Production*.

40 David Hesmondhalgh, "Bourdieu, the Media, and Cultural Production," *Media,
Culture & Society* 28, no. 2 (2006): 223.

41 Michael Wallenstein, "Netflix Series Spending Revealed," *Variety*, March 8, 2013,
https://variety.com/2013/digital/news/caa-agent-discloses-netflix-series-spending
-1200006100/.

42 "Art for Art's Sake," characterized by high symbolic capital and low economic
capital, with a small, "intellectual audience"; "Bohemia," characterized by low
symbolic capital and low economic capital, with "no audience"; "Bourgeois Art,"
characterized by moderate symbolic capital and moderately high economic
capital, with moderate numbers of "bourgeois audience"; and "Industrial Art,"
characterized by low symbolic capital and high economic capital, with a large
"mass audience."

43 An earlier version of this diagram appeared in Eve Ng, "Contesting the Queer
Subfield of Cultural Production: Paratextual Framings of *Carol* and *Freeheld*,"
Journal of Film and Video 70 (Fall/Winter 2018): 8–23.

44 Aymar Jean Christian, "Open TV Production," in *Open TV: Innovation beyond
Hollywood and the Rise of Web Television* (New York: New York University Press,
2018), 59–100; see also "Open TV Distribution," 156–211.

45 See Nellie Andreeva, "Ryan Murphy Inks Giant Deal with Netflix," *Deadline*,
February 13, 2018, https://deadline.com/2018/02/ryan-murphy-giant-overall-deal
-with-netflix-1202287851/.

46 Lesley Goldberg, "Lena Waithe Moves Overall Deal from Showtime to Amazon,"
Hollywood Reporter, July 27, 2019, https://www.hollywoodreporter.com/live-feed
/lena-waithe-moves-deal-showtime-amazon-1227446. Waithe was an executive
producer on Amazon's 2021 series *Them*, and then moved to HBO Max in November 2021 (see Kim Masters, "Inside Amazon Studios: Big Swings Hampered by
Confusion and Frustration," *The Hollywood Reporter*, April 3, 2023, https://www
.hollywoodreporter.com/business/business-news/inside-amazon-studios-jen-salke
-vision-shows-1235364913/).

47 Aymar Jean Christian, "Beyond Branding: The Value of Intersectionality on
Streaming TV Channels," *Television & New Media* 21, no. 5 (2020): 459. See also
Aymar Jean Christian, *Open TV: Innovation beyond Hollywood and the Rise of Web
Television* (New York: New York University Press, 2018).

48 Christian, "Beyond Branding," 459.

49 Brennan Carley, "HBO's Stories—and Storytellers—Are Setting the Standard for
Inclusive, LGBTQ+ Friendly Television," *Esquire*, June 30, 2020, https://www
.esquire.com/entertainment/tv/a33001811/hbo-lgbtq-shows-creators-inclusivity-we
-re-here-betty-interview-history/, para. 16. Other HBO series with strong LGBTQ
content mentioned by Carley include *Euphoria* (2019–), which has a trans woman
and a woman of color as lead characters and the central romantic pairing, *Los Espookys*
(2019–2022), with a cast of Latino characters that include a gay man, and *A Black
Lady Sketch Show* (2019–present), which features multiple queer Black women
characters.

50 See Kit Williamson, "'How I Sold My Web Series to Netflix': The Director of
'EastSiders' Explains His Secret," *IndieWire*, July 1, 2016, https://www.indiewire
.com/2016/07/eastsiders-lgbt-web-series-sold-netflix-kit-williamson-1201701822/.

51 See Tiona McClodden, "Artist Statement," *TionaM.com*, n.d., https://www.tionam
.com/artiststatement; David Murrell, "Experimental Filmmaker Tiona Nekkia
McClodden Doesn't Care if You Miss the Point," *Philadelphia Magazine*, July 6,
2019, https://www.phillymag.com/news/2019/07/06/tiona-nekkia-mcclodden/.

52 For descriptions of some of this content, see Hollis Griffin, *Feeling Normal:
Sexuality and Media Criticism in the Digital Age* (Bloomington: Indiana University
Press, 2016), 86–87, 88–89.

53 Mikelle Street, "Groundbreaking *Noah's Arc* Is Back Tonight for Special 'Rona'
Reunion," *Advocate*, July 5, 2020, https://www.advocate.com/television/2020/7/05
/noahs-arc-back-tonight-special-rona-reunion-episode.

Conclusion

1 As of 2022, there have been four versions: the first film, *Invasion of the Body
Snatchers* (Don Siegel, 1956); the first remake, *Invasion of the Body Snatchers* (Philip
Kaufman, 1978), with Donald Sutherland, then *Body Snatchers* (Abel Ferrara, 1993) and
The Invasion (Oliver Hirschbiegel and James McTeigue, 2007) with Nicole Kidman.

2 Eve Ng, "Rebranding Gay: New Configurations of Digital Media and Commercial
Culture" (PhD diss., University of Massachusetts, 2013), https://scholarworks
.umass.edu/dissertations/AAI3589112/, 312.

3 Although LGBTQ representation in U.S. media has improved in quantity and
quality over the last few decades, there have been other periods of partial regression,
such as various negative depictions of gay men during the AIDS epidemic; see, for
example, Larry Gross, *Up from Invisibility: Lesbians, Gay Men, and the Media in
America* (New York: Columbia University Press, 2001).

4 Production in Canada was allowed to resume on a province-by-province basis in
mid-2020, including in June in British Columbia, where many U.S. series now film
(see Jackson Weaver, "'Depopulating the Set': How Canada's Film Industry Is
Navigating COVID-19," *CBC News*, June 13, 2020, https://www.cbc.ca/news
/entertainment/film-industry-covid-1.5610613). In the United States, production
was permitted to resume in California on June 12 and in New York City on July 20,
2020 (see Vulture Editors, "All the Live Events, Movie Releases, and Productions
Affected by the Coronavirus," *Vulture*, September 11, 2020, https://www.vulture
.com/2020/09/events-cancelled-coronavirus.html).

5 See Mark Kennedy, "Pandemic Eats into LGBTQ Representation on Network TV,
Study Shows," *PBS*, January 15, 2021, https://www.pbs.org/newshour/arts/pandemic
-eats-into-lgbtq-representation-on-network-tv-study-shows.

6 Nellie Andreeva, "'The Handmaid's Tale' Also Suspends Production over Coronavirus," *Deadline*, March 15, 2020, https://deadline.com/2020/03/the-handmaids
-tale-shuts-down-production-coronavirus-1202883760/; Editor, "Screen: *Gentleman
Jack* Series Two Production Postponed," *Diva*, March 20, 2020, https://divamag.co
.uk/2020/03/20/screen-gentleman-jack-series-two-production-postponed/; Nellie
Andreeva, "'The Society' & 'I Am Not Okay with This' Canceled by Netflix due to
COVID-Related Circumstances," *Deadline*, August 21, 2020, https://deadline.com
/2020/08/the-society-i-am-not-okay-with-this-canceled-netflix-covid-related-no
-season-2-1203020036/; Samuel Spencer, "'Stumptown' Canceled: Why the Show Is
Ending despite Season 2 Renewal," *Newsweek*, September 17, 2020, https://www
.newsweek.com/stumptown-canceled-season-2-cancelled-abc-1532553.

7 See, for example, Reid Nakamura, "'RuPaul's Drag Race' EP on Adapting to
COVID and Evolving the Show with the Times," *The Wrap*, June 4, 2021,

https://www.thewrap.com/rupauls-drag-racc-cp-on-adapting-to-covid-and
-evolving-the-show-with-the-times/.

8 For the United States, see Graeme Bruce, "Who's Winning the COVID-19
Streaming Wars?" *YouGov*, May 26, 2020, https://today.yougov.com/topics/media
/articles-reports/2020/05/26/covid-streaming; Amy Watson, "Increased Viewership
of Major Streaming Services in the Last Month due to the Coronavirus Outbreak in
the United States as of March 2020," *Statistica*, June 18, 2020, https://www.statista
.com/statistics/1107238/svod-consumption-increase-coronavirus-us/. There was a
"pandemic bounce" in visits to pirate television and film sites as well; see Karl Bode,
"Movie and TV Piracy Sees an 'Unprecedented' Spike during Quarantine," *Vice*,
April 27, 2020, https://www.vice.com/en_us/article/5dm7xb/movie-and-tv-piracy
-sees-an-unprecedented-spike-during-quarantine.

9 See Adrian Pennington, "The State of OTT 2022," *Streaming Media*, March 26,
2022, https://www.streamingmedia.com/Articles/Editorial/Featured-Articles/
The-State-of-OTT-2022-152085.aspx.

10 See, for example, Jennifer Maas, "Netflix Loses 200,000 Subscribers in Q1, Predicts
Loss of 2 Million More in Q2," *Variety*, April 19, 2022, https://variety.com/2022/tv
/news/netflix-loses-subscribers-q1-earnings-1235234858/.

11 See, for example, "Netflix Adds More Than 7 Million Subscribers in Q4, Smashing
Previous Target," *Variety*, January 19, 2023, https://variety.com/2023/tv/news
/netflix-subscribers-earnings-q4-2022-1235493532/.

12 These are also available, like premium cable networks, as add-ons to digital
platforms such as Apple TV (Revry), Amazon Prime (Revry), Hulu (Here TV), and
paid YouTube accounts (Here TV).

13 In the United States, the average number of services subscribed to increased from
3.9 in December 2020 to 4.5 in June 2021. See Pennington, "The State of OTT
2022," para. 13.

14 Aymar Jean Christian, "The Pandemic Clears Media Pollution and Queers the
Ecosystem," *QED* 7, no. 3 (2020): 135.

15 See Lesley Goldberg, "Broadcast Pilot Season by the Numbers: Total Volume Hits a
New Low," *Hollywood Reporter*, March 9, 2022. https://www.hollywoodreporter
.com/tv/tv-news/broadcast-pilot-season-total-volume-low-1235108089/; John
Koblin, "Streaming's Golden Age Is Suddenly Dimming," *New York Times*,
December 18, 2022, https://www.nytimes.com/2022/12/18/business/media
/streaming-tv-shows-canceled.html.

16 See, for example, Alex Cranz, "The Golden Age of the Streaming Wars Has Ended,"
The Verge, December 14, 2022, https://www.theverge.com/2022/12/14/23507793
/streaming-wars-hbo-max-netflix-ads-residuals-warrior-nun. The 2018 cancelation
of lesbian writer and actor Tig Notaro's Prime Video comedy *One Mississippi* when
Amazon moved to seek "bigger, wider-audience series" was an earlier example of
this; see Dominic Patten and Nellie Andreeva, "'One Mississippi,' 'I Love Dick' &
'Jean-Claude Van Johnson' Canceled by Amazon," *Deadline*, January 18, 2018,
https://deadline.com/2018/01/one-mississippi-i-love-dick-jean-claude-van-johnson
-canceled-amazon-1202245153/, para. 3.

17 The company also faced the end of a lucrative deal with Netflix, which had also
helped make the production of low-rated series for the CW profitable for many
years. See Lesley Goldberg, "Mad about the CW Cancellations? Blame Streaming,
but Also Its Unusual Corporate Structure," *Hollywood Reporter*, May 13, 2022,
https://www.hollywoodreporter.com/tv/tv-news/the-cw-cancellations-blame
-streaming-but-also-its-unusual-corporate-structure-1235146038/.

18 Adrian Pennington noted that "27% of 2020's most popular [television series] titles"
in the United States came from outside the United States, "up from 17% in 2019."
See Pennington, "The State of OTT 2022,"

19 *2gether: The Series* is adapted from the novel *Because We . . . Belong Together* by
JittiRain, originally posted in serialized form online in 2019 by the author. *The
Untamed* is adapted from the novel *Grandmaster of Demonic Cultivation* (Chinese
魔道祖师 *Mó Dào Zǔ Shī*) by Mo Xiang Tong Xiu, originally posted to the Jinjiang
Literature City website in serialized form in 2015–2016. *Heaven Official's Blessing* is
adapted from the novel of the same name (Chinese 天官赐福 *Tiān Guān Cì Fú*) also
by Mo Xiang Tong Xiu and posted to Jinjiang Literature City in 2017. *Word of
Honor* is adapted from the novel *Faraway Wanderers* (Chinese 天涯客 *Tiānyá Kè*)
by Priest, originally posted to Jinjiang Literature City in 2010. Although the
adapted Chinese series, called *dangai*, desexualize the relationship between the two
male lead characters to comply with government censorship regulations, subtextually queer readings remain available to viewers; see, for example, Eve Ng and
Xiaomeng Li, "A Queer 'Socialist Brotherhood': *The Guardian* Web Series, Boys
Love Fandom, and the Mainland Chinese State," *Feminist Media Studies* 20,
no. 4 (2020): 479–495. In Thai BL series, the romantic/sexual character of the
relationships are clear.

20 Katherine Sender, "Real Worlds: Migrating Genres, Travelling Participants, Shifting
Theories," in *The Politics of Reality Television: Global Perspectives*, ed. Marwan Kraidy
and Katherine Sender (New York: Columbia University Press, 2012), 6.

21 See, for example, Kathryn Bromwich, "Fierce Competition: How a Brit Makeover
Saved *RuPaul's Drag Race*," *The Guardian*, November 22, 2019, https://www
.theguardian.com/culture/2019/nov/22/fierce-competition-how-a-brit-makeover
-saved-rupauls-drag-race; Sam Damshenas, "Here's How Viewers Reacted to the
First Episode of *Canada's Drag Race*," *Gay Times*, n.d. [probably July 3, 2020],
http://gaytimes.co.uk/culture/heres-how-viewers-reacted-to-the-first-episode-of
-canadas-drag-race/; Brett White, "Stream It or Skip It: 'Drag Race Holland' on
WOW Presents Plus, a Dutch Twist on a Winning Formula," *Decider*, September 17, 2020, https://decider.com/2020/09/17/drag-race-holland-on-wow-presents
-plus-stream-it-or-skip-it/.

22 See, for example, Emira Ben Amara, "The American Version of *Skam* Is Now
Out—Here's Why Countries Are Recreating the Show," *Affinity*, May 14, 2018,
http://culture.affinitymagazine.us/the-american-version-of-skam-is-finally-out
-heres-why-countries-are-replicatingteen-drama/.

23 Julia Himberg, "Revry: Making the Case for LGBTQ Channels," in *From Networks
to Netflix: A Guide to Changing Channels*, 2nd ed., ed. Derek Johnson (New York:
Routledge, 2022), 269–278.

24 "FAQ," *Revry.tv*, n.d., https://www.revry.tv/support, para. 7. Revry also has a page
for users to send their content for consideration, although it is unclear how much
user-submitted material makes it onto Revry's programming.

25 The U.S.-produced lesbian talk show *Cherry Bomb* was first hosted at AfterEllen,
which limited access to U.S. IP addresses, and then on rival site SheWired, where it
was accessible to viewers globally, though not actively marketed as such. Creator and
presenter Dalila Ali Rajah explained that the show was recorded in high enough
resolution for regular television, and five seasons aired on the Canadian channel
OutTV until 2012.

26 Hongwei Bao, "The Queer Global South: Transnational Video Activism between
China and Africa," *Global Media and China* 5, no. 3 (2020): 297–298.

27 Their study found that each of the services had distinct practices regarding the payment of up-front fees or revenue sharing once content was made available, and it was in part dependent on industry norms around film versus television series, as well as context-specific conditions such as the television industry in Israel. See Michael L. Wayne and Matt Sienkiewicz, "'We Don't Aspire to Be Netflix': Understanding Content Acquisition Practices among Niche Streaming Services," *Television & New Media* 24, no. 3 (2023): 298–315.

28 See, for example, Spencer Kornhaber, "The Coronavirus Is Testing Queer Culture," *The Atlantic*, June 10, 2020, https://www.theatlantic.com/culture/archive/2020/06/how-quarantine-reshaping-queer-nightlife/612865/; Stacy Lambe, "Pride 2020: A Guide to Virtual Events and Ways to Donate during the Pandemic," *ET*, June 25, 2020, https://www.etonline.com/pride-2020-a-guide-to-virtual-events-and-ways-to-donate-during-the-pandemic-147389. Although some early reports suggested that young queer people forced to stay at home faced additional mental health challenges, some more recent research has suggested that those who had sufficient access to online community could also take advantage of that time; see, for example, Benjamin Hanckel and Shiva Chandra, *Social Media Insights from Sexuality and Gender Diverse Young People during COVID-19* (Sydney: Young and Resilient Research Centre, University of Sydney, 2021), https://www.westernsydney.edu.au/__data/assets/pdf_file/0006/1837896/SocialMedia_LGBTQIA_YPReport_Final.pdf.

29 See Bil Browning, "Human Rights Campaign Lays Off Staff after Fundraising Drops due to Coronavirus Pandemic," *LGBTQ Nation*, April 29, 2020, https://www.lgbtqnation.com/2020/04/human-rights-campaign-slashes-staff-fundraising-craters-due-coronavirus-pandemic/.

30 Nicole Hall, "Yes, Fundraising Is Part of Our Business Model: Here's Why," *Autostraddle*, August 6, 2020, https://www.autostraddle.com/yes-fundraising-is-part-of-our-business-model-heres-why/. In contrast, the major online platforms experienced increases in advertising revenue; see, for example, Megan Graham, "Facebook, Google and Amazon Are Reaping the Benefits from Advertising's Pandemic Hot Streak," *CNBC*, April 21, 2021, https://www.cnbc.com/2021/04/21/facebook-google-and-amazon-are-reaping-the-benefits-from-advertisings-pandemic-hot-streak.html.

31 See Nico Hall, "Yes, Fundraising Is Part of Our Business Model: Here's Why," *Autostraddle*, March 15, 2023, https://www.autostraddle.com/yes-fundraising-is-part-of-our-business-model-heres-why/.

32 Marina Levina, "Queering Intimacy, Six Feet Apart," *QED* 7, no. 3 (2020): 199.

33 See staff profiles for Chris McCarthy, president of Logo and VH1, at https://press.logotv.com/executives/chris-mccarthy; Pamela Post, senior vice president of original programming and series development, at https://press.logotv.com/executives/pamela-post; and Kate Keough, senior vice president, consumer marketing for VH1 and Logo, at https://press.logotv.com/executives/kate-keough.

34 See Nellie Andreeva, "NBCU Lifestyle Group Integrates E! with Bravo, Triggering Layoffs, E!'s Betsy Slenzak Heads to Peacock," *Deadline*, September 19, 2019, https://deadline.com/2019/09/nbcu-lifestyle-group-executive-leadership-structure-combines-bravo-e-development-promotes-five-1202738669; Lesley Goldberg, "Frances Berwick Sets Senior Leadership Team at NBCUniversal," *Hollywood Reporter*, September 16, 2020, https://www.hollywoodreporter.com/live-feed/frances-berwick-sets-senior-leadership-team-at-nbcuniversal.

35 Damian Pelliccione et al., "An Interview with Revry Co-founder & CEO Damian Pelliccione," *LGBT Token*, n.d., https://lgbt-token.org/an-interview-with-revry-co -founder-ceo-damian-pelliccione/.

36 Aymar Jean Christian and Khadijah Costley White, "Organic Representation as Cultural Reparation," *Journal of Cinema and Media Studies* 60, no. 1 (2020): 137–138, 139.

37 Media and Data Equity Lab, https://www.madelab.org/.

38 Julia Himberg, "Conclusion: The Personal Is Still Political (and Profitable)," in *The New Gay for Pay: The Sexual Politics of American Television Production* (Austin: University of Texas Press, 2018), 129–138.

39 See, for example, the following ACLU map of anti-LGBTQ bills: "Mapping Attacks on LGBTQ Rights in U.S. State Legislatures," *ACLU*, last updated March 14, 2023, https://www.aclu.org/legislative-attacks-on-lgbtq-rights.

40 See, for example, Emily Waters, for the National Coalition of Anti-violence Programs, *Lesbian, Gay, Bisexual, Transgender, Queer, and HIV-Affected Hate Violence in 2016* (New York: New York City Anti-violence Project, 2017), http://avp .org/wp-content/uploads/2017/06/NCAVP_2016HateViolence_REPORT.pdf.

41 The festival had stated that it was "intended for womyn who at birth were deemed female, who were raised as girls, and who identify as womyn," thus allowing attendance by cis girls and cis women, as well as boys aged twelve and under (see statement by organizer Lisa Vogel, "Letter to the Community," *Michigan Womyn's Music Festival*, April 11, 2013, originally at http://michfest.com/letter-to-the -community-4_11_13/, archived at https://web.archive.org/web/20150330195141 /http://michfest.com/letter-to-the-community-4_11_13/). Due to this, the festival had been the target of trans rights protests for several years prior to its closure.

42 Mary O'Hara, "AfterEllen Was a Refuge for All Queer Women—until It Wasn't," *Out*, February 13, 2019, https://www.out.com/news-opinion/2019/2/13/afterellen -was-refuge-all-queer-women-until-it-wasn't.

43 See, for example, Andre Cavalcante, *Struggling for Ordinary: Media and Transgen- der Belonging in Everyday Life* (New York: New York University Press, 2018).

44 For a discussion of transphobic and/or cisgenderist commentary by prominent cis women, including the lesbian tennis player Martina Navratilova, see Gabriel Knott-Fayle, Elizabeth Peel, and Gemma L. Witcomb, "(Anti-)feminism and Cisgenderism in Sports Media," *Feminist Media Studies* (2021), https://doi.org/10 .1080/14680777.2021.1992644.

45 Writing about the 2000s, Kevin Barnhurst noted that increased media coverage in the United States about LGBTQ rights, such as that associated with Supreme Court rulings, was associated with a spike in hate crimes on the basis of sexual orientation, another grim set of evidence that the attainment of recognition for queers often comes at a cost; Kevin Barnhurst, "Visibility as Paradox: Representa- tion and Simultaneous Contrast," in *Media/Queered: Visibility and Its Discontents*, ed. Kevin Barnhurst (New York: Peter Lang, 2007), 16.

46 Editors and/or founders of the magazines *Curve* and *Diva*, the Canadian Lez Spread the Word organization producing media content for queer women, as well as websites Autostraddle, DapperQ, and Tagg Magazine, jointly published an open letter condemning "writers and editors who seek to foster division and hate within the LGBTQI community with trans misogynistic content, and who believe 'lesbian' is an identity for them alone to define" (see Ella Braidwood, "Lesbian Publications Condemn 'Vitriolic Attacks' on Trans Women," *Pink News*, December 19, 2018, https://www.pinknews.co.uk/2018/12/19/lesbian-publications-transphobia-letter/).

47 Justice Clarence Thomas wrote in his concurring opinion that "we should reconsider all of this Court's substantive due process precedents, including *Griswold*,
Lawrence, and *Obergefell*." *Lawrence v. Texas* (2003) established the right to
consensual sex between adults, including those of the same sex; *Obergefell v. Hodges*
(2015) established the right for two adults of the same sex to marry. See *Dobbs v.
Jackson* (2022), *U.S. Supreme Court*, https://www.supremecourt.gov/opinions/21pdf
/19-1392_6j37.pdf, 3.

48 See, for example, Pen America, "The 10 Most Banned Books of the 2021-2022
School Year," *Pen America*, December 21, 2022, https://pen.org/banned-books-list
-2022/.

49 See, for example, Trip Gabriel and Dana Goldstein, "Disputing Racism's Reach,
Republicans Rattle American Schools," *New York Times*, June 1, 2021, https://www
.nytimes.com/2021/06/01/us/politics/critical-race-theory.html.

50 For example, Arkansas Republican senator Tom Cotton proposed a "Stop CRT
Act" passed by the U.S. Senate in 2021, arguing that critical race theory is "un-
American" and "racist" (against white people); see Matthew Miller, "Senate Passes
Cotton's Amendment Preventing Federal Funding of Critical Race Theory,"
Washington Examiner, August 11, 2021, https://www.washingtonexaminer.com
/news/senate-passes-cotton-amendment-preventing-federal-funding-critical-race
-theory.

51 See Xiaomeng Li, "'I Feel like a "Cyber-gypsy"': BL Fanfiction Writers in China's
Changing Landscape of Fandom Culture," *Journal of Popular Culture* 56, no. 2
(2023 forthcoming). Such government actions have been interspersed with official
praise for various Chinese BL series in nationalist terms that downplay the queer
origins of the series; see Eve Ng and Xiaomeng Li, "Brand Nohomonationalism:
Chinese State *Guofeng* ('National Style') Framings of Boys Love Television Series,"
Asian Studies Review (2022 advance online publication), https://doi.org/10.1080
/10357823.2022.2142933.

52 See also, for example, Charlie Yi Zhang, "Queering the National Body of Contemporary China," *Frontiers* 37, no. 2 (2016): 1–26.

Bibliography

ACLU. "Legislation Affecting LGBTQ Rights across the Country." *ACLU*, December 17, 2021. https://www.aclu.org/legislation-affecting-lgbt-rights-across-country.

Adorno, Theodor, and Max Horkheimer. *Dialectic of Enlightenment*. Translated by John Cumming. New York: Herder and Herder, 1972.

Advocate. "OurChart.com Pulls the Plug." *Advocate*, November 22, 2008. https://www.advocate.com/news/2008/11/22/ourchartcom-pulls-plug.

Afierra. "When It Comes to Kara and Lena, the 'Supergirl' Writers Say One Thing and Do Another." *Hypable*, October 25, 2019. https://www.hypable.com/kara-lena-supergirl-season-2/.

Allen, Samantha. "AfterEllen Is Shutting Down: Is This the End of Lesbian Media?" *Daily Beast*, September 22, 2016. https://www.thedailybeast.com/afterellen-is-shutting-down-is-this-the-end-of-lesbian-media.

Amara, Emira Ben. "The American Version of *Skam* Is Now Out—Here's Why Countries Are Recreating the Show." *Affinity*, May 14, 2018. http://culture.affinitymagazine.us/the-american-version-of-skam-is-finally-out-heres-why-countries-are-replicatingteen-drama/.

Andreeva, Nellie. "NBCU Lifestyle Group Integrates E! with Bravo, Triggering Layoffs, E!'s Betsy Slenzak Heads to Peacock." *Deadline*, September 19, 2019. https://deadline.com/2019/09/nbcu-lifestyle-group-executive-leadership-structure-combines-bravo-e-development-promotes-five-1202738669.

———. "'Project Runway' to Return to Bravo." *Deadline*, May 14, 2018. https://deadline.com/2018/05/project-runway-return-bravo-lifetime-the-weinstein-co-1202390414/.

———. "Ryan Murphy Inks Giant Deal with Netflix." *Deadline*, February 13, 2018. https://deadline.com/2018/02/ryan-murphy-giant-overall-deal-with-netflix-1202287851/.

———. "'The Handmaid's Tale' Also Suspends Production over Coronavirus." *Deadline*, March 15, 2020. https://deadline.com/2020/03/the-handmaids-tale-shuts-down-production-coronavirus-1202883760/.

———. "'The Society' & 'I Am Not Okay with This' Canceled by Netflix due to COVID-Related Circumstances." *Deadline*, August 21, 2020. https://deadline.com/2020/08/the-society-i-am-not-okay-with-this-canceled-netflix-covid-related-no-season-2-1203020036/.

Anne, Valerie. "Exclusive: 'The 100' EP Jason Rothenberg on This Week's Game-Changing Episode, 'Thirteen.'" *AfterEllen*, March 2, 2016. https://www.afterellen.com/tv/476855 -exclusive-100-ep-jason-rothenberg-weeks-game-changing-episode-thirteen.

Anselmo, Diana. "Gender and Queer Fan Labor on Tumblr: The Case of BBC's *Sherlock*." *Feminist Media Histories* 4, no. 1 (2018): 84–114. https://doi.org/10.1525/ fmh.2018.4.1.84.

Arcy, Jacquelyn. "The Digital Money Shot: Twitter Wars, *The Real Housewives*, and Transmedia Storytelling." *Celebrity Studies* 9, no. 4 (2018): 487–502. https://doi.org /10.1080/19392397.2018.1508951.

Aslinger, Ben. "Creating a Network for Queer Audiences at Logo TV." *Popular Communication* 7, no. 2 (2009): 107–121. https://doi.org/10.1080/15405700902776495.

———. "PlanetOut and the Dichotomies of Queer Media Conglomeration." In *LGBT Identity and Online New Media*, edited by Christopher Pullen and Margaret Cooper, 113–124. New York: Routledge, 2010.

Bacon-Smith, Camille. *Enterprising Women: Television Fandom and the Creation of Popular Myth*. Philadelphia: University of Pennsylvania Press, 1992.

Badash, David. "Gay News Sites: Will Your Favorite Still Be There Next Year?" *New Civil Rights Movement*, September 28, 2011. http://web.archive.org/web/2016122 1072546/http://www.thenewcivilrightsmovement.com/gay-news-sites-will-your -favorite-still-be-there-next-year/news/2011/09/28/27576/.

Bagdikian, Ben. *The New Media Monopoly*. Boston: Beacon, 2004.

Baim, Tracy, ed. *Gay Press, Gay Power: The Growth of LGBT Community Newspapers in America*. Scotts Valley, CA: CreateSpace, 2012.

Baldwin, Martina, and Suzanne Leonard. "Bravo: Branding, Fandom, and the Lifestyle Network." In *From Networks to Netflix: A Guide to Changing Channels*, 2nd ed., edited by Derek Johnson, 145–153. New York: Routledge, 2022.

Bao, Hongwei. "The Queer Global South: Transnational Video Activism between China and Africa." *Global Media and China* 5, no. 3 (2020): 294–318. https://doi.org /10.1177/2059436420949985.

Barnhurst, Kevin. "Visibility as Paradox: Representation and Simultaneous Contrast." In *Media/Queered: Visibility and Its Discontents*, edited by Kevin Barnhurst, 1–20. New York: Peter Lang, 2007.

Battles, Kathleen, and Wendy Hilton-Morrow. "Gay Characters in Conventional Spaces: *Will and Grace* and the Situation Comedy Genre." *Critical Studies in Media Communication* 19, no. 1 (2002): 87–105. https://doi.org/10.1080/07393180216553.

Baym, Nancy. *Tune In, Log On: Soaps, Fandom and Online Community*. London: Sage, 2000.

Becker, Howard. *Art Worlds*. Berkeley: University of California Press, 1982.

Becker, Ron. *Gay TV and Straight America*. Piscataway, NJ: Rutgers University Press, 2006.

Bell, Matthew. "9 Ways to Fall in Love in Prague like *The Bachelorette*." *NewNowNext*, June 25, 2012. http://www.newnownext.com/9-ways-to-fall-in-love-in-prague-like -the-bachelorette/06/2012/.

Bendix, Trish. "Does LGBT Media Have a Future?" *BuzzFeed*, January 25, 2019. https://www.buzzfeednews.com/article/trishbendix/future-of-lgbt-media-out -advocate-autostraddle-into-grindr.

Berg, Madeline. "The Unlikely Savior behind MTV's Resurrection." *Forbes*, May 8, 2018. https://www.forbes.com/feature/chris-mccarthy-mtv-resurrection /#156ad59510df.

Berila, Beth, and Devika Choudhuri. "Metrosexuality the Middle Class Way: Exploring Race, Class, and Gender in *Queer Eye for the Straight Guy*." *Genders* 42 (2005).

https://www.colorado.edu/gendersarchive1998-2013/2005/08/05/metrosexuality
-middle-class-way-exploring-race-class-and-gender-queer-eye-straight-guy.

Bérubé, Allan. "'Queer Work' and Labor History." In *My Desire for History: Essays on Gay, Community, and Labor History*, edited by John D'Emilio and Estelle Freedman, 259–269. Chapel Hill: University of North Carolina Press, 2011.

Bianco, Marcie. "Lesbian Culture Is Being Erased because Investors Think Only Gay Men (and Straight People) Have Money." *Quartz*, October 6, 2016. https://qz.com /801501/afterellen-closing-lesbian-culture-is-being-erased-because-investors-think -only-gay-men-have-money/.

Bilerico Project. "About Us." *Bilerico Project*, September 22, 2007. http://bilerico .lgbtqnation.com/about/.

Bird, Elizabeth. *The Audience in Everyday Life: Living in a Media World*. New York: Routledge, 2003.

Bishop, Todd. "Inside Amazon Prime's 'Explosive' Growth: 10 Million Members and Profitable." *Geek Wire*, March 12, 2013. https://www.geekwire.com/2013/amazon -prime-10m-members-counting/.

Blevins, Jeffrey. "Source Diversity after the Telecommunications Act of 1996: Media Oligarchs Begin to Colonize Cyberspace." *Television & New Media* 3, no. 1 (2002): 95–112. https://doi.org/10.1177/152747640200300106.

Bode, Karl. "Movie and TV Piracy Sees an 'Unprecedented' Spike during Quarantine." *Vice*, April 27, 2020. https://www.vice.com/en_us/article/5dm7xb/movie-and-tv -piracy-sees-an-unprecedented-spike-during-quarantine.

Bollinger, Alex. "YouTubers Say They Have Proof That the Platform Blocks LGBTQ Content." *LGBTQ Nation*, October 1, 2019. https://www.lgbtqnation.com/2019/10 /youtubers-say-proof-platform-blocks-lgbtq-content/.

Bonilla-Silva, Eduardo. *Racism without Racists: Color-Blind Racism and the Persistence of Racial Inequality in America*. Lanham, MD: Rowman & Littlefield, 2006.

Bore, Inger-Lise K., and Jonathan Hickman. "Continuing *The West Wing* in 140 Characters or Less: Improvised Simulation on Twitter." *Journal of Fandom Studies* 1, no. 2 (2013): 219–238. https://doi.org/10.1386/jfs.1.2.219_1.

Bourdieu, Pierre. *On Television*. Translated by Priscilla Parkhurst Ferguson. New York: New Press, 1998.

———. *The Field of Cultural Production: Essays on Art and Literature*. Translated by Randal Johnson. New York: Columbia University Press, 1993.

Braidwood, Ella. "Lesbian Publications Condemn 'Vitriolic Attacks' on Trans Women." *Pink News*, December 19, 2018. https://www.pinknews.co.uk/2018/12/19/lesbian -publications-transphobia-letter/.

Branlandingham, Bevin. "Femme Pride Week Recap!!" *Queer Fat Femme*, June 10, 2009. http://queerfatfemme.com/2009/06/10/femme-pride-week-recap/.

Bravo. "The Bravo Affluencer Effect." *Bravo* (2008). Formerly up at http://www.affluencers .com.

Bromwich, Kathryn. "Fierce Competition: How a Brit Makeover Saved *RuPaul's Drag Race*." *The Guardian*, November 22, 2019. https://www.theguardian.com/culture /2019/nov/22/fierce-competition-how-a-brit-makeover-saved-rupauls-drag-race.

Browning, Bil. "Human Rights Campaign Lays Off Staff after Fundraising Drops due to Coronavirus Pandemic." *LGBTQ Nation*, April 29, 2020. https://www .lgbtqnation.com/2020/04/human-rights-campaign-slashes-staff-fundraising-craters -due-coronavirus-pandemic/.

———. "LGBT Media Shrinks Further: 365gay to Close." *Bilerico Project*, September 11, 2011. http://www.bilerico.com/2011/09/lgbt_media_shrinks_further_365gay_to_close.php.

Bruce, Graeme. "Who's Winning the COVID-19 Streaming Wars?" *YouGov*, May 26, 2020. https://today.yougov.com/topics/media/articles-reports/2020/05/26/covid-streaming.

Buozis, Michael. "Doxing or Deliberative Democracy? Evidence and Digital Affordances in the Serial Subreddit." *Convergence* 25, no. 3 (2019): 357–373. https://doi.org/10.1177/1354856517721809.

Busse, Kristina. "Fan Labor and Feminism: Capitalizing on the Fannish Labor of Love." *Cinema Journal* 54, no. 3 (2015): 110–115. https://www.jstor.org/stable/43653438.

Butsch, Richard. "Ralph, Fred, Archie and Homer: Why Television Keeps Recreating the White Male Working-Class Buffoon." In *Gender, Race, and Class in Media: A Critical Reader*, edited by Gail Dines and Jean Humez, 575–585. Thousand Oaks, CA: Sage, 2003.

Caldwell, John. *Production Culture: Industrial Reflexivity and Critical Practice in Film and Television*. Durham NC: Duke University Press, 2008.

Cameron, Kelsey. "Constructing Queer Female Cyberspace: *The L Word* Fandom and Autostraddle.com." In "Queer Female Fandom," edited by Julie Levin Russo and Eve Ng, special issue, *Transformative Works and Cultures* 24 (2017). https://doi.org/10.3983/twc.2017.0846.

Campbell, John Edward. *Getting It on Online: Cyberspace, Gay Male Sexuality, and Embodied Identity*. New York: Haworth, 2004.

———. "Outing PlanetOut: Surveillance, Gay Marketing and Internet Affinity Portals." *New Media & Society* 7, no. 5 (2005): 663–683. https://doi.org/10.1177/1461444480505601.

———. "Virtual Citizens or Dream Consumers: Looking for Civic Community on Gay.com." In *Queer Online: Media Technology & Sexuality*, edited by Kate O'Riordan and David Phillips, 197–216. New York: Peter Lang, 2007.

Carley, Brennan. "HBO's Stories—and Storytellers—Are Setting the Standard for Inclusive, LGBTQ+ Friendly Television." *Esquire*, June 30, 2020. https://www.esquire.com/entertainment/tv/a33001811/hbo-lgbtq-shows-creators-inclusivity-we-re-here-betty-interview-history/.

Carlson, Christy. "Is This because I'm Intertextual? *Law and Order, Special Victims Unit*, and Queer Internet Fan Production." In *Queer Online: Media Technology & Sexuality*, edited by Kate O'Riordan and David Phillips, 177–195. New York: Peter Lang, 2007.

Carnegie, Jim. *Television Business Report*. May 11, 2006. https://www.rbr.com/tvepaper/issue93-06-thu.html.

Carpentier, Nico. "Theoretical Frameworks for Participatory Media." In *Media Technologies and Democracy in an Enlarged Europe*, edited by Nico Carpentier, Pille Pruulmann-Vengerfeldt, Kaarle Nordenstreng, Maren Hartmann, Peeter Vihalemm, Bart Cammaerts, and Hannu Nieminen, 105–122. Tartu, Estonia: Tartu University Press, 2007.

Cashmore, Pete. "OurChart.com—*The L Word* Launching Lesbian Social Network." *Mashable*, December 18, 2006. https://mashable.com/2006/12/18/ourchartcom-the-l-word-launching-lesbian-social-network/.

Castronova, Edward. *Synthetic Worlds: The Business and Culture of Online Games*. Chicago: University of Chicago Press, 2005.

Cauterucci, Christina. "What's Left for Queer Women after AfterEllen?" *Slate*, September 23, 2016. https://slate.com/human-interest/2016/09/afterellen-site-of-record-for-queer-women-closes-leaving-void-in-lesbian-culture.html.

Cavalcante, Andre. *Struggling for Ordinary: Media and Transgender Belonging in Everyday Life*. New York: New York University Press, 2018.

Chasin, Alexandra. *Selling Out: The Gay and Lesbian Movement Goes to Market.* New York: Palgrave Macmillan, 2000.

Chin, Bertha. "Sherlockology and Galactica.tv: Fan Sites as Gifts or Exploited Labor?" *Transformative Works and Cultures* 15 (2014). http://dx.doi.org/10.3983/twc.2014.0513.

Cho, Alexander. "Default Publicness: Queer Youth of Color, Social Media, and Being Outed by the Machine." *New Media & Society* 20, no. 9 (2018): 3183–3200. https://doi.org/10.1177/1461444817744784.

Christian, Aymar Jean. "Beyond Branding: The Value of Intersectionality on Streaming TV Channels." *Television & New Media* 21, no. 5 (2020): 457–474. https://doi.org/10.1177/1527476419852241.

———. "OML and Tello Join Forces for More Lesbian Programming Online." *TubeFilter,* January 16, 2013. https://www.tubefilter.com/2013/01/16/one-more-lesbian-tello-join-forces-film-tv/.

———. *Open TV: Innovation beyond Hollywood and the Rise of Web Television.* New York: New York University Press, 2018.

———. "Open TV Distribution." In *Open TV: Innovation beyond Hollywood and the Rise of Web Television,* 156–211. New York: New York University Press, 2018.

———. "Open TV Production." In *Open TV: Innovation beyond Hollywood and the Rise of Web Television,* 59–100. New York: New York University Press, 2018.

———. "The Pandemic Clears Media Pollution and Queers the Ecosystem." *QED* 7, no. 3 (2020): 135–141. https://www.muse.jhu.edu/article/781366.

———. "The Value of Representation: Toward a Critique of Networked Television Performance." *International Journal of Communication* 11 (2017): 1552–1574. https://ijoc.org/index.php/ijoc/article/view/5697/1993.

Christian, Aymar Jean, and Khadijah Costley White. "Organic Representation as Cultural Reparation." *Journal of Cinema and Media Studies* 60, no. 1 (2020): 135–139. https://doi.org/10.1353/cj.2020.0068.

Ciriaco, Michael. "Logo's New Programming Slate Reveals Shift away from Gay-centric Shows." *Queerty,* February 21, 2012. http://www.queerty.com/exclusive-logos-new-programming-slate-reveals-shift-away-from-gay-centric-shows-20120221.

Cision. "Tapatalk Reinvents Online Forum Management Platforms with Tapatalk Groups." *Cision,* October 4, 2018. https://www.prnewswire.com/news-releases/tapatalk-reinvents-online-forum-management-platforms-with-tapatalk-groups-300724626.html.

Clifford, Stephanie. "We'll Make You a Star (if the Web Agrees)." *New York Times,* June 5, 2010. http://www.nytimes.com/2010/06/06/business/06bravo.html.

Cohen, Lizabeth. *A Consumer's Republic: The Politics of Mass Consumption in Postwar America.* New York: Vintage, 2003.

Cole, Samantha. "Tumblr Brings Back Nudity, but Not Porn." *Vice,* November 1, 2022. https://www.vice.com/en/article/xgymvj/tumblr-brings-back-nudity-but-not-porn.

Condis, Megan. "No Homosexuals in *Star Wars*? BioWare, 'Gamer' Identity, and the Politics of Privilege in a Convergence Culture." *Convergence: The International Journal of Research into New Media Technologies* 21, no. 2 (2015): 198–212. https://doi.org/10.1177/1354856514527205.

Cornucopia. "Who Owns Organic." *Cornucopia,* n.d. https://www.cornucopia.org/who-owns-organic/.

Cosgrove, Jaclyn. "Revry Wants to Be the Streaming Service for and by LGBTQ People." *Los Angeles Times,* March 15, 2019. https://www.latimes.com/business/la-fi-ct-revry-lgbtq-streaming-20190315-story.html.

Coté, Mark, and Jennifer Pybus. "Learning to Immaterial Labour 2.0: MySpace and Social Networks." *Ephemera* 7, no. 1 (2007): 88–106. https://instruct.uwo.ca/mit /3771–001/Immaterial_Labour2_0.pdf.

Croteau, David, William D. Hoynes, and Stefania Milan. "The Economics of the Media Industry." In *Media/Society: Industries, Images, Audiences*, 31–71. Thousand Oaks, CA: Sage, 2011.

D'Acci, Julie. *Defining Women: Television and the Case of* Cagney & Lacey. Chapel Hill: University of North Carolina Press, 1994.

Damshenas, Sam. "Here's How Viewers Reacted to the First Episode of *Canada's Drag Race*." *Gay Times*, n.d. [probably July 3, 2020]. http://gaytimes.co.uk/culture/heres -how-viewers-reacted-to-the-first-episode-of-canadas-drag-race/.

Day, Faithe. "Between Butch/Femme: On the Performance of Race, Gender, and Sexuality in a YouTube Web Series." *Journal of Lesbian Studies* 22, no. 3 (2018): 267–281. https://doi.org/10.1080/10894160.2018.1383800.

de Grazia, Victoria. Introduction to *The Sex of Things: Gender and Consumption in Historical Perspective*, edited by Victoria de Grazia and Ellen Furlough, 1–10. Berkeley: University of California Press, 1996.

De Kosnik, Abigail. "Should Fan Fiction Be Free?" *Cinema Journal* 48, no. 4 (2009): 118–124. https://www.jstor.org/stable/25619734.

Dobbs v. Jackson (2022). *U.S. Supreme Court.* https://www.supremecourt.gov/opinions /21pdf/19-1392_6j37.pdf.

Dominus, Susan. "The Affluencer." *New York Times Magazine*, November 2, 2008. http://www.nytimes.com/2008/11/02/magazine/02zalaznick-t.html.

Dornfeld, Barry. *Producing Public Television, Producing Public Culture*. Princeton, NJ: Princeton University Press, 1998.

Doty, Alexander. *Making Things Perfectly Queer: Interpreting Mass Culture*. Minneapolis: University of Minnesota Press, 1993.

Dow, Bonnie. "*Ellen*, Television, and the Politics of Gay and Lesbian Visibility." *Critical Studies in Media Communication* 18, no. 2 (2001): 123–140. https://doi.org/10.1080 /07393180128077.

Doyle, Vincent. *Making Out in the Mainstream: GLAAD and the Politics of Respectability*. Montreal: McGill-Queen's University Press, 2015.

Duggan, Lisa. "The New Homonormativity: The Sexual Politics of Neoliberalism." In *Materializing Democracy: Toward a Revitalized Cultural Politics*, edited by Russ Castronovo and Dana D. Nelson, 175–194. Durham, NC: Duke University Press, 2002.

Duguay, Stefanie. "He Has a Way Gayer Facebook than I Do": Investigating Sexual Identity Disclosure and Context Collapse on a Social Networking Site." *New Media & Society* 18, no. 6 (2016): 891–907. https://doi.org/10.1177/1461444814549930.

Editor. "Screen: *Gentleman Jack* Series Two Production Postponed." *Diva*, March 20, 2020. https://diva-magazine.com/2020/03/20/screen-gentleman-jack-series-two -production-postponed/.

Ehrenreich, Barbara, and John Ehrenreich. "The Professional-Managerial Class." In *Between Labor and Capital*, edited by Pat Walker, 5–45. Boston: South End Press, 1979.

Eliasoph, Nina. "Routines and the Making of Oppositional News." *Critical Studies in Mass Communication* 5, no. 4 (1988): 313–334. https://doi.org/10.1080 /15295038809366719.

Espinosa, Paul. "The Audience in the Text: Ethnographic Observations of a Hollywood Story Conference." *Media, Culture & Society* 4 (1982): 77–86. https://doi.org/10.1177 /016344378200400107.

Farmer, Brett. *Spectacular Passions: Cinema, Fantasy, Gay Male Spectatorships*. Durham, NC: Duke University Press, 2000.

Farrell, Kathleen. "Backstage Politics: Social Change and the 'Gay TV' Industry." PhD diss., Syracuse University, 2008.

Foucault, Michel. *The History of Sexuality, Volume 1*. Translated by Robert Hurley. New York: Pantheon, 1978.

Frank, Thomas. *The Conquest of Cool: Business Culture, Counterculture, and the Rise of Hip Consumerism*. Chicago: University of Chicago Press, 1997.

Fritscher, Jack. "Bear Roots Oral History: A Pioneer Maps the Genome of Bear." *JackFritscher.com*, June 20, 2000. https://www.jackfritscher.com/FeatureArticles/Articles/Intro%20Bear%20Book%202.html, para. 46.

Fuchs, Christian. "Competition and Cooperation in the Internet Economy." In *Internet and Society: Social Theory in the Information Age*, 148–212. New York: Routledge, 2008.

Gabriel, Trip, and Dana Goldstein. "Disputing Racism's Reach, Republicans Rattle American Schools." *New York Times*, June 1, 2021. https://www.nytimes.com/2021/06/01/us/politics/critical-race-theory.html.

Gamson, Joshua. "Gay Media Inc.: Media Structures, the New Gay Conglomerates, and Collective Sexual Identities." In *Cyberactivism: Online Activism in Theory and Practice*, edited by Martha McCaughey and Michael Ayers, 255–278. New York: Routledge, 2003.

———. "The Intersection of Gay Street and Straight Street: Shopping, Social Class, and the New Gay Visibility." *Social Thought & Research* 26, no. 1/2 (2005): 3–18. https://doi.org/10.17161/STR.1808.5208.

Gans, Herbert. *Deciding What's News: A Study of* CBS Evening News, NBC Nightly News, Newsweek *and* Time. New York: Vintage, 1979.

Garnham, Nicolas. "Bourdieu, the Cultural Arbitrary, and Television." In *Bourdieu: Critical Perspectives*, edited by Craig Calhoun, Edward LiPuma, and Moishe Postone, 178–192. Cambridge: Polity, 1993.

Ghaziani, Amin. "Post-gay Collective Identity Construction." *Social Problems* 58, no. 1 (2011): 99–125. https://doi.org/10.1525/sp.2011.58.1.99.

———. *There Goes the Gayborhood?* Princeton, NJ: Princeton University Press, 2014.

Gill, Rosalind. "Postfeminist Media Culture: Elements of a Sensibility." *European Journal of Cultural Studies* 10, no. 2 (2007): 147–166. https://doi.org/10.1177/1367549407075898.

Goldberg, Lesley. "Broadcast Pilot Season by the Numbers: Total Volume Hits a New Low." *Hollywood Reporter*, March 9, 2022. https://www.hollywoodreporter.com/tv/tv-news/broadcast-pilot-season-total-volume-low-1235108089/.

———. "Frances Berwick Sets Senior Leadership Team at NBCUniversal." *Hollywood Reporter*, September 16, 2020. https://www.hollywoodreporter.com/live-feed/frances-berwick-sets-senior-leadership-team-at-nbcuniversal.

———. "Lena Waithe Moves Overall Deal from Showtime to Amazon." *Hollywood Reporter*, July 27, 2019. https://www.hollywoodreporter.com/live-feed/lena-waithe-moves-deal-showtime-amazon-1227446.

———. "Mad about the CW Cancellations? Blame Streaming, but Also Its Unusual Corporate Structure." *Hollywood Reporter*, May 13, 2022. https://www.hollywoodreporter.com/tv/tv-news/the-cw-cancellations-blame-streaming-but-also-its-unusual-corporate-structure-1235146038/.

Goltz, Dustin. "It Gets Better: Queer Futures, Critical Frustrations, and Radical Potentials." *Critical Studies in Media Communication* 30, no. 2 (2013): 135–151. https://doi.org/10.1080/15295036.2012.701012.

Gorkemli, Serkan. "'Coming Out of the Internet': Lesbian and Gay Activism and the Internet as a 'Digital Closet' in Turkey." *Journal of Middle East Women's Studies* 8, no. 3 (2012): 63–88. https://doi.org/10.2979/jmiddeastwomstud.8.3.63.

Graham, Megan. "Facebook, Google and Amazon Are Reaping the Benefits from Advertising's Pandemic Hot Streak." *CNBC*, April 21, 2021. https://www.cnbc.com/2021/04/21/facebook-google-and-amazon-are-reaping-the-benefits-from-advertisings-pandemic-hot-streak.html.

Gray, Jonathan, and Amanda Lotz. *Television Studies*. Malden, MA: Polity, 2012.

Gray, Mary. *Out in the Country: Youth, Media, and Queer Visibility in Rural America*. New York: New York University Press, 2009.

Greven, David. *Representations of Femininity in American Genre Cinema: The Woman's Film, Film Noir, and Modern Horror*. New York: Palgrave Macmillan, 2011.

Griffin, Hollis. *Feeling Normal: Sexuality and Media Criticism in the Digital Age*. Bloomington: Indiana University Press, 2016.

Gross, Larry. *Up from Invisibility: Lesbians, Gay Men, and the Media in America*. New York: Columbia University Press, 2001.

Hall, Nicole. "Yes, Fundraising Is Part of Our Business Model: Here's Why." *Autostraddle*, August 6, 2020. https://www.autostraddle.com/yes-fundraising-is-part-of-our-business-model-heres-why/.

Halterman, J. "Exclusive: 'Person of Interest' EPs on Tonight's Shocking Episode." *AfterEllen*, May 31, 2016. https://www.afterellen.com/entertainment/490045-person-of-interest-exec-producers.

Hanckel, Benjamin, and Shiva Chandra. *Social Media Insights from Sexuality and Gender Diverse Young People during COVID-19*. Sydney: Young and Resilient Research Centre, University of Sydney, 2021. https://www.westernsydney.edu.au/__data/assets/pdf_file/0006/1837896/SocialMedia_LGBTQIA_YPReport_Final.pdf.

Hebdige, Dick. *Subculture: The Meaning of Style*. London: Methuen, 1979.

Heller, Dana. "Wrecked: Programming Celesbian Reality." In *Reality Gendervision: Sexuality and Gender on Transatlantic Reality Television*, edited by Brenda R. Weber, 123–146. Durham, NC: Duke University Press, 2014.

Henderson, Lisa. "Directorial Intention and Persona in Film School." In *On the Margins of Art Worlds*, edited by Larry Gross, 149–166. Boulder, CO: Westview, 1995.

———. "Queer Relay." *GLQ: A Journal of Lesbian and Gay Studies* 14, no. 4 (2008): 569–597. https://doi.org/10.1215/10642684-2008-005.

———. "'Storyline' and the Multicultural Middlebrow: Reading Women's Culture on National Public Radio." *Critical Studies in Mass Communication* 16, no. 3 (1999): 329–349. https://doi.org/10.1080/15295039909367099.

———. "The Class Character of *Boys Don't Cry*." *Screen* 42, no. 3 (2001): 299–303. https://doi.org/10.1093/screen/42.3.299.

Herring, Scott. *Another Country: Queer Anti-urbanism*. New York: New York University Press, 2010.

Hesmondhalgh, David. "Bourdieu, the Media, and Cultural Production." *Media Culture & Society* 28, no. 2 (2006): 211–231. https://doi.org/10.1177/0163443706061682.

Himberg, Julia. "Multicasting: Lesbian Programming and the Changing Landscape of Cable TV." *Television & New Media* 15, no. 4 (2014): 289–304. https://doi.org/10.1177/1527476412474351.

———. "Revry: Making the Case for LGBTQ Channels." In *From Networks to Netflix: A Guide to Changing Channels*, 2nd ed., edited by Derek Johnson, 269–278. New York: Routledge, 2022.

———. *The New Gay for Pay: The Sexual Politics of American Television Production.* Austin: University of Texas Press, 2018.

Hogan, Heather. "AfterEllen Is Shutting Down." *Autostraddle*, September 20, 2016. https://www.autostraddle.com/afterellen-is-shutting-down-352383/.

———. "Beyond Visibility: A Good Christian Girl in a Big Gay World." *AfterEllen*, September 1, 2010. Formerly up at http://www.afterellen.com/beyondvisibility/09 -01-2010, archived at https://web.archive.org/web/20121127151835/http://www .afterellen.com/beyondvisibility/09-01-2010.

———. "The Top 25 Lesbian/Bi Characters on TV (Right Now)." *AfterEllen*, November 4, 2013. Formerly up at https://www.afterellen.com/tv/201217-the-top-25 -lesbianbi-characters-on-tv-right-now, archived at https://web.archive.org/web /20181217013750/https://www.afterellen.com/tv/201217-the-top-25-lesbianbi -characters-on-tv-right-now.

Howley, Kevin. "'I Have a Drone': Internet Memes and the Politics of Culture." *Interactions: Studies in Communication & Culture* 7, no. 2 (2016): 155–175. https:// doi.org/10.1386/iscc.7.2.155_1.

Iandoli, Luca, Simonetta Primario, and Giuseppe Zollo. "The Impact of Group Polarization on the Quality of Online Debate in Social Media: A Systematic Literature Review." *Technological Forecasting & Social Change* 170 (2021): 1–12. https://doi.org/10.1016/j.techfore.2021.120924.

Iqbal, Mansoor. "Netflix Revenue and Usage Statistics (2020)." *Business of Apps*, June 23, 2020. https://www.businessofapps.com/data/netflix-statistics/.

Itay, Hod. "Logo Chief Chris McCarthy on How the Network Returned to Its Gay Roots: Why Bravo Is Not Competition." *The Wrap*, April 8, 2015. https://www .thewrap.com/logo-chief-chris-mccarthy-on-how-the-network-returned-to-its-gay -roots-why-bravo-is-not-its-competition/.

Jenkins, Henry. *Convergence Culture: Where Old and New Media Collide.* New York: New York University Press, 2006.

———. "Convergence? I Diverge." *Technology Review*, June 1, 2001. https://www .technologyreview.com/2001/06/01/235791/convergence-i-diverge/.

———. "Searching for the Origami Unicorn: *The Matrix* and Transmedia Storytelling." In *Convergence Culture: Where Old and New Media Collide*, 93–130. New York: New York University Press, 2006.

———. *Textual Poachers: Television Fans and Participatory Culture.* London: Routledge, 1992.

Jenkins, Henry, Gabriel Peters-Lazaro, and Sangita Shresthova. "Popular Culture and the Civic Imagination: Foundations." In *Popular Culture and the Civic Imagination: Case Studies of Creative Social Change*, edited by Henry Jenkins, Gabriel Peters-Lazaro, and Sangita Shresthova, 1–30. New York: New York University Press, 2020.

Jones, Mia. "De-butching Female Cops on TV's Crime Dramas." *AfterEllen*, November 23, 2010. Formerly up at http://www.afterellen.com/TV/2010/10/de-butching -female-cops-on-tvs-crime-dramas/, archived at https://web.archive.org/web /20111204001932/http://www.afterellen.com/column/pop-theory-3.

Joyrich, Lynne. "Epistemology of the Console." *Critical Inquiry* 27, no. 3 (2001): 439–467. https://www.jstor.org/stable/1344216.

———. "Queer Television Studies: Currents, Flows, and (Main)streams." *Cinema Journal* 53, no. 2 (2014): 133–139. https://doi.org/10.1353/cj.2014.0015.

Kafka, Peter. "AMC to Twitterers: Please Don't Market 'Mad Men' for Us." *Business Insider*, August 26, 2008. http://www.businessinsider.com/2008/8/amc-to-twitterers -please-don-t-market-madmen-for-us.

Kelly, Shannon. *Hot Topics: Reality TV.* Detroit: Lucent Books, 2013.

Kennedy, Mark. "Pandemic Eats into LGBTQ Representation on Network TV, Study Shows." *PBS*, January 15, 2021. https://www.pbs.org/newshour/arts/pandemic-eats -into-lgbtq-representation-on-network-tv-study-shows.

Kingsbury, Henry. *Music, Talent, and Performance: A Conservatory Cultural System.* Philadelphia: Temple University Press, 1988.

Kirkland, Catherine. "For the Love of It: Women Writers and the Popular Romance." PhD diss., University of Pennsylvania, 1984.

Knott-Fayle, Gabriel, Elizabeth Peel, and Gemma L. Witcomb. "(Anti-)feminism and Cisgenderism in Sports Media." *Feminist Media Studies* (2021 advance online publication). https://doi.org/10.1080/14680777.2021.1992644.

Kohnen, Melanie. *Queer Representation, Visibility, and Race in American Film and Television: Screening the Closet.* New York: Routledge, 2016.

Kona Equity. "Revry Inc." *Kona Equity*, December 14, 2022. https://www.konaequity .com/company/revry-inc-4395709467/.

Kornhaber, Spencer. "The Coronavirus Is Testing Queer Culture." *The Atlantic*, June 10, 2020. https://www.theatlantic.com/culture/archive/2020/06/how-quarantine -reshaping-queer-nightlife/612865/.

Kovacoglu, Emrah. "False Rumor: We Are Not Shutting Down!" *AfterEllen*, September 21, 2016. https://www.afterellen.com/general-news/514543-false-rumor-not -shutting.

Lafayette, Jon. "Fuse, Dropped by Comcast, Blasts Operator." *Multichannel News*, December 31, 2018. https://www.multichannel.com/news/fuse-dropped-by-comcast -blasts-operator.

———."Fuse Appoints Leonard Senior VP, Content Strategy." *Next TV*, July 11, 2016. https://www.nexttv.com/news/fuse-appoints-leonard-senior-vp-content-strategy -157922.

Lagerwey, Jorie. "Bravo Brand Motherhood: Negotiating the Impossibilities of Post-feminism." In *Postfeminist Celebrity and Motherhood: Brand Mom*, 51–72. New York: Routledge, 2017.

Lambe, Stacy. "Pride 2020: A Guide to Virtual Events and Ways to Donate during the Pandemic." *ET*, June 25, 2020. https://www.etonline.com/pride-2020-a-guide-to -virtual-events-and-ways-to-donate-during-the-pandemic-147389.

Lee, Hye-Kyung. "Participatory Media Fandom: A Case Study of Anime Fansubbing." *Media, Culture & Society* 33, no. 8 (2011): 1131–1147. https://doi.org/10.1177 /0163443711418271.

Lee, Michael J., and Leigh Moscowitz. "The 'Rich Bitch': Class and Gender on the *Real Housewives of New York City.*" *Feminist Media Studies* 13, no. 1 (2012): 64–82. https://doi.org/10.1080/14680777.2011.647971.

Levina, Marina. "Queering Intimacy, Six Feet Apart." *QED* 7, no. 3 (2020): 195–200. https://www.muse.jhu.edu/article/781374.

Leyshon, Andrew, Peter Webb, Shaun French, Nigel Thrift, and Louise Crewe. "On the Reproduction of the Musical Economy after the Internet." *Media, Culture & Society* 27, no. 2 (2005): 177–209. https://doi.org/10.1177/0163443705050468.

Li, Xiaomeng. "'I Feel like a "Cyber-gypsy"': BL Fanfiction Writers in China's Changing Landscape of Fandom Culture." *Journal of Popular Culture* 56, no. 2 (2023 forthcoming).

Light, Alan. Post 35, "***Gay-Friendly DVD's, Version 5***" thread. *Home Theatre Forum*, May 31, 2001. https://www.hometheaterforum.com/community/threads/gay -friendly-dvds-version-5.17406/page-2.

Lisotta, Christopher. "The Golden Girls, Their Timelessness and Their Very Gay Legacy." *Queerty*, April 14, 2016. https://www.queerty.com/the-golden-girls-their -timelessness-and-their-very-gay-legacy-20160414.

Lockett, Dee. "*Brown Girls* Is Now an Emmy-Nominated Show Well Ahead of Its HBO Debut." *Vulture*, July 13, 2017. https://www.vulture.com/2017/07/brown-girls-emmy -nominated-well-ahead-of-its-hbo-debut.html.

Lookadoo, Kathryn L., and Ted M. Dickinson. "Who Killed @TheLauraPalmer? Twitter as a Performance Space for *Twin Peaks* Fan Fiction." In *Television, Social Media, and Fan Culture*, edited by Alison F. Slade, Amber J. Narro, and Dedria Givens-Carroll, 337–351. Lanham, MD: Lexington.

Lothian, Alex. "Living in a Den of Thieves: Fan Video and Digital Challenges to Owner- ship." *Cinema Journal* 48, no. 4 (2009): 130–136. https://www.jstor.org/stable/25619736.

Lotz, Amanda. *Portals*. Ann Arbor: Michigan Publishing, University of Michigan Library, 2017. http://dx.doi.org/10.3998/mpub.9699689.

———. *The Television Will Be Revolutionized*. 2nd ed. New York: New York University Press, 2014.

———. *We Now Disrupt This Broadcast: How Cable Transformed Television and the Internet Revolutionized It All*. Boston: MIT Press, 2018.

Lovelock. Michael. "'Is Every YouTuber Going to Make a Coming Out Video Eventu- ally?': YouTube Celebrity Video Bloggers and Lesbian and Gay Identity." *Celebrity Studies* 8, no. 1 (2016): 87–103. https://doi.org/10.1080/19392397.2016.1214608.

———. *Reality TV and Queer Identities: Sexuality, Authenticity, Celebrity*. New York: Palgrave Macmillan, 2019.

Lutz, Catherine, and Jane Collins. *Reading* National Geographic. Chicago: University of Chicago Press, 1993.

Maas, Jennifer. "Netflix Loses 200,000 Subscribers in Q1, Predicts Loss of 2 Million More in Q2." *Variety*, April 19, 2022. https://variety.com/2022/tv/news/netflix-loses -subscribers-q1-earnings-1235234858/.

Manchester, Katherine. "12 'Natural' Brands, Owned by Giant Corporations—Here's the Breakdown." *Groundswell*, January 30, 2015. https://groundswell.org/12-natural -brands-owned-by-giant-corporations-heres-the-breakdown.

Mann, Denise. "Does 'Heroes 360' Represent NBC's Blistering Vision of the Future?" *Flow TV*, July 10, 2009. http://flowtv.org/2009/07/does-heroes-360-represent-nbcs -blistering-vision-of-the-futuredenise-mann-university-of-california-los-angeles/.

———. "It's Not TV, It's Brand Management TV: The Collective Author(s) of the *Lost* Franchise." In *Production Studies: Cultural Studies of Media Industries*, edited by Vicki Mayer, Miranda Banks, and John Caldwell, 99–114. New York: Routledge, 2010.

Marcie. "Pop Theory: Is the 'Cotton Ceiling' Theory All Fluff?" *AfterEllen*, June 11, 2012. Formerly up at http://www.afterellen.com/content/2012/06/pop-theory -cotton-ceiling-theory-all-fluff, archived at https://web.archive.org/web /20120613173822/http://www.afterellen.com/content/2012/06/pop-theory-cotton -ceiling-theory-all-fluff.

———. "Pop Theory: The Butch in 2012." *AfterEllen*, June 18, 2012. Formerly up at http://www.afterellen.com/content/2012/06/pop-theory-butch-2012, archived at https://web.archive.org/web/20120620202205/http://www.afterellen.com /content/2012/06/pop-theory-butch-2012.

———. "Pop Theory: What's (Legally) in a Choice?" *AfterEllen*, December 1, 2011. Formerly up at http://www.afterellen.com/column/pop-theory-3, archived at https://web.archive.org/web/20111204001932/http://www.afterellen.com/column /pop-theory-3.

Martin, Alfred L. Jr. "Introduction: What Is Queer Production Studies/Why Is Queer Production Studies?" *Journal of Film and Video* 70, no. 3–4 (2018): 3–7. https://doi .org/10.5406/jfilmvideo.70.3-4.0003.

———. "Queer (In)frequencies: SiriusXM's OutQ and the Limits of Queer Listening Publics." *Feminist Media Studies* 18, no. 2 (2018): 1–15. https://doi.org/10.1080 /14680777.2017.1315735.

Mayer, Vicki. *Below the Line: Producers and Production Studies in the New Television Economy.* Durham, NC: Duke University Press, 2011.

Mayer, Vicki, Miranda Banks, and John Caldwell. *Production Studies: Cultural Studies of Media Industries.* New York: Routledge, 2009.

McCabe, Janet, and Kim Akass, eds. *Quality TV: Contemporary American Television and Beyond.* New York: I. B. Tauris, 2007.

McClodden, Tiona. "Artist Statement." *TionaM.com*, n.d. https://www.tionam.com /artiststatement.

McCroy, Winnie. "Wish There Was a Netflix for Lesbians? Tune into Tello!" *Edge*, March 27, 2015. https://www.edgemedianetwork.com/news/national//174055.

Media and Data Equity Lab. https://www.madelab.org/.

Metcalf, Mitch. "ShowBuzzDaily's Top 25 Monday Cable Originals (& Network Update): 4.13.2015." *ShowBuzzDaily* [April 2015]. http://www.showbuzzdaily.com /articles/showbuzzdailys-top-25-monday-cable-originals-4-13-2015.html.

———. "Updated: ShowBuzzDaily's Top 150 Friday Cable Originals & Network Finals: 4.21.2017." *ShowBuzzDaily* [April 2017]. http://www.showbuzzdaily.com/articles /showbuzzdailys-top-150-friday-cable-originals-network-finals-4-21-2017.html.

———. "Updated with Broadcast: ShowBuzzDaily's Top 150 Thursday Cable Originals & Network Finals: 9.8.2016." *ShowBuzzDaily* [September 2016]. http://www .showbuzzdaily.com/articles/showbuzzdailys-top-150-thursday-cable-originals -network-finals-9-8-2016.html.

Miller, Brandon. "'They're the Modern-Day Gay Bar': Exploring the Uses and Gratifications of Social Networks for Men Who Have Sex with Men." *Computers in Human Behavior* 51 (2015): 476–482. https://doi.org/10.1016/j.chb.2015.05.023.

Miller, Matthew. "Senate Passes Cotton's Amendment Preventing Federal Funding of Critical Race Theory." *Washington Examiner*, August 11, 2021. https://www .washingtonexaminer.com/news/senate-passes-cotton-amendment-preventing -federal-funding-critical-race-theory.

Moody, Annemarie. "Cartoons on the Bay: Pulcinella Awards 2008." *AWN*, April 14, 2008. https://www.awn.com/news/cartoons-bay-pulcinella-awards-2008.

Moore, Candace. "Liminal Places and Spaces: Public/Private Considerations." In *Production Studies: Cultural Studies of Media Industries*, edited by Vicki Mayer, Miranda Banks, and John Caldwell, 125–139. New York: Taylor & Francis, 2009.

Morimoto, Lori, and Louisa Ellen Stein. "Tumblr and Fandom," in "Tumblr and Fandom," edited by Lori Morimoto and Louisa Ellen Stein, special issue, *Transformative Works and Cultures* 27 (2018). http://doi.org/10.3983/twc.2018.1580.

Mowlabocus, Sharif. *Gaydar Culture: Gay Men, Technology and Embodiment in the Digital Age.* Farnham, UK: Ashgate, 2010.

Moylan, Brian. "Introducing the Cast of the 'Gay Housewives of New York.'" *Gawker*, June 2, 2010. https://gawker.com/5552861/meet-the-cast-of-the-gay-housewives-of -new-york.

Mulshine, Paul. "Man-Boy Love." *Heterodoxy* 2, no. 10 (1994): 10–11. Formerly up at http://archive.discoverthenetworks.org/Articles/1994%20September%20Vol%20 2%20No2.pdf, archived at https://web.archive.org/web/20210607162315

/http://archive.discoverthenetworks.org/Articles/1994%20September%20Vol.%20 2%20No2.pdf.

Munt, Sally, Elizabeth Bassett, and Kate O'Riordan. "Virtually Belonging: Risk, Connectivity, and Coming Out On-line." *International Journal of Sexuality and Gender Studies* 7, no. 2/3 (2002): 125–137. https://doi.org/10.1023/A:1015893016167.

Murrell, David. "Experimental Filmmaker Tiona Nekkia McClodden Doesn't Care if You Miss the Point." *Philadelphia Magazine*, July 6, 2019. https://www.phillymag .com/news/2019/07/06/tiona-nekkia-mcclodden/.

Nabi, Robin, Erica Biely, Sara Morgan, and Carmen Stitt. "Reality-Based Television Programming and the Psychology of Its Appeal." *Media Psychology* 5 (2003): 303–330. https://doi.org/10.1207/S1532785XMEP0504_01.

Nader, Laura. "Up the Anthropologist: Perspectives Gained from Studying Up." In *Reinventing Anthropology*, edited by Dell Hymes, 284–311. New York: Random House, 1969.

Nakamura, Reid. "'RuPaul's Drag Race' EP on Adapting to COVID and Evolving the Show with the Times." *The Wrap*, June 4, 2021. https://www.thewrap.com/rupauls -drag-race-ep-on-adapting-to-covid-and-evolving-the-show-with-the-times/.

Naughty North. Header box text. http://thenaughtynorth.blogspot.com.

New York Times. "Webdenda: People and Accounts of Note." *New York Times*, June 19, 2006. https://www.nytimes.com/2006/06/19/business/media/19adco-webdenda.html.

Newman, Michael. "New Media, Young Audiences and Discourses of Attention: From *Sesame Street* to 'Snack Culture.'" *Media Culture & Society* 32, no. 4 (2010): 581–596. https://doi.org/10.1177/0163443710367693.

Ng, Eve. "Contesting the Queer Subfield of Cultural Production: Paratextual Framings of *Carol* and *Freeheld*." *Journal of Film and Video* 70 (Fall/Winter 2018): 8–23. https://doi.org/10.5406/jfilmvideo.70.3-4.0008.

———. "Rebranding Gay: New Configurations of Digital Media and Commercial Culture." PhD diss., University of Massachusetts, 2013. https://scholarworks.umass .edu/dissertations/AAI3589112/.

Ng, Eve, and Xiaomeng Li. "A Queer 'Socialist Brotherhood': The *Guardian* Web Series, Boys Love Fandom, and the Mainland Chinese State." *Feminist Media Studies* 20, no. 4 (2020): 479–495. https://doi.org/10.1080/14680777.2020.1754627.

———. "Brand Nohomonationalism: Chinese State *Guofeng* ('National Style') Framings of Boys Love Television Series." *Asian Studies Review* (2022 advance online publication). https://doi.org/10.1080/10357823.2022.2142933.

O'Brien, Anne, and Páraic Kerrigan. "Gay the Right Way: Roles and Routines of Irish Media Production among Gay and Lesbian Workers." *European Journal of Communication* 35, no. 4 (2020): 355–369. https://doi.org/10.1177/0267323120903684.

obsession_inc. "Affirmational Fandom vs. Transformational Fandom." *Dreamwidth*, June 1, 2009. http://obsession-inc.dreamwidth.org/82589.html.

O'Hara, Mary Emily. "AfterEllen Was a Refuge for All Queer Women—until It Wasn't." *Out*, February 13, 2019. https://www.out.com/news-opinion/2019/2/13/afterellen -was-refuge-all-queer-women-until-it-wasn't.

Ohmann, Richard. "The Shaping of a Canon: U.S. Fiction, 1960–1975." *Critical Inquiry* 10, no. 1 (1983): 199–223. https://www.jstor.org/stable/1343412.

Older than Netfic. "A New History of Fandom Purges." *Tumblr*, October 15, 2019. https://olderthannetfic.tumblr.com/post/188360541394/a-new-history-of-fandom -purges.

Ono, Kent. "Postracism: A Theory of the 'Post-' as Political Strategy." *Communication Inquiry* 34, no. 3 (2010): 227–233. https://doi.org/10.1177/0196859910371375.

Ortner, Sherry. "Studying Sideways: Ethnographic Access in Hollywood." In *Production Studies: Cultural Studies of Media Industries*, edited by Vicky Mayer, Miranda Banks, and John Caldwell, 175–189. New York: Routledge, 2009.

Papacharissi, Zizi, and Jan Fernback. "The Aesthetic Power of the Fab 5: Discursive Themes of Homonormativity in *Queer Eye for the Straight Guy*." *Journal of Communication Inquiry* 32, no. 4 (2008): 348–367. https://doi.org/10.1177/0196859908320301.

Parsemain. Ava. "Queering and Policing Gender: The Pedagogy of *RuPaul's Drag Race*." In *The Pedagogy of Queer TV*, 95–117. London: Palgrave, 2019.

Patten, Dominic, and Nellie Andreeva. "'One Mississippi,' 'I Love Dick' & 'Jean-Claude Van Johnson' Canceled by Amazon." *Deadline*, January 18, 2018. https://deadline.com/2018/01/one-mississippi-i-love-dick-jean-claude-van-johnson-canceled-amazon-1202245153/.

Pelliccione, Damian, Alia J. Daniels, Christopher Rodriguez, and LaShawn McGhee. "An Interview with Revry Co-founder & CEO Damian Pelliccione." *LGBT Token*, n.d. https://lgbt-token.org/an-interview-with-revry-co-founder-ceo-damian-pelliccione/.

Pennington, Adrian. "The State of OTT 2022." *Streaming Media*, March 26, 2022. https://www.streamingmedia.com/Articles/Editorial/Featured-Articles/The-State-of-OTT-2022-152085.aspx.

Perez, Ruben Jr. "Fuse Announces Fall 2019 TV Lineup." *Entertainment Rocks*, August 14, 2019. https://www.entertainmentrocks.com/fuse-announces-fall-2019-tv-lineup/.

Perryman, Neil. "*Doctor Who* and the Convergence of Media: A Case Study in 'Transmedia Storytelling.'" *Convergence: The International Journal of Research into New Media Technologies* 14, no. 1 (2008): 21–39. https://doi.org/10.1177/1354856507084417.

Phillips, David. "Negotiating the Digital Closet: Online Pseudonymity and the Politics of Sexual Identity." *Information, Communication, and Society* 5, no. 3 (2002): 406–442. https://doi.org/10.1080/13691180210159337.

Powdermaker, Hortense. *Hollywood, the Dream Factory: An Anthropologist Looks at the Movie-Makers*. London: Secker & Warburg, 1951.

Power, Shannon. "Forget Netflix, There's a New Asian Streaming Service That's 100% LGBTI." *Gay Star News*, July 21, 2017. https://www.gaystarnews.com/article/forget-netflix-theres-new-streaming-service-100-lgbti/.

Prudom, Laura. "Queer Eye Season 2: Why Netflix's Reboot Is TV's Most Inspiring Show." *IGN*, June 15, 2018. https://www.ign.com/articles/2018/06/15/netflixs-queer-eye-reboot-is-the-ultimate-feel-good-binge.

Puar, Jasbir. *Terrorist Assemblages: Homonationalism in Queer Times*. Durham, NC: Duke University Press, 2007.

Pullen, Christopher. *Straight Girls and Queer Guys: The Hetero Media Gaze in Film and Television*. Edinburgh: Edinburgh University Press, 2016.

Queerty. "William Sledd Was Going to Be Bravo's YouTube Star." *Queerty*, February 2, 2010. https://www.queerty.com/william-sledd-was-going-to-be-bravos-youtube-star-then-everything-fell-apart-20100202.

Radar Online. "'We Can Fictionalize the Footage!': Secret Bravo Contract Exposes How 'Reality' TV Shows Are REALLY Made." *Radar Online*, September 23, 2013. https://radaronline.com/exclusives/2013/09/real-housewives-new-jersey-secret-bravo-contract-exposes-reality-tv-shows-really-made-documents/.

Radway, Janice. *A Feeling for Books: The Book-of-the-Month Club, Literary Taste, and Middle-Class Desire*. Chapel Hill: University of North Carolina Press, 1997.

Ramos, Dino-Ray. "Comcast Drops Fuse after a Decade: Channel Exec Calls Decision Is 'Surprising and Troubling.'" *Deadline*, December 30, 2018. https://deadline.com /2018/12/comcast-drops-fuse-jennifer-lopez-michael-schwimmer-1202527319/.

Reid, Joe. "ICYMI, Netflix Is Coming to Eat Bravo's Lunch." *Primetimer*, August 26, 2020. https://www.primetimer.com/features/netflix-is-coming-to-eat-bravos-lunch.

Rentschler, Carrie, and Samantha Thrift. "Doing Feminism in the Network: Networked Laughter and the 'Binders Full of Women' Meme." *Feminist Theory* 16, no. 3 (2015): 329–359. https://doi.org/10.1177/1464700115604136.

Reuters. "Bravo Tops Survey of Gay-Friendly Companies." *Reuters*, May 13, 2008. http://www.reuters.com/article/2008/05/13/industry-gay-dc-idUSN1343338320080513.

Revry. "FAQ." *Revry.tv*, n.d. https://www.revry.tv/support.

———. "Questions." *Revry.tv*, n.d. https://www.revry.tv/support.

Reyes, Mariel Soto. "Hulu Is Rolling Out a Download Option for Ad-Free Subscribers on iOS." *Business Insider*, October 9, 2019. https://www.businessinsider.com/hulu -gives-ad-free-users-content-download-option-2019-10.

Romano, Aja. "The Archive of Our Own Just Won a Hugo. That's Huge for Fanfiction." *Vox*, August 19, 2019. https://www.vox.com/2019/4/11/18292419/archive-of-our-own -wins-hugo-award-best-related-work.

Rosenblum, Emma. "How Andy Cohen Became Bravo's Face." *New York Magazine*, January 8, 2010. http://nymag.com/arts/tv/features/63010/.

Rosten, Leo. *Hollywood, the Movie Colony, the Movie Makers*. New York: Harcourt Brace, 1941.

Rubin, Gayle. "Thinking Sex: Notes for a Radical Theory of the Politics of Sexuality." In *Pleasure and Danger: Exploring Female Sexuality*, edited by Carole Vance, 267–312. New York: Routledge, 1984.

Rudnick, Bret Ryan. "An Interview with Robert Tapert." *Whoosh* 52 (2001). http:// whoosh.org/issue52/itapert1b.html.

Russo, Vito. *The Celluloid Closet: Homosexuality in the Movies*. New York: Harper, 1987.

San Filippo, Maria. "Before and after AfterEllen: Online Queer Cinephile Communities as Critical Counterpublics." In *Film Criticism in the Digital Age*, edited by Mattias Frey and Cecilia Sayad, 117–136. New Brunswick, NJ: Rutgers University Press, 2015.

Sass, Erik. "Q.Digital Rolls Up LGBT Media Cos." *Media Post*, September 29, 2015. https://www.mediapost.com/publications/article/259347/qdigital-rolls-up-lgbt -media-cos.html.

Scolari, Carlos A. "Lostology: Transmedia Storytelling and Expansion/Compression Strategies." *Semiotica* 195 (2013): 45–68. https://doi.org/10.1515/sem-2013–0038.

Scott, D. Travers. "Queer Media Studies in the Age of the E-invisibility." *International Journal of Communication* 5 (2011): 95–100. http://ijoc.org/ojs/index.php/ijoc/article /view/1055/510.

Scott, Suzanne. *Fake Geek Girls: Fandom, Gender, and the Convergence Culture Industry*. New York: New York University Press, 2019.

———. "Repackaging Fan Culture: The Regifting Economy of Ancillary Content Models." *Transformative Works and Cultures* 3 (2009). https://doi.org/10.3983/twc.2009.0150.

Sender, Katherine. *Business, Not Politics: The Making of the Gay Market*. New York: Columbia University Press, 2004.

———. "Dualcasting: Bravo's Gay Programming and the Quest for Women Audiences." In *Cable Visions: Television beyond Broadcasting*, edited by Sarah Banet-Weiser, Cynthia Chris, and Anthony Freitas, 302–318. New York: New York University Press, 2007.

————. "Evolution, Not Revolution." In *Business, Not Politics: The Making of the Gay Market*, 24–63. New York: Columbia University Press, 2004.

————. "Feeling Real: Empirical Truth and Emotional Authenticity." In *The Makeover: Reality Television and Reflexive Audiences*, 105–135. New York: Columbia University Press, 2012.

————. "Gay Readers, Consumers and a Dominant Gay Habitus: 25 Years of the *Advocate* Magazine." *Journal of Communication* 51, no. 1 (2001): 73–99. https://doi.org/10.1111/j.1460-2466.2001.tb02873.x.

————. "Real Worlds: Migrating Genres, Travelling Participants, Shifting Theories." In *The Politics of Reality Television: Global Perspectives*, edited by Marwan Kraidy and Katherine Sender, 1–11. New York: Columbia University Press, 2012.

————. *The Makeover: Reality Television and Reflexive Audiences*. New York: Columbia University Press, 2012.

Serrano, Pedro Angel. "Queer Hip-Hop Musicians Struggle against the Gaystream." *Radio 4 All*, October 3, 2003. https://www.radio4all.net/index.php/program/7910.

Shield, Andrew. "'I Was Staying at the Camp, and I Met This Guy on Grindr, and He Asked Me to Move in with Him': Tourists, Immigrants, and Logistical Uses of Socio-sexual Media." In *Immigrants on Grindr: Race, Sexuality and Belonging Online*, 111–142. London: Palgrave Macmillan, 2019.

Shifman, Limor. *Memes in Digital Culture*. Boston: MIT Press, 2014.

Shu, Catherine. "YouTube Updates Its Policies after LGBTQ Videos Were Blocked in Restricted Mode." *Tech Crunch*, June 20, 2017. https://techcrunch.com/2017/06/19/youtube-updates-its-policies-after-lgbtq-videos-were-blocked-in-restricted-mode/.

Silverstone, Roger. *Framing Science: The Making of a BBC Documentary*. London: British Film Institute, 1985.

SLK. "The Good Life." *Ausxip*, 2000. https://www.ausxip.com/interviews/mgood.html.

Smith, Erin Copple. "'Affluencers' by Bravo: Defining an Audience through Cross-promotion." *Popular Communication* 10, no. 4 (2010): 286–301. https://doi.org/10.1080/15405702.2012.715327.

Smith, Reiss. "The 'Netflix of Queer Content' Launches across Asia despite Gay Sex Bans." *Pink News*, January 2, 2020. https://www.pinknews.co.uk/2020/01/02/gagaoolala-lgbt-streaming-service-asia/.

snicks. "The History of U.S. Daytime Gay Soap Kisses." *AfterElton*, August 16, 2012. Formerly up at http://www.afterelton.com/tv/2012/08/gay-soap-kisses-oltl-atwt-dool, archived at https://web.archive.org/web/20120817223703/http://www.afterelton.com/tv/2012/08/gay-soap-kisses-oltl-atwt-dool.

Spencer, Samuel. "'Stumptown' Canceled: Why the Show Is Ending despite Season 2 Renewal." *Newsweek*, September 17, 2020. https://www.newsweek.com/stumptown-canceled-season-2-cancelled-abc-1532553.

Stanley, Alessandra. "Sex and the Gym: 'Work Out' and the Gaying of Bravo." *New York Times*, July 19, 2006. http://www.nytimes.com/2006/07/19/arts/television/19watc.html.

Stilwell, Jessica. "Fans Without Pity: Television, Online Communities, and Popular Criticism." Master's thesis, Georgetown University, 2003.

Street, Mikelle. "Groundbreaking *Noah's Arc* Is Back Tonight for Special 'Rona' Reunion." *Advocate*, July 5, 2020. https://www.advocate.com/television/2020/7/05/noahs-arc-back-tonight-special-rona-reunion-episode.

Taylor, T. L. *Play between Worlds: Exploring Online Game Culture*. Cambridge, MA: MIT Press, 2006.

Terranova, Tiziana. "Free Labor: Producing Culture for the Digital Economy." *Social Text* 18, no. 2 (2000): 33–58. https://www.muse.jhu.edu/article/31873.

The Retroist. "Reddit Has a Crazy *Game of Thrones* Community That Welcomes Fans' Biggest Fear." *Geek*, June 22, 2016. https://www.geek.com/games/reddit-has-a-crazy -game-of-thrones-community-that-welcomes-fans-biggest-fear-1658848/.

Thornton, Sarah. *Club Cultures: Music, Media and Subcultural Capital*. Hanover, NH: University Press of New England, 1996.

Thrasher, Steven. "What Tumblr's Porn Ban Really Means." *The Atlantic*, December 7, 2018. https://www.theatlantic.com/technology/archive/2018/12/tumblr-adult -content-porn/577471.

Tongson, Karen. *Relocations: Queer Suburban Imaginaries*. New York: New York University Press, 2011.

Tuchman, Gaye. *Making News: A Study in the Construction of Reality*. New York: Free Press, 1978.

Turow, Joseph. *Breaking Up America: Advertisers and the New Media World*. Chicago: University of Chicago Press, 1997.

———. *Niche Envy: Marketing Discrimination in the Digital Age*. Boston: MIT Press, 2006.

Usher, Nikki, and Eleanor Morrison. "The Demise of the Gay Enclave, Communication Infrastructure Theory, and the Transformation of Gay Public Space." In *LGBT Identity and Online New Media*, edited by Christopher Pullen and Margaret Cooper, 271–287. New York: Routledge, 2010.

Vaid, Urvashi. *Virtual Equality*. New York: Anchor, 1995.

Valerie Anne. "Exclusive: 'The 100' EP Jason Rothenberg on This Week's Game-Changing Episode, 'Thirteen.'" *AfterEllen*, March 2, 2016. https://www.afterellen .com/tv/476855-exclusive-100-ep-jason-rothenberg-weeks-game-changing-episode -thirteen.

Vavrus, Mary. *Postfeminist News: Political Women in Media Culture*. Albany: State University of New York Press, 2002.

Villarreal, Daniel. "YouTube Changes Its Policy on Anti-LGBTQ Hate Speech, but Will It Work?" *LGBTQ Nation*, October 1, 2019. https://www.lgbtqnation.com /2019/12/youtube-changes-policy-anti-lgbtq-hate-speech-will-work/.

Vogel, Lisa. "Letter to the Community." *Michigan Womyn's Music Festival*, April 11, 2013. Originally at http://michfest.com/letter-to-the-community-4_11_13/, archived at https://web.archive.org/web/20150330195141/http://michfest.com/letter-to-the -community-4_11_13/.

Vulture Editors. "All the Live Events, Movie Releases, and Productions Affected by the Coronavirus." *Vulture*, September 11, 2020. https://www.vulture.com/2020/09 /events-cancelled-coronavirus.html.

Wagmeister, Elizabeth. "Bravo Unveils New On-Air Look, Logo in Brand Refresh (Exclusive)." *Variety*, February 6, 2017. https://variety.com/2017/tv/news/bravo-new -logo-and-tagline-1201977500/.

Wallenstein, Andrew. "Bravo Tops Survey of Gay-Friendly Companies." *Hollywood Reporter*, May 13, 2008. https://www.hollywoodreporter.com/news/bravo-tops -survey-gay-friendly-111589.

Wallenstein, Michael. "Netflix Series Spending Revealed." *Variety*, March 8, 2013. https://variety.com/2013/digital/news/caa-agent-discloses-netflix-series-spending -1200006100/.

Walters, Suzanna Danuta. *All the Rage: The Story of Gay Visibility in America*. Chicago: University of Chicago Press, 2001.

Warner, Michael. *The Trouble with Normal: Sex, Politics, and the Ethics of Queer Life*. New York: Free Press, 1999.

Waters, Emily. *Lesbian, Gay, Bisexual, Transgender, Queer, and HIV-Affected Hate Violence in 2016*. New York: New York City Anti-violence Project, 2017. http://avp .org/wp-content/uploads/2017/06/NCAVP_2016HateViolence_REPORT.pdf.

Watson, Amy. "Increased Viewership of Major Streaming Services in the Last Month due to the Coronavirus Outbreak in the United States as of March 2020." *Statistica*, June 18, 2020. https://www.statista.com/statistics/1107238/svod-consumption -increase-coronavirus-us/.

Wayne, Michael L., and Matt Sienkiewicz. "'We Don't Aspire to Be Netflix': Understanding Content Acquisition Practices among Niche Streaming Services." *Television & New Media* (2022 advance online publication). https://doi.org/10.1177 /15274764221100474.

Weaver, Jackson. "'Depopulating the Set': How Canada's Film Industry Is Navigating COVID-19." *CBC News*, June 13, 2020. https://www.cbc.ca/news/entertainment /film-industry-covid-1.5610613.

Weber, Brenda R., ed. *Reality Gendervision: Sexuality and Gender on Transatlantic Reality Television*. Durham, NC: Duke University Press, 2014.

Weldon, Glen. "New 'Queer Eye' Is a Reboot, Not a Retread." *NPR*, February 7, 2018. https://www.npr.org/2018/02/07/583676372/new-queer-eye-is-a-reboot-not-a -retread.

Westenfeld. Adrienne. "The 10 Most-Banned Books in America." *Esquire*, May 5, 2022. https://www.esquire.com/entertainment/books/g39908103/banned-books/.

Westerfelhaus, Robert, and Celeste Lacroix. "Seeing 'Straight' through *Queer Eye*: Exposing the Strategic Rhetoric of Heteronormativity in a Mediated Ritual of Gay Rebellion." *Critical Studies in Media Communication* 23, no. 5 (2006): 426–444. https://doi.org/10.1080/07393180601046196.

White, Brett. "Stream It or Skip It: 'Drag Race Holland' on WOW Presents Plus, a Dutch Twist on a Winning Formula." *Decider*, September 17, 2020. https://decider .com/2020/09/17/drag-race-holland-on-wow-presents-plus-stream-it-or-skip-it/.

Williamson, Kit. "'How I Sold My Web Series to Netflix': The Director of 'EastSiders' Explains His Secret." *IndieWire*, July 1, 2016. https://www.indiewire.com/2016/07 /eastsiders-lgbt-web-series-sold-netflix-kit-williamson-1201701822/.

Wimberly, Jason. "Logo's *Fire Island* Contributes to Gay America's Moral Decline." *Advocate*, March 9, 2017. https://www.advocate.com/commentary/2017/3/09/logos -fire-island-contributes-gay-americas-moral-decline.

Yee, Nick. "The Labor of Fun." *Games and Culture* 1, no. 1 (2006): 68–71. https://doi .org/10.1177/1555412005281819.

Zhang, Charlie Yi. "Queering the National Body of Contemporary China." *Frontiers* 37, no. 2 (2016): 1–26. https://doi.org/10.5250/fronjwomestud.37.2.0001.

Zhao, Jing Jamie, Ling Yang, and Maud Lavin. Introduction to *Boys' Love, Cosplay, and Androgynous Idols: Queer Fan Cultures in Mainland China, Hong Kong, and Taiwan*, edited by Maud Lavin, Ling Yang, and Jing Jamie Zhao, xi–xxxiii. Hong Kong: Hong Kong University Press, 2017.

Zwicky, Arnold. "HoYay!" *Linguist List*, January 20, 2005. http://listserv.linguistlist .org/pipermail/ads-l/2005-January/044924.html.

Index

ABC, 11, 152n43; LGBTQ content, 11–12, 53, 79, 94, 163n52

Abraham, Michael (Downelink co-founder), 30, 36

access to technology, 8, 9, 22, 35–36, 177n35

advertising: advertisers, 24, 61, 71, 93, 99; on digital media, 30, 63, 64, 71, 80, 110, 112, 115, 182n30; on LGBTQ media, 9, 47, 63, 64, 84, 97, 111, 136, 164n59, 167–168n7; as professional experience of cultural producers, 38–39; on television, 11, 87, 120, 122

Advocate, The magazine, 9, 24, 70, 151n33, 159n7, 168n11

Affluencer magazine, 28, 86

affluencers, 86, 93, 102–103

AfterEllen: content, various, 10, 19, 22, 44–46, 47, 48, 55, 62, 88, 93, 95–97, 97–98, 100, 120, 124–127; *passim*, 130, 158n51, 159n14, 159n15, 160n18, 162–163n51, 172n61, 172n71; content, web series, 53–54, 56, 57–61, 62, 120, 124–127; *passim*, 129, 181n25; establishment, 31, 36, 52–53, 115; and independent producers, 112–114; ownership and purchase by Logo, 2, 5, 22, 30, 41, 71–72, 80, 112–113, 115, 164n63; producer discourses, 44–46, 47, 49; sale to Evolve media, 62, 72; as site of LGBTQ community, 9–10, 55, 65, 67–69, 70, 72, 75, 112; staffing, 32, 34, 35, 36–37, 38, 39, 40–42, 49, 99, 100, 115, 141–143, 154n76, 156n18, 157n44; staff trajectories after departing, 50; transphobia, 72, 138; users, 17, 22, 69–70, 163n51, 163n54, 165n69

AfterElton (TheBacklot): absorption by NewNowNext, 62; content, 10, 44, 47, 48, 53–54, 55, 56–57, 61, 62, 96–97, 97–98, 100, 120, 124–127; *passim*, 129, 130, 158n51, 159n14, 159n15, 160n21, 162–163n51, 172n60; establishment, 31, 36; and independent producers, 113; ownership and purchase by Logo, 2, 5, 30, 41, 80, 115, 164n63; producer discourses, 47; rebranding as TheBacklot, 62; as site of LGBTQ community, 9–10, 55, 65, 67–68, 70, 72, 75, 112; staffing, 32, 34, 35, 36–37, 38, 39–40, 41, 42, 49, 66, 115, 141–143, 156n18, 157n44; staff trajectories after departing, 50; users, 69, 163n54

A List, The: Dallas (Logo, 2011), 78, 95

A List, The: New York (Logo, 2010), 126, 127; content, 104; and Logo's rebranding, 78, 91, 94–95; participants, 66; reception, 119–120

Amazing Race, The (CBS, 2001–present), 12; LGBTQ participants, 79, 94

Amazon Prime, 62, 182n30; LGBTQ content, 2, 64, 105, 134, 161n39, 180n12, 180n16; LGBTQ producers, 128, 178n46; subscriptions, 121, 177n36

Anyone But Me (Tina Cesa Ward, 2008–2011), 60, 113, 126, 127

203

"peak TV", 12, 53, 109, 120–121
Planet Green: LGBTQ content, 118
PlanetOut, 9, 61, 78, 159n7, 168n11
Pluto TV, 105, 161n39
Polly, John (LogoONLINE/LogoTV and
NewNowNext editor): commentary about
LGBTQ community and identity, 95;
commentary about Logo, 95; commentary
about NewNowNext, 97; after departing
Logo, 50; at LogoONLINE/LogoTV, 29,
34, 37; professional background, 37, 40;
recruitment of contributors for Logo's
websites, 37
positionality, researcher, 17–18, 22
post-feminist discourses, 101. See also
feminism
post-gay discourses, 4, 20, 101, 137
post-network television. See under television
industry
post-racial discourses, 101–102
Pride.com, 9, 70, 159n7, 163n56
Pride TV (South Africa), 64
Primetimer, 74, 166n81
Prime Video. See Amazon Prime
production culture. See under cultural
producers
production studies, 13, 15–16; queer
production studies, 16. See also cultural
producers; field of cultural production
(cultural field)
professionalization. See under cultural
producers
Project Runway (Bravo, 2004-), 85, 91, 103,
126, 127; LGBTQ participants, 28, 47–48,
84, 156n16
Puar, Jasbir, 82, 102

queer activism. See LGBTQ activism/
activists, in the community
Queer as Folk (Showtime, 2000–2005), 12,
88, 94, 99, 101, 120
queer community. See LGBTQ community/
interaction
Queer Comrades, 135
"queer dispersal" (Alfred Martin Jr.), 55, 82
Queer Eye (Netflix, 2018–), 30, 105
Queer Eye (Queer Eye for the Straight Guy)
(Bravo, 2003–2007), 126, 127; and Bravo's
brand, 1, 4, 13, 77, 78, 80, 117, 129–130;
content, 83–84, 105, 118, 129, 167n5;

digital content, 28, 62; LGBTQ
participants, 4, 83–84, 156n16; spin–offs,
83, 135, 169n28; viewers, 84, 118
queer media. See LGBTQ media
queer media production. See LGBTQ media
production
queer production studies, 16
"queer relay" (Lisa Henderson), 50,
150n13
queer subcultures. See under subcultures
Queerty, 10, 28, 73, 120, 165n73, 165n74

race: Black Lives Matter, 105; and gaystream
program categories, 93; George Floyd
protests, 136; post-racial discourses,
101–102; racial inequality and racism, 13,
82, 99, 101, 105, 136, 139, 184n50; racially
diverse content, 11, 46, 63, 86, 88, 89, 94,
100, 104, 108, 111, 113, 117, 127, 128, 134,
170n45, 178n49. See also under cultural
producers; fandom
Rajah, Dalila Ali (AfterEllen video
contributor): as African American,
157n44; Cherry Bomb web series, 39,
59–60, 66, 113, 157n45, 181n25;
commentary about LGBTQ media
production, 113
Real Housewives series, 66, 91, 105, 117, 126;
and Bravo's brand, 77, 129; content, 94–95,
103; development, 85–86; LGBTQ
participants, 170n42; multiple series, 103,
170n41; production, 176n25; spin-offs,
170n41
reality television, 11, 12–13, 20, 66, 102;
LGBTQ participants, 4, 13, 20, 28–29, 45,
66, 78–79, 81, 83–85, 86–87, 94–95, 99,
102, 103, 104–105, 109, 116–118, 123–129;
passim, 138, 170n42; LGBTQ viewers,
118–120, 164n62, 169n30; perceived
authenticity of participants, 105, 119–120.
See also individual shows
Real L Word, The (Showtime, 2010–2012),
58, 118, 119, 164n62
rebranding: Bravo, 25–26, 78, 80–81, 82–85,
86–87, 103, 170n37; Logo, 61, 78, 80–81,
89–90, 103, 156n24, 157n30. See also
dualcasting; gaystreaming
Reddit, 74, 166n80
Reid, Joe (Television Without Pity
recapper), 105, 166n81

About the Author

EVE NG is an associate professor in the School of Media Arts and Studies and the Women's, Gender, and Sexuality Studies Program at Ohio University. She is the author of *Cancel Culture: A Critical Analysis* and has published articles in journals including *Communication, Culture & Critique, Development and Change, Feminist Media Studies, Feminist Studies, International Journal of Communication, Journal of Film and Video, Journal of Lesbian Studies, New Review of Film and Television Studies, Popular Communication, Television & New Media*, and *Transformative Works and Culture*. She is as an associate editor of *Communication, Culture & Critique* and serves on the editorial board of the *Journal of Lesbian Studies* and *Transformative Works and Culture* and on the Strategic Planning Task Force of the International Communication Association.